FATHER OF
THE BENSONS

FATHER OF
THE BENSONS

The Life of Edward White Benson
Sometime Archbishop of Canterbury

GEOFFREY PALMER and NOEL LLOYD

Lennard Publishing

First published in 1998 by
Lennard Publishing
a division of
Lennard Associates Ltd
Mackerye End, Harpenden
Herts AL5 5DR

A catalogue entry is available from the British Library.

ISBN 1 85291 138 7

Jacket design: Design 2 Print
Production Editor: Chris Hawkes

Printed and bound in Great Britain by
Butler & Tanner, Frome and London

CONTENTS

This book is for
Rosemary and Adrian Stephenson

ACKNOWLEDGEMENTS

W e would like to thank Allan Downend and the E.F. Benson Society most sincerely for their generosity in putting at our disposal the Benson diaries which they hold. We are also grateful to Lynda Lee for lending us *The Life Work of Edward White Benson*, by J.A. Carr (1898) and Derek Gibbons for finding *'Church Bells' Life of Archbishop Benson* (1896), rare books, both of which have provided much valuable material. Thanks also to Cynthia and Tony Reavell of the Tilling Society for encouragement and support and also to the Rev. Harry Matthews, Headmaster of Heath Mount Preparatory School which Eustace Miles attended over 120 years ago!

Among the books consulted were the two-volume work by A.C. Benson on his father, his books on Maggie and Hugh Benson, *The Trefoil*, *Beside Still Waters*, and his Genealogy of the Benson family; also E.F. Benson's books of family reminiscences, *Our Family Affairs*, *Mother*, *As We Were* and *Final Edition*. David Newsome's A History of Wellington College and On the Edge of Paradise were sources of vital information. R. St. C. Talboy's A Victorian School and George F.H. Berkeley's My Recollections of Wellington College put the school's first Master and its past in a different light. The Wellington College Register gave us many essential facts. The biography of Charles Kingsley by his wife was useful, as was Elizabeth Wordsworth's Glimpses of the Past, Georgina Battiscombe's Life of Elizabeth Wordsworth, and Ethel Smyth's As Time Went On. Betty Askwith's Two Victorian Families was re-read with pleasure and profit. Our biography of E.F. Benson was always at hand. Edward White Benson's own works were a rich ore in revealing important aspects of his character and of his own religious beliefs.

BACKGROUND

The name Benson comes from the Scandinavian 'Björnson', 'Son of the Bear'. As such it has little romance about it, and certainly nothing patrician; it is an honest, unpretentious name which befitted the Yorkshire yeomen who bore it for hundreds of years. Edward White Benson came from a family which had no connection the Bensons of more southerly counties, from whom occasionally an eminent member emerged, though not one of them achieved the greatness that this descendant of 'the rude forefathers of the hamlet' did. For an Archbishop of Canterbury, in the nineteenth century, to have his roots, not in academe or a gentle birthright, but in folk scarcely higher then peasants, was unthinkable – until it happened; and when it did the Archbishop's antecedents were so blurred by the mists of time that acceptance or non-acceptance was never an issue. By the time ha had risen to such positions in Education and the Church there was no-one to question his fitness to hold them, despite his lowly beginnings. And the Archbishop himself with his stately presence, ardent spirit and commanding looks could easily have had forebears as patrician as his appearance suggested.

As far as can be discovered from registers the earliest known members of the Benson family were forest rangers, tenants of Fountain Abbey before the dissolution. As long ago as 1348 John Benson held a toft or homestead from the Abbey at Swinton-by-Masham. Another branch of the family had migrated to Ribblesdale and held the grange of Copman-Howe (later Capon Hall) between Settle and Malham. A Robert Benson held the lodge at Bridghouse in Nidderdale early in the fourteenth century, and another Robert, probably his son, held the grange a few miles further up Nidderdale, near Ramsgill.

The first Benson to emerge with flesh on his bones was Thomas, who, in 1480, was forester at the Branga (of Banger House), a forest lodge between Thornthwaite in the parish of Pateley Bridge and Dacre. He was succeeded by his son who acquired the freehold of the property at the suppression of the greater monasteries, which saw the end of the importance of Fountain

Abbey; and the possession of Banger House descended in the direct line until 1802, when William Benson died.

The next Benson to emerge from obscurity was Christopher, born in 1793, commonly known as 'Old' Christopher, an affectionate and patriarchal title given to him by the people of the dale. He married Bridget Clarke and settled in Pateley Bridge.

'Old' Christopher was the real founder of the Benson family fortunes; up till then they had lived the traditional Dalesman life on their own small estates. As a rule they married early, had large families and lived to a ripe old age. They were little different from their neighbours; it was a proud, enclosed, thoughtful and humerous community, having little or nothing to do with the outside world of towns, commerce and urban practices. Due to the number of endowed grammar schools in the Yorkshire dales the Bensons were decently educated.

How 'Old' Christopher augmented his modest patrimony is not clear, but he certainly prospered, and died owning a good deal of land round Pateley Bridge. Among a small number of properties he bought was the Crown Inn, the principal posting-house in the village, worth some £3,000 a few years after his death. He also established a business as a factor with merchants in York, the staple of his business being the dairy produce he raised on his own estate and also bought from neighbouring farmers. And so this mercantile enterprise marked the break-up of the old quiet and self-contained Dalesman life. The Bensons were now well-to-do landowners and merchants.

'Old' Christopher died in 1765 at the age of 52. One of his sons, Christopher, was a merchant in a substantial way of business in York. He died in 1802 and in his will assessed his property at about £12,000, in addition to an estate at Huntingdon, near York. As his wife had died before him his property was divided between his two daughters, Ann and Eleanor. Ann married William Sidgwick, a mill-owner, of Stonegappe and Skipton, and Eleanor married her first cousin, White Benson, son of one of Christopher's younger brothers.

White Benson was born at Ripon in 1771. He was called White because in the year of his birth his father inherited an estate left to him by Francis White, the Chapter Clerk of Ripon Cathedral, for no better reason than that they had often been partners in games of whist.

White Benson was the grandfather of the future Archbishop: William Sidgwick was the grandfather of Mary Sidgwick, later to become the Archbishop's wife;thus they were second cousins, and this fact was to have a bearing on the nature of the relationship between them.

White Benson was not an altogether satisfactory husband for Eleanor (who was a considerable heiress), with whom he had eloped at the age of

16. He had a brilliant mind and an attractive nature but Eleanor's father had not approved of the match and his doubts seem to have been well founded, for White wasted both his own and his wife's property. He attempted to sell her land at Pateley in order to pay his debts and his own father bought it in order to save further depreciation of the family property. White was a Lieutenant in the 6th Royals, Warwickshire, which was commanded by the Duke of Gloucester, and the young officer was able to boast of his friendship with his Colonel when he served with him in the Irish Rebellion of 1798. He was a fashionable officer, extravagant and addicted to gambling at high stakes, thus dissipating more of the family resources. He also lent money freely in order to buy popularity, and did not often see a return of the loans. He had a mild taste in literature, and in Huddersfield he published a volume of verse at his own expense. It was called *Poems and Ballads*, and they were principally indebted to Ossian and Miss Burney.

He left the army while still a young man with the rank of Captain and, after living in Ireland for some months, joined the family business in Pontefract. He died in 1806, after falling from a horse, leaving his widow and young son, Edward White, in strained circumstances.

Edward White Benson, born in 1800, had great natural gifts, but being a rather sickly boy was educated privately by Dr. Sollitt of York, who gave him a good grounding in scientific subjects. Dr. Sollitt was a great chemist, notable astrologer and framer of horoscopes. On one occasion he tried to practise a spell to raise the Evil One. He marked out a circle with mystic pentagrams, then said the Lord's Prayer backwards. Suddenly he heard his name called from outside the locked door and the sounds of bumping and crashing. He unlocked the door and in the next room he found the furniture splintered and broken and the crockery smashed. Panic-stricken, the doctor made a bonfire of his black books and gave up magic completely. So too did his pupil, and ever afterwards, Edward White Benson followed only the path of orthodoxy. His mother sold their house in York lived in various parts of the country, in the hope of finding health for the frail child.

Mrs White Benson married again, the Rev. Stephen Jackson, Vicar of Sheldon in Warwickshire, and by him had two daughters, Lucy and Mary Anne. Her wanderings with her son came to an end and they settled down to a more humdrum life. Edward kept up his scholarship, reading and writing voraciously, and was much involved with chemical experiments, spending many hours in his home-made laboratory. He was specially interested in the manufacture of colours, white lead and cobalt.

Although his father had been so shockingly extravagant, Edward possessed a modest competence, enough to enable him to carry on with his experiments without having to find further employment. Even so, it was a risky undertaking to get married, though Harriet Baker was ready to accept that risk, and they were married on August 28, 1826. The Baker family were staunch Unitarians and it was with some reluctance that Harriet joined the Church of England to be more acceptable as wife to a strongly Evangelical husband.

Edward and Harriet moved to Birmingham and took a house in Lombard Street, then in a pleasant suburb with an abundance of trees and gardens. Later in the century it lost its rural aspect when factories were built all around.

Edward tired to supplement his income as a chemical manufacturer and as a writer, but he was not very prolific. He published two books: *Education at Home* in 1824, and *Essays on the Works of God* in 1827, and he also contributed to scientific journals, Dr. Ure's *Dictionary of Chemistry* and the *Penny Cyclopaedia*.

Edward's chief discoveries were the nitric acid dipping bath for electrotyping purposes; a method of producing soda carbonate; the production of white lead and cobalt; and improvements in photography; and he was known, probably not accurately, as the first man in England to make Lucifer matches.

Whatever talents Edward had in scientific accomplishments he lacked in business affairs. Other people made fortunes out of some of his inventions, but somehow they slipped through his fingers and he was content to potter about in his not entirely professional way. he produced eight children between 1829 and his death in 1843, the eldest of whom would be a future Archbishop of Canterbury.

CHAPTER ONE

EDWARD White Benson, son of Edward White Benson the unsuccessful chemist, was born on July 14, 1829, at No. 72, Lombard Street, Birmingham. When young he was called White rather than Edward to distinguish him from his father. Harriet was the next to be born, in 1831, but she died at the age of nineteen. Eleanor arrived in 1833, Christopher in 1835, Emmeline in 1837, Ada in 1840, Charles and William, twins, in 1842. William died as a baby.

White Benson himself in his turn fathered six children. His sister Eleanor married Thomas Hare, an Assistant Charity Commissioner and author of a book advocating a change in parliamentary representation. Christopher, paralysed as a child, was never able to walk and for most of his life lived at Wiesbaden in Germany where he took pupils and married the daughter of Professor Walker of Oxford. Emmeline married the Rev. George Girdlestone Woodhouse and bore him eight children. Ada was the clever one. She became Headmistress of High Schools in Oxford, Norwich and Bedford, married Andrew MacDowall and had two children. Charles, the surviving twin, was the odd man out of the family. He was slight and delicate and had few manly qualities. Though he was very sociable, a great reader of fiction and lover of plays, there were no academic achievements for him; for many years he was the manager of the Oakley Slate Quarries at Portmadoc in North Wales, dying at the age of 51. A dandy, with his bowler hat, cameo tie-ring and smart suit, his walk was tittupping and his laugh was shrill.

The young White was baptised when he was eight months old, privately in St. Martin's Church, Birmingham. Three other children were baptised at the same time, with only their parents and sponsors present. No other member of the family was invited to the ceremony because White's father considered that public christenings were scandalous. At St. Martin's Church they were held every Sunday, and babies and children up to the age of ten were arranged round the Communion rail and sprinkled from the font with a watering-can; an irreligious act, the high-minded chemist considered.

One of young White's earliest recollections was intensely frightening. One evening he was looking out of his nursery window in Lombard Street which faced the laboratory at the end of the garden when there was a muffled explosion and all the glass in the laboratory windows cracked and flew out and a great burst of white smoke enveloped the building. The noise brought his mother rushing out of the house and down the garden path and a minute later the terrified boy saw her and the laboratory assistant supporting his father, his face covered with blood, back to the house. Some detonating powder had exploded and wrecked the room. His father was in shock for a long time but as he had instinctively put up his hands to his face just in time he saved his eyesight. What made the impression on White's mind so permanent was the fact that a short time before he had himself been in the laboratory watching his father conducting the experiment.

The elder Edward's business remained in a rocky state for some time, so to augment his income he accepted the post of manager at an extensive and prosperous alkali works at Stoke, near Droitwich; a new factory which was said to have the tallest chimney in England. This meant that the family had to leave Birmingham. They moved to Wychbold, a small village near Droitwich, and bought a low-timbered house called Ivy Cottage. The house was overshadowed by tall trees and had a large garden, at the bottom of which was a stable, inevitably turned into a laboratory.

Wychbold was only a couple of miles from the alkali factory and Edward gladly walked there and back every day, savouring the country air and the peacefulness of his surroundings. When the family began to increase they moved from Ivy Cottage to nearby Brook House, a simple grange of red brick, consisting of a parlour, dining-room, a bookroom (which soon became a laboratory) and a few bedrooms. There was a pleasant garden and a brook which ran across the fields at the bottom.

Young White remembered vividly the church at Upton, near Wychbold, partly because its shape was so unusual, and partly because of the extraordinary behaviour of the clerk, who was the village shoemaker. The church had no aisles and the middle passage led to the chancel in which there was a 15-feet high three-decker pulpit. The pews on either side of the passage were either long or square; the Bensons had a square one. The musicians sat in the gallery and played the clarinet, flute, violin and cello. The clerk was dressed all in black, except for a white tie, a wig and horn-rimmed spectacles which gave him an owlish look. He would announce a hymn or a psalm, the fiddle played the tune once, then all the musicians struck up. But only the clerk sang the words, in a strong braying voice, oblivious of time or tune. No other member of the small congregation joined in – the farmers grinned behind their hands, Edward White Benson stood motionless and grim-faced. His family longed to giggle but did not dare to move a muscle; their father, though pious and unworldly, was a forceful character, and the behaviour of his children was for him a pointer to his strong Evangelical beliefs. He was a total abstainer from strong drink; in all his many illnesses he absolutely refused all alcoholic stimulants. Only once, when he was in a state of semi-consciousness, did a doctor pour brandy down his throat.

He always dressed smartly. Everything had to be of the right shape, colour and size; if there had been male models in those days he would have portrayed a country business gentleman perfectly. His dress suit was black, so was his stock, but a white-frilled front showed over his waistcoat, and a bunch of seals dangled from his fob. His pantaloons were black, but his stockings white. He wore pumps in the house and high boots out of doors. His ensemble was completed by a beaver hat and black gloves. White became infected with his father's dandyism and when he grew up was always careful about the cleanliness, cut and appearance of his clothes; so much so that he often irritated his own children with his finicky ways. He would 'tut-tut' at untidiness and brush a reproving hand across a dusty collar – unnecessary gestures when the children were in the middle of a game.

The young White was, as his father had been, a rather delicate child, thin and pasty-looking, but when he had spent a long holiday with his cousin, the Rev. William Sidgwick, who was curate at Rampside, near Barrow-in-Furness, followed by others with Sidgwick cousins in Yorkshire, he returned home so brown and well that his parents announced that it was silly to call him White and Edward was substituted. But it was a temporary measure, and it was not until he went to Rugby as a Master that he was finally called Edward.

White was not a conventionally good child; he could be disobedient, but there was nothing mean or malicious in his naughtiness, and it was easy to forgive the little boy with his pleading blue eyes.

His great-aunt, Mrs William Sidgwick, daughter of Christopher Benson of York, was rather a *grande-dame* who inspired a respect mixed with fear rather than love. She lived at Skipton, in the Castle, and White spent some happy holidays there, doted on by her middle-aged bachelor sons, Christopher and James. William Sidgwick, White's cousin, left Rampside to become Headmaster of Skipton Grammar School. His elder brother, John Benson Sidgwick, senior partner in the High Mills, lived in a lonely house on the moors at Stonegappe. He married Sarah Greenwood and they had seven children. John Sidgwick's claim to fame rests on the fact that Charlotte Brontë acted as governess to his children for a few months in 1839. According to her own account she was treated very unkindly, but it is well-known that the Sidgwicks were a very benevolent couple, and they would not knowingly have caused pain to anyone. Certainly one of the children in later life recorded that he threw a Bible at Miss Brontë, but he could not have been more than four years old at the time. The truth is that Charlotte did not like children, had no imagination or skill in managing them, and in her morbid condition took everything as a slight. If she was asked to walk to church with the family she thought she was being ordered about like a slave; if she was not invited she was being excluded from the family circle and she sulked. A family of angels would not have found favour with Charlotte Brontë at that period. There is no record that White Benson ever met Charlotte Brontë. He did visit Stonegappe when he was about five, but that was some years before Charlotte's arrival. He stayed there for some time and, dressed in frocks and pinafores by the children's nurse, did lessons with the children in their schoolroom; learning verses from the Bible and listening reverently to John Benson Sidgwick as he discoursed on religious matters.

There were days at the seaside and games in the hayfield. On one of his later visits there occurred an incident that shocked him deeply and was the cause of his hatred of shooting. While out with a shooting party he heard the heart-rending cry of a hare, wounded but not killed, and he was immediately sick. His sensitive nature hated cruelty of any sort, and he vowed he would never take up a gun for sport. He kept that vow until he was an old man, never allowing his children to read books about hunting or shooting. Eventually his rigid views were relaxed, even to the extent of making over the shooting at Addington Park to Arthur.

White began his first serious lessons when he was about seven. His father had his own idiosyncratic ideas about education and how children should be schooled. In order to train his son to regard time seriously and develop a responsible attitude to work he did not draw up a timetable of lessons, but left it to the boy's own commonsense to prepare his work himself, so that he could repeat it to his father at breakfast the following day. If things had not gone well and White could not decline his Latin grammar properly, Edward would declare that a father was the worst kind of teacher for a child and threaten to send him away to school. But the next morning he had forgotten the threat and the regular process was repeated. After the breakfast catechism White would often accompany his father to the works, and there he would be free to ramble about and talk to the workmen, asking them questions about their work and their families, and listening intelligently to what they had to say. He never lost his love of conversation with simple people, even though in later life his patience as a listener often wore thin, especially when talking to prosy clerics.

After these visits White would return home alone for an early dinner, then for the rest of the day he could do his lessons where and when he liked. He would usually shut himself up in the book-room and try to work, but he was easily distracted, principally by the great number and variety of books that filled the shelves, and also by his childish need to chatter to anyone who would listen. One of his allies was his Aunt Mary Anne, who often stayed with the Bensons and was always ready to listen to his readings from Shakespeare or the poets.

One winter afternoon White, then about ten years old, was found by his mother perched on top of the library steps reading *A Midsummer Night's Dream*. She advised him to get on with his studies, but the boy, fascinated by the story, turned page after page, until he came to an engraving of Bottom wearing the ass's head. The picture struck him dumb with terror. He could only see a real monster, not a character in a play, and he gazed at it with shuddering horror. What if he met it in the lane outside the house when it was dark... Eventually he gained the courage to close the book and return it to its place; but for weeks the picture haunted him and gave him terrible nightmares. It was not for years that he dared to open that copy of Shakespeare again.

White Benson's two besetting sins at that early stage of his development were idleness and lying, and in spite of the many beatings he received they continued to worry his parents. His lies were in fact expressions of his vivid imagination. They were not told in order to escape trouble. He was a very talkative child and would prattle away to strangers and tell them the most outrageous stories. His sister Harriet, to whom he was devoted and who was a much more reserved child, was renowned for never telling a lie, and in later years White wished fervently that his own character had been as blameless.

It was about this time that White's father, mindful of his growing family and still inadequate income, decided to capitalise on some of his chemical experiments, and in 1838 obtained a patent for the manufacture of cobalt and persuaded a group of friends to enter into partnership with him. They founded the British White-Lead Company and built a large factory on Birmingham Heath. Edward Benson's health, never robust, began to decline, but for a time he was able to walk daily from his house in Winson Green to the works. When the walk grew too exhausting the family moved first to Spring Hill in Birmingham and then into a small house in the factory grounds which had been built for a manager; and here White spent his life until he left King Edward's School in Birmingham, where he had been a scholar since the age of 11. His surroundings were not as grim as they might have been. The factory was in the country with plenty of open space around, and there was a canal nearby on whose banks grew a profusion of wild flowers.

The initial success of the white-lead business did not last. More capital was needed but not forthcoming, and in 1842 the company failed. The worry of it exacerbated Edward White's ill-health and within a year he had died from an internal cancer after a great deal of suffering.

Apart from natural grief there was panic in the family. Harriet Benson had a large family to bring up, feed and educate, and no money to do it on. All her income had ceased with her husband's death, and thoughts of a penniless future became unbearable. The situation was relieved somewhat when Edward's partners put a proposal to her. Her immediate difficulties would be solved and she was grateful to them, but she did not realise that eventually things would work out to her disadvantage.

They offered her the house free for her use during her lifetime and would grant her a small annuity in lieu of Edward's income as a partner. This would end when she died. Harriet was naïve in business matters, and the partners did not mean to cheat her, but for her the arrangement could not have been a worse one. Being healthy she presumed that her death was many years off, and she hoped that she could save a little money in the years to come. Although the works were closed she had the house and the children had the run of the disused buildings. The family's standard of living went down drastically, though there was no actual hardship and there was hope for the future.

White Benson was 14 years old when the change in the family fortunes came about. During his early teens he had become more and more religious-minded, delighting in ritual and the aesthetics of religious observance rather than in the spiritual aspects. He had developed into a serious, rather priggish boy, always conscious of his status as the eldest member of the family. He gathered around him a number of like-minded friends and together they would say the Canonical Hours every day in a little room, formerly an office, in the now-deserted factory, that he had established as an oratory. It contained a table, draped in a cloth, and stools for kneeling, brass rubbings from nearby churches hung from the walls and on the table stood a wooden cross, made by an old carpenter. It was typical of the boy's critical faculties that he complained to the workman that he had rounded off the ends of the cross instead of leaving them square.

The story of the oratory is redeemed by White's human response to the surreptitious visits made by his sisters when he was at school. He was furious – it was *his* chapel and only he and those he chose could worship there, in preparation for his future as a clergyman, so one day he perched a booby trap on top of the slightly opened door and a pile of books descended on Emmeline's head.

White Benson was, of course, a day boy at King Edward's School, the Headmaster being James Prince Lee, once a Master at Rugby under

Arnold and later Bishop of Manchester. He had been happy during his first year there, having a kind and just teacher, the Rev. George Moyle, who later became the Headmaster of Chudleigh School. The strict discipline that Moyle enforced did not worry White; it even increased his popularity. White used to say that, apart from Prince Lee, he owed more to Moyle than to any other teacher at the school because he had to work so hard. But in his second year he came up against a cold, unfeeling teacher who made him wretched and caused his rebellious spirit to flare up. It was at this critical period of his life that his father died, leaving him bereft of affection and wise counsel; and for a time he was plunged into deep unhappiness.

It was fortunate that the friends he made at school helped him back to self-respect and stability. One of the most intimate was Joseph Barker Lightfoot, an accountant's son and a future Bishop of Durham. He was a year older than White. The two boys lived near each other and met on the way to school.

Whoever arrived first at the meeting-place would put a stone in a hole in a wall if he had no time to wait for the other, as a signal that he had been there so that the other did not wait in vain. On half holidays the boys took long walks together, exploring the neighbourhood and discussing with the solemnity of youth their readings in theology and planning their futures in the service of religion. White at this time was an odd mixture of youth and age. He could laugh and run, make jokes and behave as a teenage boy, and then almost in the next breath put on the airs of a grown up and lay down the law about theological matters that he barely understood but attacked or defended with stubborn persistence. This aspect of his character was fostered by the atmosphere and conventions of the school. Religion, the classics, obedience, discipline and morality were the requirements of King Edward's and most other schools of the time. What was frowned on was independence of thought and speech, the questioning of conventional ideas or rebellion against authority, however unjustly it acted.

Another friend from King Edward days was Brooke Foss Westcott, also older than White, and also to become Bishop of Durham after Lightfoot's death in 1889. As a senior boy in the First Class he was allowed to lean his head on his hand when the class was gathered round Prince Lee's desk, and White was duly awestruck. Frederic Wickenden, afterwards a Prebendary at Lincoln, was also regarded by White with great affection. He was a delicate boy, son of a surgeon, devoted to art and antiquities. Neat and precisely dressed, he was full of laughter and interested in games.

In 1842 White Benson appeared in print for the first time in a way that did not do him much credit, however innocent his intentions. He and a friend named Henry Palmer, admiring some questions on the Gospel of St. Matthew that one of the Masters gave as a weekly exercise, copied them down, and eventually had them printed in a small booklet which they intended to be sold 'for the use of schools' – a typically grandiose schoolboyish idea, the only objection to it being that the questions were not theirs to publish in the first place. The project cost them four pounds. It was not long before authority interfered and the distribution of the booklet was stopped. Somehow the chastened pair managed to find the money to pay the printers, and the scheme came to a sorry end, but not before there was an exchange of acrimonious letters between the 'editors', in which the words 'rogue' and 'fool' were bandied. Fortunately the friendship between the boys survived the hiccup of plagiarism.

White's mother gave him a member's ticket for the Free Library at Birmingham and he became a frequent visitor, reading avidly as he walked home after school. On one occasion he discovered Newman's No. 90 of *Tracts for the Times*, and was intrigued to learn something that his mother's strong protestantism would not approve of. When she had examined what he was reading she said quietly, 'I don't care for the book, nor for the people who write such things, but I don't want to stop you reading what you choose. Only you ought to think – would your father have approved of it?'

With a flash of stubbornness he retorted, 'Yes, mother, I have thought of that and I think he would wish me to be acquainted with what is going on in the Church.'

His mother capitulated without a struggle. 'Very well, White, then I haven't another word to say,' and White continued to make his choices from the library unhindered.

When he was in his 16th year an incident occurred which nearly changed the course of his life. A friend of his father's, a partner in a commercial house in Birmingham, knowing that Mrs Benson's means were becoming more straitened the older her children grew, wrote to her and offered to take White into his business, with the prospect of an eventual partnership, and adding an enticing sentence – 'It is as good as making his fortune.'

Mrs Benson's first reaction was to agree to allow White to take up the offer and leave school immediately. All their problems would be solved, she thought. But she was not a hasty woman and before presenting White with a *fait accompli* she consulted her husband's half-brother, William Jackson, who had become a Fellow of Worcester College and Bampton Lecturer. He in turn wrote to Prince Lee and asked for his advice, and the Headmaster strongly advised against the proposed course of action. He was confident, he said, that White would never make a man of business but would do far better if he stayed at school and went on to university. His glowing tributes to White's scholarly abilities helped Mrs Benson to decide to turn down her friend's offer. The financial sacrifice this would cause was alleviated by the promise of William Jackson and John Benson Sidgwick to pay White's expenses at school, and to see that, when the time came, he would be given a good start at university and lack for nothing.

So White continued to shine at school and fulfil the promises his teachers made for him. He read the whole of Livy, Herodotus and Thucydides, and made copious notes on every page of the textbooks in copybook handwriting. His quick and retentive memory enabled him to read poetry and prose in Greek, Latin and English; he could recite most of the psalter by heart and a large part of it in the Latin version. On half holidays he would walk with a few intimate friends from Birmingham to Coventry to examine its churches and old buildings which he sketched with a sure touch, and having previously read up the history of the places they visited made an admirable guide.

At school he laid the foundations of his remarkable knowledge of liturgy and church ritual, and gained a love of ceremonial order and dignity. Once asked what he would like to be he said, 'I should like to be a Canon and recite the daily offices in my Cathedral.'

Through the accounts written in later life by the friends he had made at school, White Benson seems to have something of a saint. Modest and courteous, considerate of others, with a high standard of thought and conduct, he had a winning smile and sympathetic manner. There was a feeling among his friends that when he was around there was something higher, purer and more spiritual in their midst which influenced them to lead a better life. He was the personification of 'whatsoever things are pure, whatsoever things are lovely...' An irreverent schoolfellow once said to him, 'And how is the Benson Etheriality?' which only provoked a brave, forgiving smile.

To be fair to White Benson these memories of a saintly schoolboy written to his son Arthur after the Archbishop's death in 1896 could well have been clouded by the distance in time and the imperfect recollections of elderly churchmen. Even so, they are likely to have been basically truthful. White was most of the things his early friends declared, but it is a pity they missed out his stubbornness and refusal to entertain views other than his own; and his scorn for those who lacked his own high standards. R.M. Moorsom, one of his schoolfellows, admitted that White Benson fell a little short of the ideal by his lack of enthusiasm for games. He did not play cricket, football, hockey, racquets or fives; not even rounders, although he had the courage and determination to do have done well if he had joined in. Then it gradually dawned on his friends that, as his father had died and he was head of the family, he had made early preparations to work to support his mother, sisters and crippled brother; and enjoyment of games had to be put aside for the rigours of hard work. Even at that early age he had chosen duty rather than enjoyment. So eventually his friends recognised his nobility and respected him all the more.

For his Headmaster, James Prince Lee, he had an almost romantic attachment, and talked about him continuously. Lee was a profoundly stimulating teacher who exercised a fascination on each of his pupils as he formed their literary tastes and religious feelings. 'To "do" is important,' Lee would say, 'but to "know" is equally imperative.' Besides being a classical scholar he was widely read in contemporary writers such as Scott and Wordsworth. He had been a Craven Scholar and Fellow of Trinity. His teaching methods were old-fashioned: he insisted on very close analysis of words and the defining of nuances, and failed to acknowledge that the best writers use words instinctively rather than deliberately; and although his pupils enjoyed the intellectual exercise, Lee's methods tended to turn out stylists, observant and compressed, but without the simplicity and lucidity of Virgil or Homer. On White Benson the result was not altogether fortunate. His style became uneasy, crabbed and over-elaborate, full of fanciful words and strained meanings. He was simple and telling in extempore speaking but in written work, because of compression and excision, the effect was stilted and clumsy.

Lee suffered from ill-health, particularly neuralgia and inflamed eyes, and he was a laudanum addict. He was in constant pain when he taught, but his efforts only increased the boys' devotion. He did much to enliven their intellectual tastes and gave them leisure time to pursue their own interests, but he could not bear contradiction or correction and was unfitted to deal with the expression of independent thought. His severity to wrong-doers lacked understanding or compassion, and his furies were as passionate as his religious convictions. Still, as White Benson, after his unhappy start at the school, never transgressed again, he did not come into conflict with his revered Headmaster.

In 1847 Lee became the first Bishop of Manchester, an unhappy appointment as it turned out, but it had been pressed on him by the strong wish of the Prince Consort, and he held it until his death. The task of collecting subscriptions towards a testimonial was undertaken by White, who spent several hours concocting a circular that, when printed, was to be given to all 500 boys in the school.

'O happy Lightfoot,' White wrote to his friend at Cambridge on Lee's departure, 'happy all that enjoyed his latest teaching and miserable me, that shall come back next half-year and see another in his place.' That place was taken by the Rev. E.H. Gifford, afterwards Archdeacon of London, another man of great scholarship which he had the knack of sharing with his pupils and which earned him their respect.

Joseph Lightfoot was by now at Trinity College, Cambridge. He was a good-natured, though rather silent man. With his big mouth and slight squint, which a monocle did nothing to hide, his appearance was somewhat grotesque. His laughter was rich and gutteral and ended with an explosive cry. The two friends corresponded fervently and at inordinate length on the many fascinating arguments that were sweeping through religious and educational circles. Among them were the 'mistaken and dangerous opinions' of Dr. Arnold of Rugby, the dichotomy of the Roman Church being the true church in Italy but in error in England; the meanness of humanism, the poverty of the doctrines of Socrates, and the dark and anarchical mind of Aeschylus when he wrote, 'Once dead, there is no resurrection.'

In one letter White grew enthusiastic about the formation of a small Society for Holy Living, the founder members being Lightfoot and himself. Others, carefully vetted, would be welcome. It was to be a secret society, but with no new tenets – no seeking for new truths. Particularly they would renounce the vain pomp and glory of the world. 'Have we ever attempted this?' White asked plaintively. Another noble objective of the Society was to preach the Gospel to the poor, so that God need not say, 'My people perish for lack of knowledge.' They would also seek to alleviate the conditions of the poor and those upon whom the shadow of death darkly and coldly rested in Christian England. Their highest aim, however, would be to promote the spiritual unity of the Church. But all those noble objectives were not to be striven for for their own sake – all was to be done for Christ's sake, to the glory of God. And there, White declared passionately, was the difference between morality and religion. 'If we do any work for its own sake, instead of God's, that work is none of His, and He will not prosper it, for He will not have man presume to do His work by other than His means.' White's beliefs at this time were a strange mixture of arrogance and humility. The Society evidently did not get off the ground, for no more was heard about it.

White met his new Headmaster in Birmingham while helping his old one to pack his books preparatory to moving to Manchester, and cautiously approved of him. 'He is certainly a very young man indeed,' he wrote to Lightfoot early in 1848, 'and rather bashful in his manner. He was exceedingly liked at Shrewsbury and particularly for his justice. This is very promising for us who require so firm a hand.' But Mr Gifford fell horribly in the estimation of both White and the new Bishop when, over lunch, they were discussing the Consecration Sermon which had caused a disturbance in Birmingham. Unluckily he said he that believed instances might be found in the Greek Testament of the present passive used for the perfect, so that they should not take all for Gospel clearly. There was a silence and countenances fell, but the Bishop saved the lunch from utter ruin by the Greek quotations that streamed from him like light from the sun, and the new Headmaster was put in his proper place.

Between White Benson and Joseph Lightfoot there was a great difference of opinion which spilled over in their letters concerning the respective merits of Tractarianism and Evangelicalism; sometimes one, sometimes the other, attracted them at different times, and both were caught up in confusion and doubt as to where it was leading them. White spoke of Evangelicalism in harsh terms, and Lightfoot thought him uncharitable; then Lightfoot modified his opinions and spoke gratefully of the writers of the Oxford Tracts and their efforts against the absurdities of the Evangelical system, particularly the exaltation of preaching to the detriment of prayer. This declaration alarmed White and he threatened that if Lightfoot turned Tractarian again they would not stand much chance of working together in the future, even though he did not believe they were ever intended to be separate. White acknowledged that his own ideas were vague and indefinite, especially after having heard Newman speak. 'He is a wonderful man,' he wrote, 'and spoke with a sort of Angel eloquence. Sweet, flowing, unlaboured language in short, pithy and touching sentences.' Newman's style of preaching reminded White of Arnold, and his emaciated appearance and feeble voice were impressive. His sermon on the parable of the sower was spell-binding, and White's heart yearned towards the old man – until he linked the name of the Lord Jesus Christ with the Holy Mother of God, and joined together 'Jesu!' and 'Maria!' White tried to be fair and accept that Newman was only labouring in another part of the Lord's Vineyard, but found it impossible to believe that he had not committed the sin of those who have left their first love. White was further saddened during the Loretto Litany, when Newman's chanting was careless; and his overall opinion of the preacher was that he was a flawed saint to whom it would be impossible to give complete allegiance.

In his reply to that letter Lightfoot was unusually censorious. Even though his own feelings were moving away from Protestant dissent towards the High Church and the faith held by the confessors and martyrs of old, he expressed his disapproval of White's visit to St. Chad's to hear Newman; to take part in an act of worship which was schismatical and heretical at the same time, with the excuse that there was no other place of worship nearby.

White Benson left King Edward's School for good in the summer of 1848, and the friends' long, argumentative but loving letters came to a temporary end. He took a holiday tutorship with a family named Wicksted, tenants of Abergeldie Castle in Ballater, Aberdeenshire. His letters during this period were chiefly to his mother and sister Harriet, describing his surroundings, the weather, his experiences while fishing for salmon, and the services at the kirk. Naturally he disapproved of the latter. 'Dearest English church, how much do thy services surpass even this reformed Kirk of Scotland – to say nothing of the inferiority of the building!' There was no Communion table, no font, nothing holy or Christian-looking. The place was arranged just like a theatre, the gallery and pulpit in a half octagon, and 'the floor is covered all over with pews'. There were no Psalms, no Lessons, no Gloria, not even the Lord's Prayer, and the Minister wore a gown rather than a surplice. White did grant, however, that the Minister was well-loved and esteemed, and the full congregation, many of them having walked seven or eight miles to attend, spoke volumes for the good he had done. To his sister he made a request for a pair of white kid gloves – by return of post – as the Highland Ball was to be held next week.

In the same letter he chided Harriet for not telling him of the tide of feeling or the vows of holiness she must have experienced during her Confirmation and First Communion – not, of course, that he wanted her to expose 'the thoughts that lie too deep' for words. She had apparently enthused in her letter on all the external details of the service, even down to Mr Latimer's cap and Miss Chavasse's ticket, but the spiritual details were painfully missing.

He attended the Highland Games which preceeded the Highland Ball, the men of the party travelling to Invercauld on Highland ponies, the ladies in a carriage. The Queen and Prince Albert were present at the proceedings, together with the Princess Royal and the two Princes; and before the games started they were presented with bouquets. Highland soldiers were everywhere, with spiked shields, swords and Lochaber axes.

White described the young Prince of Wales as a 'fair little lad, rather of slender make, with a good head and a remarkably quiet and thinking face, above his years in intelligence, I should think'.

The Queen was the most plainly dressed woman there, according to White; Prince Albert was 'horribly padded and belted', and the Princess Royal was a plain child with a will and temper of her own. White justified his long gossipy letter about the royals, how they were dressed and whom they chatted to, only because he thought his mother would be interested. He did not wish to be thought of as a 'vulgar observer of great folk'.

After the excitement of the Highland Gathering and the Ball there was little else of import to record, and soon it was time for Cambridge.

CHAPTER TWO

WHITE Benson was elected to a Subsizarship at Trinity College in 1848. Before he took up residence there he paid his first visit to London, staying with the Lightfoots in Vauxhall. He had vowed that, in his anxiety to get to Cambridge, he would not stay in the capital a moment longer than necessary; in the event, however, he stayed two extra days, almost dumb with admiration of the wonderful things he saw. Two which impressed him by their size were the colossal head of Rameses II in the British Museum (which he mistakenly called the Memnon Head) and the Victoria Tower. He considered the Thames wondrous and mysterious yet practical and business-like (though he thought the Mersey was finer). The Tower of London, St. Paul's, Somerset House, Westminster Abbey, the great warehouses of the South Bank – all filled him with astonishment. 'Surely,' he wrote in a diary which he discarded after two pages of entries, 'England cannot be in decline as so many of those whom I know tell me, when her metropolis is full of such true, such liberal, such refined feeling: witness the crowds with which the British Museum was filled admiring, the mighty company that yesterday knelt in Westminster worshipping. Doubtless there is high and holy work for heads and hearts and hands in the generation to come. If I work not in it, with it, for it, heavy and deserved will be my condemnation.'

His first rooms in College were attic rooms at the top of the staircase on the north side of the Gate leading from the New Court to the Bridge and Avenue. He had to live on very slender resources, even though his Subsizarship was supplemented by one or two small Exhibitions from Birmingham. His mother helped him as best she could, but the other children were growing up and their education also had to be thought of. She was reluctant to ask any of her better-off relations for help, having a Victorian lady's dislike of mentioning money matters, so was prepared to undergo real privation. She cut down on staff and did the household chores herself, helped by her two oldest daughters. Luxuries were out of the question, and even necessities often dismissed as inessentials. At one time she thought she might restart her husband's business with one of his patents for the production of colours, but when White heard of the plan he came down on it firmly. It was a most distasteful project, he stormed. If his family was 'in trade' his sisters' marriage prospects would be ruined and his own career in the Church would be more difficult to achieve. 'I trust that the scheme may be abandoned once and for all,' he ordered, and his mother gave in to his vehement disapproval. Poverty and loss had not made White at all humble, but rather forceful and intransigent.

White was not being unreasonable, according to the climate of the time. Society was rigidly stratified: aristocracy was either high-minded or dissolute; the landed gentry was deeply committed to religion, Evangelical, Tractarian or Modernist; trade was not nearly so involved, though paying respectful lip service to religious observance; and the mass of people, the poor and the destitute, did not matter. Social conscience was not a strong force. Emphasis was placed on salvation, the road to Heaven, the reward in the next world for the faith that in this world withstood hardship and misery. So White was content to remain in the stratum that God had been pleased to put him, not willing to have the family name demeaned by a mother running a business, even though he did not mind her scrubbing and polishing and scrimping over food in order to keep the family going. His own efforts to economise were entirely admirable. In spite of living amidst a large circle of more or less wealthy friends, he was adamant in his refusal to extend to them the hospitality he would have wished in return for that which he received. It could have been an unbearably miserable time but his strength of character gave him joy in the knowledge that he was doing the right thing. His first year at Cambridge cost him a little over £90.

He read hard, both mathematics and Classics, slept as little as possible and gave up all recreations except bathing. During breaks in study he walked about the neighbourhood exploring churches. The only indulgence he allowed himself was a Sunday breakfast with Lightfoot at which they ate veal and ham pie. After breakfast it was back to religion and the reading of passages from the Fathers. Cyprian's *De Unitate* made a great impression on White and led to a lifelong obsession with the Saint. White's mathematical coach was a profound Evangelical, a fact which did not make White regard him charitably in the first place, and his decidedly eccentric ways of teaching made him an absurd figure. He was always in bed when his pupils arrived, and when finally he was roused he dressed slowly, singing hymns as he did so and occasionally he poked his head round the bedroom door to give the bored young men another problem to solve while they were waiting. White afterwards said that as a result of such coaching he went into the Trigonometry paper of the Mathematical Tripos so little prepared that he did not even know the meaning of *pi*. At the time of the Tripos he was suffering from one of his frequent colds and was allowed to do the paper lying on a sofa in the Senate House.

White was happier with the geology lectures of Professor Sidgwick, his second cousin, who tried to impress him with the belief that his real bent was for geology rather than theology. But White was not to be deflected from his determination to become a clergyman.

His chief friends at Trinity were still those he had made at school: Lightfoot, Westcott, Hutchinson, Ellis and Wickenden. Then there were Henry Bradshaw, Arthur Duke Coleridge, Arthur Gordon and Prince Frederic of Schleswig-Holstein Nöer, a fellow Commoner of Trinity. Nearly 20 years later White remembered the Prince when he was choosing names for his third son, and he was christened Edward Frederic. By then Prince Frederic had abandoned politics, dropped his princely style and was living quietly in exile. Other friends included James Atlay, later Bishop of Hereford, Professor Sidgwick, W.C. Mathison and Francis Martin, Bursar and afterwards Vice-Master of Trinity. He wrote home frequently; his mother was regaled with the details of his daily activities, the furniture of his room, his eating habits and the success of his efforts to economise. To his sister Harriet, however, he was stern and fatherlike. Once she wrote to him about the structure and arrangements of a cathedral she intended to visit. He replied on Christmas night, 1848, and not only did he send her elaborate notes and diagrams of the building, but could not resist continuing his letter with strong warnings against the influence of her Unitarian uncles. They would not, he admitted, deliberately seek to proselytise her, but inadvertently she might be within hearing distance of some expression discordant with the feelings she was accustomed to regard 'our God incarnate'. She was to pray fervently that any false doctrine she accidentally heard did not sink into her mind, that no heretical seed be lodged there, to lie for a time and then ripen. In February, 1849, a letter from Harriet made him positively incoherent. She was staying with one of her uncles in Bolton and told White she had been teaching in a Unitarian Sunday School. 'It made me jump to hear,' he wrote. 'Can you at all content yourself with saying merely, "Jesus Christ" without some expression of love in worship in word or deed. Hold fast what thou hast that no man take thy Crown. Do! Do! Do! Be up and doing – and is the feeling of love of God – so that you would be even a doorkeeper in His house rather than be prosperous in sin – is this a constant feeling?'

When Harriet had solved this syntactical mystery she had to put up with one more little bit of advice. 'Take care of your stops and capital letters...' When White was not preaching he was teaching.

In April, 1849, he was elected to a full Sizarship and not long after that he moved upwards again to become a scholar of Trinity. He managed to get some tutoring work and therefore was able to give more financial help to his mother. But now she, who usually obeyed him in all important matters, took a decision without consulting him. She invested much of what small capital she had in a railway company – in the year when George Hudson, the Railway King, crashed, frightening shareholders and causing flotations to collapse. So her investment left her much poorer than when she had so blithely made it.

White's 16-year-old sister Eleanor wrote to congratulate him on his upward move and wrote, 'What a fine, clever fellow you are, you will soon be Archbishop of Canterbury, and would deserve to be, should you not?' One feels that White would not have disagreed with her. Now that his circumstances had improved he was able to tell his mother that the self-denial he was practising was less painful.

Another letter to his mother in October of the same year was a light-hearted account of his first meeting with the little girl who, years later, was to become his wife. 'Tell Charlie [his eight-year-old brother] that a sweet little girl, our Cousin Minnie, made me quite ashamed of a … little boy, our brother … for Minnie is only a month or two older than that little boy, and she reads a great deal and learnt a lay of Macaulay's for pleasure, and knows both Bible history and English history well, to say nothing of geography, and writing and drawing – Oh! Charlie. Moreover she passed a good examination with me in Latin grammar, to the end of the pronouns.' Poor Minnie was actually a very attractive little girl and not a dreadful swot, but at that time White was only interested in her scholastic attainments and not in her personality. She was 'sweet' because she knew so much, not because she was affectionate and cheerful.

Apart from the death of his father White Benson had not suffered any major domestic catastrophe, but one was to occur at the end of May in 1850, a couple of months before his 21st birthday. The house in the lead works was in a most insanitary condition, as many houses were in those days, and nobody took much notice of smells, foul-tasting water, headaches and upset stomachs; they were an accepted part of living and Mrs Benson was no more aware of that danger than any other housewife. It was not until all the children went down with fever that she became alarmed. Harriet was the most affected and the doctor diagnosed typhus when he saw the eruption of spots on her abdomen, and noted her depressed vitality and bouts of delirium. Mrs Benson wrote to White telling him the children were unwell, but she minimised the seriousness of their illness, not wanting to interrupt his studies and alarm him unduly; but when Harriet failed to make any progress she wrote again, and her anxious words grieved him.

'Do you think,' he said in reply, 'that instead of my coming down to you, you yourself should come up here for a week and bring one of those who is under ten years old – (that would be half fare on the railway). This place is so beautiful and fresh now, that I think it would restore the health of the most confirmed invalids.' He went on. 'Prayers for your restoration in my heart mingled with prayers that He will not suffer me so to abuse the health and happiness and prosperity that He gives me here (for in these, my dear Mother, I know that you rejoice), that it might be necessary for Him to visit my offences with the rod, and my scourges hereafter.' It seems that White's concern for his own health, physical and moral, took a somewhat higher place than that of his family. He even ended his letter with a kind of joke. 'And now, as I should have said formerly if I had been an old Roman, and as I now say heartily, as I am not, Edward W. Benson to his own dear Mother and all hers wishesh health...'

Two days later he was writing home again, saying that he wished he could say anything that would comfort the invalids, but they would comfort each other best, though they must remember that 'true comfort is of the Comforter'.

But prayers and pious sentiments did not work, and Harriet grew rapidly worse and died very suddenly. Joseph Lightfoot, who had been informed first, broke the news to White, who was at that moment writing another comforting letter to Eleanor, wishing that they could all visit him at Cambridge, and threatening to go home himself and see what was happening, in spite of all injunctions to stay away. His letter changed tack immediately and he wrote at length of how David knew sorrow and how his Psalms revealed how fully he was comforted; how Luther sought comfort after the death of his daughter by thinking of the death of Christ; and now they must trust God had so clothed Harriet in His robes that she entered boldly before the Throne of Almighty God. He gave his sister the most glowing of testimonials – how full of grace and praise her spent years were, how little she displayed of common passions, how obedient and truthful she was, how the lessons of Christ's doctrine had leavened her whole heart. He acknowledged the humanity of Harriet by admitting that she had not yet come to an age when religious feeling is very actively displayed (and of course she misplaced her commas), but the general picture he gave was of a little saint.

Having posted the letter he hurried off to Birmingham and arrived home to find another ghastly shock awaiting him. His mother, worn out from her devoted nursing of the children, had on the previous day laid out Harriet's body herself and had made all the arrangements for the funeral. Then she went to bed, but about midnight she got up, lit a night lamp and went in to have a last look at the wasted little body. She returned to her bed, eventually fell asleep and during the night died from heart failure, her head upon her hand. The next morning she was discovered dead and cold, and it was then that White arrived, not having known that his mother had been ill. It took all his faith to withstand this further blow, but his faith was enough. After the double funeral he set to work to investigate the family finances. He found that what he had been told, but had not properly realised, was that his mother's only income, apart from a few hundred pounds which had been invested, had been an annuity, now, of course, cut off abruptly. The shares turned out to be almost worthless, and his calculations led him to the grim realisation that all the money they had to face the future with, when all expenses had been paid, was just over a hundred pounds.

This appalling situation brought all the family rallying round with extraordinarily generous offers. His half-uncle William Jackson immediately put enough money at his disposal to see to his most pressing needs, and the orphans eventually went off to various relations. Eleanor and Ada were looked after by Mrs William Sidgwick, the widow of his father's first cousin; the others went off to Manchester to stay with their Uncle Thomas until more permanent arrangements could be made. Christopher Sidgwick of Skipton, White's cousin, also gave generous financial help. He wrote to White, deploring the fact that he had spent a fortune on building and endowing a church at Skipton while Mrs Benson had been getting by on a most inadequate income; but, he explained, when he had visited White's father on his deathbed, he had been given to understand that his family was amply provided for. Like her other relations he thought that her income came from invested money.

White wrote to Prince Lee, the Bishop of Manchester, to tell him of the family tragedy and talked about 'the heavy affliction with which it has pleased God to visit us'. Then he made an extraordinary decision about the future of Charlie, his youngest brother. 'An uncle resident in Manchester has offered liberally to take my younger brother, a child nearly eight years old – and maybe one of his sisters – and bring him up as his own child for some years to come. He undertakes not to instil into the child any Unitarian principle, and says that I can freely exercise my influence by visit or by letter, and hereafter decide on the boy's school; meantime he will have to attend the meeting-house, and grow up with the greatest respect for his uncle and aunt – this I say from knowledge of his character – and naturally for their opinions also, with all the power of early association full upon him. The question then becomes – is it possible for a lad so placed to grow up a Churchman? and, on the other hand, is it right to reject the means of maintenance for him which God in His providence lays before us?'

White decided it was right to reject the means of maintenance, and not risk the possible pollution of his little brother's faith with the taint of

Unitarianism. Thomas Baker's reply to the rejection, in a scornful and cold way, put White firmly in his place as a self-righteous bigot. Baker wrote: 'I remark your observations upon the inducements which moved you to decline my proposal as to Charlie. I consider that you will be hereafter be bound to provide for his future as he would have been provided for had he been with me. The view you have taken of my religious opinions has caused me deep regret. I had hoped that your own good sense and the conclusions you might have drawn from your observations of the characters of various members of the family who entertain opinions similar to my own, would have preserved you from such narrow and debasing sentiments, and me from the reflections consequent upon them. As I have been wrong in such anticipations I do not see how you can expect from us any sympathy in pursuing an education which has so far taught you not to regard us as friends, but as a class whose influence, beyond a very small range, is to be avoided. I could say very much more on this subject, perhaps I may sum it up by observing that I have self-respect and religious principles, in both of which there is a duty. Of this, in my several conversations with you, you seem to be unmindful.'

White's reply was white-hot with a passionate defence of his decision to refuse Charlie a safe and comfortable haven in Manchester with an uncle and aunt who would so willingly have become loving substitute parents to a bewildered orphan. He thanked his uncle for his kindness towards the children as well as for the 'uncommon candour' with which he had told him what he thought of his opinions. Eleanor and Ada, still not fully recovered, were staying with their aunt and uncle, and White recognised what trouble they might be causing in such a quiet home and was therefore doubly grateful. Then he went on to reply to the part of the letter which had caused him great surprise, great pain and much reflection to what it might forebode. He asked his uncle's pardon most sincerely if he had violated or offended his self-respect and religious principles, then went on to propound his own, in great detail, stating those points of Christian doctrine and practice which seemed to bear upon the future of his youngest brother.

'Beside the Eternal Father whom you worship with us, I, according to the unchanging Creed of the Catholic Church, believe that there is in the Godhead a second Person, His Eternal Son, and a third person, the Holy Ghost; that the second of These having assumed on earth, and now retaining in Heaven a human existence in addition to his Divine, and having here done certain acts affecting our eternal state, is entitled to a distinct and peculiar worship ... shall conclude every Service, every discourse, with ascriptions to praise to Him with the Father and the Holy Ghost – with what conscience or with what countenance if memory should

ever suggest that in one person's case, and his the dearest that could ever
be, I had robbed those Divine Persons of the worship and the praise that
should have proceeded from his heart, his mind, his lips, his whole life?
Whom could you more rightly blame as hypocrite than him whose
professions should have been so loud, whose acts so discrepant? This is a
very serious matter; and I hope you will not think bitterly either of the
young man's presumption, or the young Churchman's bigotry. Bigot (so-
called) thus far, a conscientious Catholic must ever be...'

It was a very long and very sincere letter and sheds much light both on
the strong and the insufferable sides of his nature. There were bounds
which he could not allow his religious convictions to seep through; he
could not but decline to submit to the influence of someone who did not
share them anyone over whom he had control. So that was that. Young
Charles was removed from the pernicious influence of Unitarianism and
White was able to return to Cambridge with a clear conscience but
wondering uneasily as to how he could assume resposibility for his brothers
and sisters in the years to come, for his uncles and aunts could not be
expected to bear the burden for ever.

His worries were soon brought to an end, in a most unexpected way –
God's answers to his prayers, he did not doubt. Looking and feeling
desolate he was crossing the Great Court when he met Francis Martin, the
Bursar, who, though he only knew the young student slightly, had heard of
his family troubles, and felt sorry for him. They talked for a few minutes,
one extending condolences, the other receiving them with proper respect,
then the older man invited White to his rooms, and further talk resulted
in the beginning of a warm friendship.

Francis Martin was unmarried, childless, a fierce gruffness hiding his
affectionate nature, and wealthy, and he could not have entered White's
life at a better time. White responded to the older man's devotion with a
cool and respectful liking and did nothing to show that his own nature did
not have the same warmth and spontaneity. For many years White was a
favourite son to Francis Martin, whose feelings even extended to White's
brothers and sisters, for whose education he made himself responsible;
and he left the Bensons a large part of his fortune when he died in 1868,
at a time when White Benson had been married for nine years, and had
fathered five of his six children. He had named his eldest son Martin after
his benefactor.

Francis Martin was a fervent Evangelical. He had taken high honours
in Classics and mathematics and from Bursar he became Vice-Master of
Trinity and a dominant influence in the College for many years.
Questions would no doubt be asked these days as to the depth of the
fervour between the two men, but there seems little point delving into the

relationship with the purpose of finding any homosexual bonding. It seems clear that the older man fell in love with the younger, for White Benson was very handsome with a splendid head, mobile mouth and very blue eyes. He often put his arms around White's shoulder, stroked his hand and fondled his hair, but the younger man did not fall in love with the older though he was willing to accept both the devotion and all the advantages that went with it.

When White had got over the first shock of his mother's and sister's deaths he slowly re-entered the life of the College, especially the religious life, though for months afterwards he frequently dreamed of them both, once that Harriet had recovered from her fever, and once that Emmeline and Ada had both caught the disease; dreams from which he awoke trembling and troubled. One of his few diversions was an interest in the supernatural and, together with Lightfoot, Westcott and Hort, founded the Ghost Club. The future Archbishop was always more interested in physical phenomena than he cared to admit, and passed on that interest to at least two of his sons. One of the first mediums, a Mrs Hayden, visited England from America as early as 1852, and her séances were no doubt discussed at Trinity with great interest. In 1878 the Dialectical Society came into being and a committee was formed to investigate Spiritualism. In 1882 the British National Spiritual Alliance, influenced by a group of scientists and scholars at Trinity, discussed the foundation of a Society for Psychological Research, and the first number of the Society's Proceedings was published in 1883. Henry Sidgwick, White Benson's future brother-in-law, was the first President. Thus the Ghost Club was the acorn from which the Society for Psychical Research eventually grew, from the amateur fumblings of White and his friends through the lifelong enthusiasm and dedication of Henry Sidgwick.

Henry Sidgwick had been a member of the Ghost Club while at Trinity as an impoverished student of 17. In 1859, when he was 21, he was made a Fellow. The following year he had his first meeting with a medium who puzzled him because she seemed to levitate a table. But on the whole he was not impressed by the lady. After ten years of interior struggle between evolution and religion he resigned his Fellowship, since it could only be held by *bona fide* members of the Church of England, and he no longer considered himself to be one. In order not to lose him the College made him a Lecturer in Moral Science. Later he became a Praelector in Moral and Political Philosophy, and later still Knightsbridge Professor. In April 1876, White Benson married him to Eleanor Balfour, sister of Arthur, both workers in the field of Psychical Research, and she continued her interest after Henry's death in 1900. Eleanor Sidgwick did not die until 1937, after a lifetime's cool and lucid influence over the subject and the society dedicated to the investigation of paranormal matters.

CHAPTER THREE

E ARLY in 1851 White visited his Uncle William at Exeter. He went over Exeter Cathedral with his Aunt Lucy and was much impressed by its magnificence. They also walked over the hills and saw Dartmoor and the beautiful windings of the Exe up towards Exmoor. He was very reluctant to leave his Uncle's house where everyone was kind and everything was beautiful; though he was horrified to find that William and his wife had given up their open carriage and dismissed their manservant in order to contribute so very largely to Eleanor's schooling and the other children's welfare. On his return to Cambridge he went to church and was encouraged by the 'very voice of my dear Lord': 'Seek ye first the Kingdom' and 'Why take ye thought?', which considerably lessened his anxiety about the future of his brothers and sisters, especially as Francis Martin was only too anxious to help.

Another walk with Lightfoot brought criticism on his head from his best friend, who told him he was getting extravagant notions of indulgence and enjoyment, the very reverse of his former ascetic virtues. White took the observation well and jokingly represented himself in the future as a threadbare half-starved country clergyman with a large family, the results of his self-indulgences, being visited by a pompous, well-fed old tutor of his College called Lightfoot...

When Mr Martin gave him £100 in a bank account for the young ones, and for Charles in particular, as a way of keeping his own birthday, White made the strange comment in his diary that kindness was flowing in so thick and fast that he would easily forget to be grateful. Mr Martin told him repeatedly to go to him for all things, as if he were his father, for pleasures and well as necessities, and emphasised his own unworthiness to assist the family.

White Benson took little interest in politics and only read newspapers as a duty. He was attracted to history, particularly the traditions of ancient history and resemblance in modern movements to their forms in the past. But, above all, it was the rituals and dogma of religion that fascinated him, rather than the simplicity of the Christian message. He was considered a

High Churchman in matters of ritual but had leanings towards liberal views in religious matters. He was, in fact, largely indifferent to ecclesiastical party differences. He was a regular attender of the Chapel Services at Trinity and tried always to say the Canonical Hours in his rooms, alone or with a friend. His mind was thoroughly liturgical and his happiest hours were spent in church, and in later days he would lengthen the daily service in his private Chapel so much that the household was thoroughly inconvenienced by his enthusiastic excesses.

On Commemoration Day, 1851, he delivered a speech in praise of George Herbert in the Hall of Trinity College and for this he received a silver cup, and was commended by Dr. Whewell, the Master of Trinity. In fact so highly was the speech regarded that the following year it led to a window being installed to commemorate George Herbert.

White never won a University Scholarship or a Browne Medal, though he did become a Senior Optime in mathematics and Senior Chancellor's Medallist, which made up for his other scholastic disappointments. Two men who stimulated him in his undergraduate days were Professor Blunt, a former curate to Bishop Heber, in the Lecture room and Dr. Harvey Goodwin, later Bishop of Carlisle, in the pulpit. Both exercised an influence that led to his complete refusal to entertain the smallest particle of religious doubt. It is common for the devout to pass through a period of questioning, if not of rebellion, after the certainties of childhood have broken up; after which there is either a return to religious convictions or a complete break with the religious past; but in White Benson's case there never was such a period. His faith was innate. From his earliest years he had been an ardent believer and remained so for the rest of his life. Never once, even at the deaths of his mother and his sister, and that of a dearly beloved son, did his belief in the dogmas of the Christian Church waver for an instant. The natural reactions of grief and inability to understand the Divine purpose fully passed him by. To his younger brother, Christopher, crippled from birth, he wrote, 'You do not say anything, my dear boy, about a regular study of the Scripture – do you find any difficulty in the way of doing this?' And he went on to ask, 'And how can we hope to dwell happily for ever beyond the grave with *Those* whom we care not to know and love on this side of it, our Maker, Saviour, Sanctifier?'

In the Long Vacation of 1851 he joined a reading party in the Lake District, led by Mr Mathison, Tutor of Trinity. His diary for this period, which lasted nearly two months, contains the most minute descriptions of natural scenery, and of visits to Arnold's house, Wordsworth's Grasmere, Robert Southey's grave in Grosthwaite Church, Scafell, Rydal Water and Hartley Coleridge's cottage. Not as much reading was done as they had intended. Except when the weather was extremely wet they were out most of the day visiting churches, walking, boating on the lakes, bathing in pools and streams, collecting ferns and falling down steep hills. White loved it all, sketched and wrote in his diary page after page of ecstatic comments. Even when it rained some of the most enthusiastic readers donned mackintoshes, plaids and horsecloths and strode out, returning sodden but in good spirits. White plunged into the Mirror Pool in Rydal Head and 'shrieked and shrieked with delight'. His not always felicitous prose sometimes turned into poetry when he was particularly moved. 'Here's tansy for you, and a head of clover and that bright red bush and that wild aster. Here's the many-headed white-flower on little tufts, geraniums with spiky seeds and fantastic leaves, here's a harebell, and more yet, and lastly some sage, light, sweet euphrasy, and then the two delicate little ferns that Potter put into my hand for the make up of the cluster...'

After climbing up Scardale Fell and seeing Windermere in all its length they scampered down 'jumpy, jerky, wally-shally, boggy-joggy, splashy rushy, thumpy, zany, coky boasty, bathy, warmy, coolly, freshy', which must have been the most surreal sentence that White ever concocted.

At one point he was deeply moved by a flock of herons 'rising into the golden sunlight above the hills, I could not tell from whence, and sailing on the glorious arches of their wings, on and on – always alone, and each as he came down with outstretched neck and pendant legs ready to settle, taking one last sweep down, then up, on to the summit of the tall Scotch fir, to take a survey of the realm, and, as another approached, plunging into the thick heads of lower trees with a loud goodnight to his neighbours...' His diary entry finished with the curious reflection: *My Heavenly Father careth for them. I am of more value than many herons.*

Halfway through August Francis Martin arrived to join the party and was universally welcomed. His health was rather delicate and he could not join in all the expeditions, but he boated and bathed with great enjoyment. On one occasion he sat with White in his bedroom reading Terence. He frequently seized White's hand or played with his hair. 'I do not worthily return his affection,' White wrote. 'I find myself hardly able to understand it.' But though puzzled, and a little embarrassed, he allowed his benefactor to express his love without drawing away, though 'how unlike him shall I be if my lot resembles his, in affectionateness'.

One of the few anecdotes of White's Cambridge days to show him as human, reckless and capable of intense feeling outside religious matters, occurred on a Degree day in 1850, when a West African undergraduate named Crummell, of Queen's, appeared in the Senate House to take his degree. Black people were unusual enough in those days, and a black university student even rarer. Somebody in the gallery called out, 'Three groans for the Queen's nigger!' There was a shocked silence. Then an undergraduate in the front of the gallery, who had not up to then been taking much interest in the proceedings, became scarlet with indignation, and shouted, in a voice that rang through the whole building, 'Shame, shame! Three groans for you, sir!,' followed by 'Three cheers for Crummell!' The cheers were given heartily by the assembled company and the original offender had to stoop down and hide himself from the storm of hisses and groans that erupted all around him. Crummell's champion was Edward White Benson, whose reputation for righteousness was thereby enhanced.

In 1852, after the Tripos, White went for a long visit to Yorkshire, to stay with various relations, and then to Mrs William Sidgwick, his widowed cousin, at Bristol, where a large party was gathered. The Classical Tripos list was to be published on March 25, and White was as nervous as he had ever been, pretending to his friends that they must be satisfied if he came fourth or fifth on the list, but secretly hoping that he might be bracketed second. Never, though, did he imagine that he might beat or even equal Macnaghten, the favourite. On the Monday evening, during tea, 'a gentleman from Cambridge' was announced, and Francis Martin appeared, muffled in a greatcoat and swathed in scarves, his hat and carpet-bag in one hand, the other extended in greeting. After hearty handshakes and breathless enquiries after the company's healths White's spirits suddenly plummeted, certain that his benefactor had come to break the bad news about his place in the Tripos list and to cushion the blow that would be made public the next day.

Mr Martin saw the crestfallen look on the young man's face and hurried to blurt out the reason for his visit. 'I've come to bring you news from Cambridge – good news! You've got the Senior Medal, and, yes, you've beaten Macnaghten!'

By this time they were in the dining-room, and his cousins were crowding round them, pawing at Mr Martin and asking what the Medal was, and its significance.

'Why, the highest of the University honours,' he exclaimed proudly, 'the last and the greatest!'

White, realising that he was not in a dream, executed an extraordinary series of leaps and bounds, and then had to catch hold of the door to support himself. Mr Martin was relieved of his carpet-bag and outer clothes, and Frisk, the dog, alarmed by the commotion, was dissuaded from shaking White's trouser leg furiously.

Never again would he enjoy such an evening, White decided, for it was the reward of long labour against hope. Brother and sisters, aunts and cousins, all had eyes full of stars, and Mr Martin clasped his hand and folded it into all manner of shapes till it felt quite numb. Best of all, his little cousin Minnie put her arms round his neck, stroked his hair and patted his forehead, her gentle affection arousing strange feelings in his breast, so that he blushed and the palms of his hands felt hot.

That night he laid his head on his pillow with the calm and happy feeling that God had blessed him, and he prayed that the day's bright gleam would be the forerunner of a light that God had lit for him to shine through his future years.

During the rest of the week that White was with the Sidgwicks he and Minnie were constant and close companions. They read poetry together and White was struck by the depth of her thought, how her eyes would flash at some fine passage, her striking voice and gestures as she read. One evening, after the other members of the household had retired, he told Minnie's mother that if Minnie grew up the same sweet, clever girl she presently was, she would make such a wife as he had often said he should most pray for himself. At first Mrs Sidgwick was not encouraging and suggested that he would meet somebody older who would have all the qualities he hoped for Minnie. 'I know that Minnie will grow up in love with me,' he insisted, 'and who can ever love me better than that?'

He and Mrs Sidgwick had many midnight conferences and gradually she became reconciled to her little daughter eventually marrying the tall, eager student. White left the Sidgwicks happy that his plan had received official blessing.

His little brother Charles stayed with him for a week when he returned to Cambridge. Though ten years old he looked about seven, and was a most sensitive child. He always kissed White last thing at night and first thing in the morning, and the refusal of a kiss after a Latin lesson brought on a flood of tears. 'Save him, good Lord,' White prayed.

CHAPTER FOUR

WHITE returned to Cambridge intending to study hard. He read German and liked Uhland but detested Heine. He cultivated his friendship with Prince Frederic and enjoyed his amusing conversation and knowledge of the Classics. He took a few pupils but preferred to saunter in the Backs during the summer mornings of 1852, carrying a book which more often than not he forgot to open. He berated himself for his laziness, but decided that it was a natural reaction from the years of hard work that had led up to his recent degree. However, before he could bring himself to renounce his new life of leisure, events made the decision for him.

One morning, leaning out of a window of his rooms in Trinity's New Court, he saw Dr. Goulburn, the Headmaster of Rugby School, whom he knew by sight, strolling up the avenue of limes. Then there was a knock on his door, and on opening it he found the Headmaster standing on the threshold. 'I'm Dr. Goulburn of Rugby, and I'd like you to join my staff,' was the unexpected and unceremonious introduction. The offer was decidedly congenial, the more so when White heard the terms of his appointment. He would assist the Headmaster with the sixth form but would only have one hour's teaching a day. He would have the 50 or so Schoolhouse boys as private pupils and as much time to read for his Fellowship as he needed.

After consulting his friends he decided to accept, one attraction of the offer being that he would be teaching Arnold's sixth form, in Arnold's library; another that he would be able to take on himself completely the education of his brothers and sisters, thus ridding himself of the obligation he felt towards both his relations and Francis Martin. A further example of serendipity was the fact that his cousin, William Sidgwick's wife, was intending to move from Bristol to Rugby so that her sons Henry and Arthur could attend the school; and as his sister Ada lived with them there was another link between the two families. Above all, there was Minnie, aged twelve, for whom he felt such an oddly turbulent tenderness, and now he would be able to woo her properly. It had been tacitly agreed that he should be allowed to speak to Minnie about marriage, though he believed that she already knew something of his intentions. She was sitting on his knee when he asked her if she thought it would ever come to pass that they would be married. Instantly, tears fell down her cheeks, and he thought for a moment that he had scared her. He told her that he would never love anyone as he would love her. Minnie, pretty, plump and docile, flattered but artless, intimated in her kittenish way that she would wait until she was grown up and then give him her hand. From that moment her suitor and her mother both took it for granted that the agreement was a solemn and binding promise, and Minnie felt trapped. She admired White, she revered him, she was not afraid of him as many people were, but did she love him? She could not make up her mind. She was happy when she knew he was happy, but she was not less happy when she was not with him. She had allowed him one kiss in the garden and that weighed heavily on her conscience.

After a short stay in lodgings on the Dunchurch Road, White went to live with the Sidgwicks in the suburbs. The house was called Blue House, from the colour of its bricks, and had a large garden which contained many elm trees. Apart from Mrs Sidgwick, her family and Ada Benson, Mrs Sidgwick's sister, Henrietta Crofts, lived there. She was a lady of decidedly masculine appearance with a deep voice to match. She occasionally suffered from moods of dark depression which cast a blight on the household. The Sidgwick's eldest son, William, was shortly to go to Oxford on a scholarship. Henry and Arthur were being good scholars at Rugby; then Edward Benson, having finally decided to drop the name 'White', joined them; and the household became an extraordinary amalgam of strong characters, each seeking to dominate the others in one way or another. Edward was a natural bully, Miss Crofts morbidly jealous; Mrs Sidgwick, good natured but fussy, infuriated everyone by her habit of 'talking people round' and making things worse than ever; and Ada Benson was as strong-minded as her brother Edward. It was a miracle that the household did not explode, but on the whole there were remarkably few *contretemps*.

In those days Rugby was a quiet country town set amid pasture land, rich in wood and water and great grassy fields. The school buildings were well-proportioned, of a somewhat Puginesque Gothic, better without the later incongruous additions and the flimsy Chapel Tower. Edward Benson felt an immediate *rapprochement* with both school and town, and quickly settled down to a régime that suited him and gave him great contentment. He had only the first lesson in school, so he was able to devote most of the morning reading for his Fellowship. In the afternoons he would ride all over the countryside, sometimes accompanied by Minnie on her pony, and in the evenings worked with individual pupils. Frequently he had to take the sixth form for Dr. Goulburn, which he found very pleasant. His only disagreement with the Headmaster was the latter's low estimate of the innate goodness of boys. Dr. Goulburn believed that their tendency was towards evil rather than good; Edward was convinced that the opposite was the case, however often a boy might fall from grace. That apart, it was an idyllic existence for Edward, made more so by the stimulating society of many of his colleagues, a remarkable body of men who later held distinguished positions in education and the Church – Headmasters of such schools as Marlborough, King Edward's School, Birmingham, and Haileybury; or high in the Church as Dean of Canterbury; and in university life as Professor of Poetry at Oxford, Professor of Greek at Durham University, and Vice-Provost of Oriel College, Oxford.

Edward kept a spasmodic diary at Rugby, summarising the events of months in merely a few lines. In March, 1853, he recorded the happiness of a holiday with his sister in Exeter, where his uncle William Jackson was living, and of a few days with Prince Frederic at Combe, and of his last seven weeks at Cambridge, reading Chaucer with Mr Martin, enjoying his summery rooms in the deep shade of the avenue. Then came his unexpected appointment to Rugby; and the term came to a delightful end by the visit to Cambridge of his aunt, sisters Eleanor and Emmeline, Miss Crofts, Henry Sidgwick and most welcome of all, Minnie. This was the seal of his Cambridge life.

During his first term at Rugby, Edward returned to Cambridge for his Fellowship examination, the result of which he said was 'satisfactory', and in January of 1854 he was ordained by the Bishop of Manchester at Bury.

It was a curious examination. He presented himself, as instructed, to the Rectory of the Bishop's Chaplain, a country clergyman, and was shown into the Chaplain's presence; but he, it seems, did not catch his visitor's name and, after a few preliminaries during which it was established that a candidate for Orders was sitting before him, asked him the date of the Call of Abraham. Edward looked blank and confessed that he had no idea. The Chaplain then asked him the date of Solomon's birth. Again Edward pleaded ignorance. 'Very bad, sir, most reprehensible ignorance,' was the severe reprimand. 'What did you expect? The sequence of the events of Bible history is a necessary part of a clergyman's knowledge.' He then asked another date of which Edward was ignorant. By this time the Chaplain was glowering fiercely. 'What College do you belong to?'

'Trinity,' said Edward, wondering at the charge of ignorance.

'What degree?'

'Eighth Classic.'

'Any university distinction?'

'Senior Chancellor's Medallist and Fellow of Trinity...'

The Chaplain's frown turned into a genial smile. 'Oh,' he said, 'you are Mr Benson, mentioned in this letter from the Bishop of Manchester. I beg your pardon, I did not catch your name. We may consider the examination at an end,' and he handed Edward a sealed document which had been lying on a side table. When Edward opened it he read that he had passed a most creditable examination. He never did discover whom he had been mistaken for, or why he had passed the examination before a single question had been asked, but he hoped that some unfortunate candidate knew the date of Solomon's birth.

Edward did not enjoy his second half year at Rugby as much as the first. His health was giving him much concern; he suffered from weakness and debility, headaches and depression, the first appearance of the trouble that was to plague him for the rest of his life. His doctor said it was likely to be two years before he fully recovered. Although he did not allow his school work to be affected by illness he was able to do very little work for himself. With his Headmaster's permission he gave up his first lesson completely and confined himself to his private pupils and lectures on composition to the fifth and second fifth forms. He became rather gloomy about the state of scholarship in the school. He believed that something ailed the place but could not put his finger on the cause, except that Dr. Goulburn's low opinion of his charges' qualities, he thought, must have something to do with the malaise.

In 1853 Edward's health improved. He returned to his theological reading with with great energy, in particular studying Hippolytus, the Greek father, with a view to producing a new edition of his work. His enthusiasm resulted in two articles in the *Journal of Classical and Sacred Philology* the following year.

In the holidays he travelled assiduously, visiting Rome with Lightfoot and spending many hours every day at the city's churches and galleries; and in France he visited most of the important cathedrals. He identified and catalogued the hundreds of statues at Rheims, and started a collection of pictures, photographs and engravings of sacred subjects and ecclesiastical buildings, arranging them meticulously in portfolios. This patient labour was symptomatic of the young man's attitude to work which always remained with him. Nothing was too small or unimportant to escape his eager eyes, his love of accuracy and attention to detail.

In Rome he and Lightfoot were presented to the Pope, Pio Nono. The most formal wear they had with them were frock coats, so to avoid offending protocol they used safety pins to turn the garments into dress coats. Edward described the ceremony in St. Peter's in great detail in a letter to Minnie Sidgwick in terms that were almost poetic. He was very impressed by the service, the Pope under his canopy, the Cardinals in their white and scarlet, the Pope's clear and sonorous voice, the glorious singing, and the procession with the Pope, tiara on his head, sitting in a great chair borne on the shoulders of 16 men in scarlet robes, making the Sign of the Cross over the heads of the people on his progress through the church, while the tapers burned on the altar, and the great circle of lamps glowed round the tomb of the Apostle. 'How strangely are good and evil mixed in this complicated earth,' was his final comment.

Nearly a month later he wrote to Minnie again, after attending Vespers at St. Peter's. 'I like very much to be present at those services in which one can join heartily like Vespers, which consist mainly of Psalms, Lessons and Collects. It helps one to feel that there is a Holy Catholic Church, though its skirts are so sadly rent – and it is good, I think, that we should try to feel this, and in spite of all its sins and shortcomings of the Church in this or that country, there is still one Lord and one Baptism.'

All his letters to Minnie were as solemn as those he wrote from Rome, written as though she were a theological student his own age, all as from a teacher to a pupil; didactic, grave, humourless. One wonders how a little girl, concerned with a little girl's occupations, received the missives. No doubt she read them dutifully and tried to understand them, then folded them carefully and put them away, trying not to think of the next one that would shortly arrive. Minnie's mother was more interested in her lodger's communications to her daughter and tried to impress upon Minnie how good it was of Edward to take so much interest in her and give her the benefit of his great knowledge. She emphasised to her how grateful she should be and hinted of a future state when she would be a permanent recipient of such noble sentiments.

A year later Edward wrote to Minnie's mother, 'It has been very good for me to live at Rugby, and to be with you. I am sure I feel gentler and more even, and as if I had advanced a little, though alas! it is very little, in the wisdom which is above. But above all thank God that he has given me one little heart to be so much mine now, and to grow more and more mine daily all our lives, as mine is already hers wholly, and I doubt not, but trust in Him that He will teach us how to do each other good, and build each other up, both by softening and strengthening, and that to your joy also.'

Edward was 27 when he wrote that not altogether literate letter: Minnie was 15. She was by this time aware of her future, and trying not to dread it. Pressured by her mother, flattered by Edward's attentions, there was nobody in the family to listen to her doubts and fears. From the age of 12 until she was 18 life was a long preparation for marriage to the young schoolmaster who was kind but severe, patronising and often disapproving. Knowing that her future had been settled, Minnie felt obliged to fit herself for a destiny for which she did not feel worthy. She knew that she must grow to love her husband-to-be and she did her best. Only to her diary, to be seen by no eyes but her own, did she confess that the real Minnie was not the one Edward believed he knew.

If only she could have confided completely in her mother the strain would have been much less, but she could not for, as she told her diary: 'Mother rather feared than loved.' And again: 'A terrible time. Dreary, helpless ... the strain on my conscience and the position towards Edward and Mama ... I lacked courage to bear his dark looks, but I see now I did not love him.' 'Lessons with Edward – so dreaded – architecture and physical geography.'

Edward's unease at the way things were going at Rugby found expression in a letter to Lightfoot, written in September, 1856. 'All things in the scholastic way go worse and worse. One lives in perpetual provocation to unlovingness, unchristian talk, distaste at one's place, and disobedience to those in command. And I for one am not strong enough to conquer all this, and be the stronger, as some men might be. Alack, alack! Oh for a Rhemish or a Roman Stall!'

He was not seriously thinking of turning Roman Catholic, although there were aspects of Catholicism that appealed to him, especially the music at High Mass and the eloquence of the Priests in the pulpit; and he wished that somehow all branches of the Christian faith could unite, that all 'good men' could be of the same religion. But he was too much attached to the Church of his fathers to contemplate leaving it. His postscript to the letter to Lightfoot was: 'I am thinking of being ordained Priest at Christmas, if possible at Cambridge, i.e., at Ely. Will you not also?'

In 1857 Edward's health began to worry him again, and his friends became concerned. Neuralgia attacked him constantly and nervous prostration left him weak and depressed. Dr. Sharpe advised him to leave Rugby altogether and to give himself a long rest, wisely realising that the school was to blame for much of his weakness. He went to Cambridge and had talks with Francis Martin and his Trinity friends: and he was offered a Lectureship with the prospect of a Tutorship soon afterwards. The idea appealed to Edward and he accepted gratefully; but the change from school to university never actually came to pass.

The reason lay in a bottle of medicine. In those days neuralgia was treated with quinine, port wine and heavy feeding. Edward overate and overdrank reluctantly, and drugged himself morning and night with quinine – with the result that nausea and a muzzy head gave him sleepless nights and drowsy days, but no relief from pain. Then Dr. Sharpe tried a new remedy – a powerful sedative which seemed to stroke away the pain as though by an invisible hand. The relief was so enormous that Edward proclaimed himself cured, and was able to give up the unsuccessful remedies.

To add to his newfound confidence Dr. Goulburn retired, and was succeeded by Dr. Temple who, through the tenderness of his nature, energy, and devotion to the tasks which faced him, brought a completely different approach to the running of the school; and he became Edward's lifelong friend. Edward and Rugby were at one again, and life regained its savour, though he was still unsettled about his future plans. If anyone could make him stay at Rugby it would be Temple, 'a grand man to look at, and a grander to hear,' he wrote to a friend, the Rev. J.T. Pearce. 'I never so heard a man speak evidently out of his own very heart, and his face quite haunts me. I feel intensely drawn to him; he is clearly one who hates "policy" and thinks nothing of lucre or place, but solely of right. He is the man to improve us all.' All the same, Edward believed that his days at Rugby were coming to an end, though he would do nothing precipitous. He was, he said, 'as motionless at present as the body in the first law of motion. Bide where I am. Spring to the rope and perhaps miss all...'

Edward enjoyed teaching when he was in good health and spirits, and though the idea of returning to Trinity appealed, it would mean an indefinite postponement of his marriage to Minnie. His salary at Trinity would fall far short of what he was earning at Rugby. A Headmastership was what he would most like but public school plums were few and far between. He had already missed Westminster School, the Headmastership of which was in the gift of the Masters and Fellow of Trinity. His willingness to accept the post had been delicately passed to the Fellows, and everybody expected that he would be appointed, but to his surprise and that of most of the College, the post was offered instead to an old Etonian, the Rev. C.B. Scott, who stayed at Westminster until 1883. This disappointment had followed one two years earlier when he was turned down by Bishop Tait, newly appointed to London, who had been looking for a Domestic Chaplain.

Edward's eventual move from Rugby was as unexpected, exciting, and fearful as he could ever have imagined.

CHAPTER FIVE

I N 1853 it was decided that a fund which had been set up to perpetuate the memory of the Duke of Wellington, who had died the year before, should be used to found a college for the sons of Officers, the site to be on a remote area on the borders of Windsor Forest, not far from Wokingham on the Hampshire border. A mile away Broadmoor, the criminal lunatic asylum, was being built.

The Prince Consort was an enthusiastic supporter of the plan and he busied himself with all the details of both buildings and administration. Just before Edward had decided to leave Rugby, even without future prospects, he was offered the Mastership of the new College and he accepted it without a second thought. He had to see the Council of Wellington College in the House of Lords, where he heard that his appointment had been agreed upon; the Council would ante-date his salary for three months, and he would also receive £200. His letter of suggestions for running the school was discussed and almost every point was accepted without dissention. The Prince Consort was Chairman of the Governors; Lord Derby was a member of the council and chatted to Edward graciously; and Lord Lansdowne and Mr Sidney Herbert, ex-Secretary of War, were equally pleasant. But it was Prince Albert who impressed Edward the most – 'a Prince of Princes' he called him. The Prince had seen him several times before the interview, and each man formed a high opinion of the other. One of Prince Albert's suggestions was that Edward should undertake a tour of Germany and Prussia in order to study the methods of education in their military schools. Edward agreed with alacrity.

He wrote to Minnie from Potsdam on July 6, 1858, and described his visit to Baron Stockmar and his dinner with the Prince and Princess Frederic William, the future King and Queen of Prussia. The Princess, opposite whom he sat, kept him talking incessantly so that he was not able to eat a great deal, and after dinner she chatted about Balmoral and the people who worked on the estate. 'Fancy this party of seven Germans, and one English lady who spoke German as fluently as they did, all of them talking in English the whole dinner in compliment to me, a stranger and poor schoolmaster,' he concluded.

But on the whole Edward found the tour rather dull. His main impression was that English Classical schools were vastly superior to their German equivalents, and that our run of scholars was superior in sense, feeling and scholarship. However, their conceit was unbounded. They knew little of English education but refused to give up the fictitious notions that they held about it.

After a three-month engagement Edward White Benson and Mary Sidgwick were married on June 23, 1859, at the Old Church at Rugby by Dr. Temple, who had replied to Edward's invitation by saying that he would come from Pekin to have the pleasure of giving him his wife. Edward was 30, and Minnie 18.The honeymoon was spent in Switzerland.

Minnie's confidences to her diary reveal the agony of the disastrous time which provided such a bad start to the marriage, and the shame of the first night in a Paris hotel, but in the context of the time it would have been thought creditable that never once did she let the mask of cheerful complaisance slip. 'An utter child,' she wrote, 'with no stay on God. 12 years older, much stronger, much more passionate, and whom I didn't really love. How evidently disappointed he was – trying to be rapturous – feeling so inexpressibly lonely and young, but how hard for him!' And she cried every time she was alone.

Edward was a passionate man; in love, in temper, in enthusiasms. He had thought of Minnie as a 'remedy against sin' all during the years of his courtship, and had kissed her future pillow every night after setting up her photograph against it – 'a pillow that now swells up quite plump and innocent close to mine, but won't do so long.'

'The nights,' Minnie wrote from the depths of her unhappiness. 'I can't think how I've lived...'

The official version of the marriage of Edward and Minnie was that it was happy, tranquil, a close companionship of body, mind and spirit. There was not a single thought or plan that he did not share with her, and from first to last her whole life and energies were devoted to him. He consulted her about everything and depended on her judgment; every word he wrote he submitted to her criticism. She supplied the buoyant vitality that he needed during his moods of depression. She was his stability, his rock. To their families and friends their relationship was an authentic love story. But the truth was different. Minnie was a Victorian bride, bound by convention to submit to the male, unable to express her doubts and unhappiness, pretending love where there was none, putting up with Edward's selfishness and lack of imagination, going through the motion of unquestioning obedience, rebelling only in her thoughts and in the pages of her diary, where she recorded the names of various young women to whom she had become attracted, sighing wistfully over the delicious times she had had with Emily, Annie and Katie: the first recordings we have of the true picture of Minnie's deep-down sexual inclinations.

The honeymoon ended in July and Edward and Minnie had returned to England, staying first at her mother's house in Rugby, then moving to the Master's Lodge at Wellington. 'I would have died, rather than that anyone would have thought for a moment I wasn't happy,' Minnie wrote and went about in public with a contented smile on her plump face, trying hard to live up to Edward, to educate herself so that she could talk intelligently to him and his intellectual friends. She wrote notes on Church architecture assiduously, tried to learn German, and read books which gave her mental indigestion. She carried out her household duties eagerly, though not very efficiently, provoking sighs and sarcasm from Edward over extravagance and unpaid bills, and she kept her diary.

Wellington College, designed by John Shaw, was built upon rising ground with a wide view to the south over a tract of heather in which brick kilns were visible. On either side was a sandy hill, Edgebarrow on the east and Ambarrow on the west, both covered with Scotch firs. A Mr Gibson had presented 12 acres to the Governors, and they in 1863 bought another 150 acres. The College grounds were bordered by large estates belonging to prominent local residents, between them a road climbed to a high plateau called the Ridges, from where there was a glorious view over the wooded plain of Hampshire. The Ridges was Edward's favourite walk; under its northern slopes ran an ancient Roman road called the Devil's Highway, where once he found some coarse pottery which turned out to be early British.

One could step out of the College gates and walk for hours along sandy paths among aisles of pine trees. The air of the entire countryside was fresh and sweet, laden with the aromatic scent of the firs blowing over the heather. A marsh to the north of the College was turned into three lakes which served as bathing pools. Rhododendrons flourished all around and an avenue of Wellingtonias led to the main approach of the College.

The Foundation Stone was laid on June 2, 1856, by Queen Victoria and she opened the College on January 29, 1859. At the beginning there were 70 boys, called Foundationers. The first Head Boy was John Boughey, who held the post for three years and became the first holder of the Queen's Medal. (He later rose to the rank of Major-General and died at the age of 87). 36 boys joined the school in the second term of 1859, 29 in the Lent Term, 1860, 14 in the Summer Term and 51 in the Michaelmas Term. After every evening service, Minnie, a sedate matron of 18, used to shake hands with each of the boys and wish them goodnight. The boys wore a uniform that Prince Albert had suggested; dark green jacket with brass buttons, plaid trousers and a cap like that of a postman of the period. But the uniform was eventually given up. It was unpopular from the beginning, and became more so when two of the boys were mistaken for ticket collectors at the local railway station.

Dr. Temple came from Rugby to help Edward get settled in and arrange the school. He examined the boys as to their scholastic accomplishments, and was distressed to find that many of them were real duffers, and the lowest form was filled to overflowing. It was an inauspicious beginning to Edward's 'seminary of sound learning and religious education'. There is a story (apocryphal) that on the first day Edward harangued the boys so fiercely that they all ran away that same evening.

Queen Victoria did not pay another visit to the College until November, 1864, on a fine warm day when the school had grown in numbers and was prospering. She was dressed in deepest mourning – it was only three years since the Prince Consort had died – though she was in good spirits, smiled when she entered a dormitory that was in the process of being cleaned, and laughed at the idea of the confectioner's shop being regarded as a necessity. But she disapproved of armchairs. She kissed the two Benson boys, thus winning their parents' hearts. Only once did she show grief, when she saw the Foundation Stone which Albert had laid in one of the Chapel walls. Her popularity soared when she asked for a week's holiday for the boys.

The school outgrew its original design, and its reputation for cultivating scholarship and winning university distinctions grew steadily. The curriculum became ever more classical and Rugby customs and traditions were introduced. There were far fewer difficult and backward boys than there were at the beginning of Edward's régime. Edward, his physical troubles in abeyance, was immensely energetic. His work began at half past six each morning and did not end until after midnight. Every Sunday he preached in the Chapel, he taught the sixth form and examined the school regularly and rigorously. He was very conscious of his responsibility for the boys' welfare, but because of his autocratic nature, unwavering principles and inability to tolerate contradiction or criticism, his relations with the Governors and Masters were sometimes strained. He was also a harsh disciplinarian and had a volcanic temper. His beatings were famous for their severity. General Sir Ian Hamilton remembered to his dying day in 1947, at the age of 94, that he had been caned every day for weeks for being late for Chapel or classes. The colours of the bruises on his body, blue, green, yellow and dark purple made his friends gasp when he displayed them in the dormitory.

Strangely, Edward was not aware of the terror he could inspire. For him punishment promoted goodness; it was his Christian duty to administer the cane when wrongdoing had been perpetrated. Even when the rebukes were verbal rather than physical they were terrifying enough to make Masters as well as boys burst into tears. Remorse quickly followed, however, and often he asked forgiveness of the boy he had just beaten. There was a generous and courteous side to him to which boys naturally responded, but on the whole he was not popular. Boys were irritated that he knew so much about them, and they suspected him of prying. They were bored by what they thought were the silly and unnecessary rules he formulated, and by the way he exaggerated the sinfulness of petty offences. Nothing escaped his vigilant eye – a bread crust on the gravel, a cap lying in the court, even an open door that should have been closed, all were the occasions for moralising and recriminations. Any evasion of duty on the part of senior boys who were given prefectorial powers brought dire penalties. A Prefect was not to be late for early school. There was no punishment if the offence happened once. The second time brought a punishment of 1,000 lines, the third brought demotion to the fifth form for a week, the fourth demotion for the rest of the half. The Prefects were never late...

Another apocryphal story that circulated among outsiders was that barbed wire was fixed around the tops of the dormitory partitions in order that the purity of adolescent boys should not be sullied. The idea may have been mooted but it was never put into practice.

The Masters were inspected and supervised as diligently as were the boys. He regarded smoking as ungentlemanly and self-indulgent, and forbade it in the study, common room, Masters' quarters and in the grounds. The story is told of a Master and a boy who, unknown to each other, met accidentally behind a haystack in order to indulge in the forbidden practice. Each had the opportunity to betray the other, but each agreed to silence for his own sake. Loyalty and admiration were accorded the Master in great quantity, but affection was not included in the way he was regarded. To succeed at Wellington a boy had to be respectful, hard-working, obedient and humourless.

Edward had begun to suffer from acute bouts of mental depression, though he tried to hide them from those around him; and Minnie had to bear the burden of trying to persuade him out of them. He never attended a meeting of the Governors without being sure beforehand that he was going to be dismissed. He thought everything was going wrong; the boys were being sullen and rebellious and the Masters were guilty of incompetence and disloyalty. He was as a rule so buoyant and optimistic that these occasional but severe lapses were all the more worrying. Nowadays a physical basis for his moods would be investigated and treatment prescribed, but then such a condition was part of God's plan and submitted to with as good a grace as possible.

When Edward was first installed at Wellington all questions regarding the running of the estate, together with the commisariat, catering and domestic arrangements, were in the hands of Mr Chance, Secretary to the Governors, and a Steward, both of whom were responsible to the Governors, not to the Master. Edward was fretted by the dual control; it offended his autocratic nature. So he drew up a manifesto on the subject and sent it to the Governors, not all of whom looked upon him with favour. He half expected to be asked to resign and was surprised when every point of his proposal was accepted. One of the Masters was appointed Bursar, but Edward was able to inspect the books regularly, and dealt leniently with the Bursar's inexperience.

One of the first things that Edward did, when the school's finances were secure, was to agitate for the building of a new Chapel, and he promised that substantial contributions from some of his friends would be forthcoming. There was little dissent from the Governors, thrilled that they would be associated with a new and beautiful building; and Gilbert Scott was asked to prepare plans for a Chapel of brick in the Early English style. The plans were inspected at every stage by Edward, and his interferences led to arguments with the Governors, the architect and even the carvers of the flowers on walls and pillars. Edward had to compromise several times when expense became the overriding consideration. On July 12, 1861, on Speech Day, the Prince Consort laid the Foundation Stone of the Chapel. In December he died and the 14th Earl of Derby became President. During this year the Sanatorium (actually a hut) was built. The Earl and Edward found themselves at one on most matters concerning the school. The Vice-President was Colonel Talbot, afterwards Sergeant-at-Arms of the House of Lords, but he and Edward, of similar temperaments, frequently found themselves at loggerheads. Owing to the rapidly growing number of boys, originally intended to be 300 at most, but ultimately reaching 500, the additions necessary to the Chapel caused it to become a shapeless, formless building, not the Chapel of exquisite proportions and fine details of which Edward had been the inspiring director. However, he eventually became reconciled to the changes. There was nothing in his whole Wellington life in which Edward took such constant delight as the Chapel and the services at which he presided. He preached there every Sunday morning, not from a pulpit but from a small desk on the chancel steps. He composed his sermons between ten in the morning and 12 noon. Obviously the material had been simmering in his mind all week, but the pressure of composition was terrific and the firm closing of his study door at 10 o'clock, after the first early service on Sunday, was a demand for privacy that would brook no interference. Sometimes he wrote his sermons sitting at a rustic table in a summer house where he had a view of the heathery moorland towards Sandhurst. Very often the last sentences were being written while the chapel bell was ringing.

The texts that Edward chose were, for the most part, from the Old Testament – Exodus, Numbers, Daniel, Proverbs and Psalms were the most popular. A few came from the Epistles, but hardly any from the Gospels. He had nothing to say that was simple or down-to-earth. He dealt with the most abstruse ideas and arguments that were above the heads of all but the most intellectual. There was no understanding of boyish faults, occasional apathy, forgetfulness, boredom, high spirits or just plain naughtiness. The ideals he promulgated were the highest, the most rigid and unassailable that only a saint could attain. Not once did he talk about the good Samaritan, the Sermon on the Mount, the woman taken in adultery, the prodigal son. Never did he talk about what Jesus had said and done. Never was humanity understood as a condition of life. 'Stop being human,' it seemed that he urged. 'Be perfect as your Father in Heaven is perfect. The Christian can accept nothing less.'

There was no room in Edward's creed for laughter, enjoyment or any action that did not aspire to the realities beyond the earth. Faults that were habitual and constant, even those that were committed only rarely, showed the strength and the capabilities of evil. There was no joy that was not connected with the life of the spirit. Two months of sloth could ruin a whole career; a simple bad habit could close the door of honour for ever. Some deep subtle untruthfulness, or some baseness unknown to the world, could work its way into and rot the very soul. The world was nothing but a battlefield, the struggle had to be renewed daily, hourly. There were two principles within each soul, one godless and defying, the other whose eyes were lit with the eternal light. And Sunday after Sunday the boys of Wellington were fed with the narrow commands of a merciless and unforgiving creed that, in spite of their rolling periods and Edward's compelling tones, painted sin as a haze before them with pleasure, ease, gain and success attending the enemy. 'Sin will overcome faith, or faith will slay sin. Kneel before the Holy Altar and choose.' There must be no enjoyment for its own sake, no laughter that was spontaneous and unrestrained; no action that was not performed for the highest motives; all activities and energies must be directed towards the effort to become perfect.

His sermons were delivered with a terrible sincerity and a blazing conviction that he must persuade his boys to find the way, the truth and the life by following the path by rules he had laid down, with no allowance for question or dissent. And the boys, eyes shining, or eyes glazed over, suppressing yawns, renewing resolutions, sat motionless, the very picture of pilgrims on the way to Paradise.

His services and the religious teaching he instituted at Wellington gave rise to further troubles with the Governors, who were not very knowledgeable Churchmen. Some of them accused him of being High Church; others called him Latitudinarian. After he had presented a copy of *Essays and Reviews* to the Masters' Library, a letter in *The Record* accused him of presenting the book to the boys' library. Edward replied indignantly that the room was not accessible to the boys and that Masters should be able to study works of various tendencies. The Editor called this explanation an evasion that Christians would not accept, but the book remained in the library.

Edward's ecclesiastical views at this time were hard to define. He was devoted to Christian art and tradition, and used ancient forms of devotion and hymns from Breviary and Missal. Yet he permitted evening Communions (being careful not to tell the Bishop) and once shocked a Master by mentioning the Mass in favourable terms. To make things more complicated he was a great friend of both Charles Kingsley and Dr. Temple. Edward defended himself from his critics by affirming that he was neither High, Low, nor Broad Church; and that the school services were little different from those held at Eton, Harrow and Rugby, except that theirs were more choral.

Charles Kingsley, the Rector of Eversley, and Edward were firm friends, even though they differed on many points of church politics. Kingsley, like F.D. Maurice, was a Christian socialist, also a novelist and journalist. In 1860 he was appointed Professor of Modern History at Cambridge. Later he became Canon of Chester, then Chaplain to Queen Victoria. He was one of the most remarkable and prolific writers of his age. Edward's stormy life at Wellington was made more bearable by Kingsley's good nature, warmth and enthusiasm. The rectory at Eversley was an easy walk from Wellington, and the two men met frequently and went for long walks. When he had a sudden desire for tobacco Kingsley produced clay churchwarden pipes from where he had previously hidden them in furze bushes or holes among tree roots.

Charles Kingsley was in his forties; he had flashing eyes, a beak-like nose and, when he was not stammering, a sonorous voice. On weekdays he wore a grey coat and knickerbockers, big boots, a flannel shirt and a black tie. His gifts to the Benson children were fascinating: West Indian nuts, red seeds, and Indian feather ornaments. Once regarded as a revolutionary socialist, he was now an enlightened liberal, a poetic idealist, a prince of country parsons. The children loved him, and knew *Westward Ho!* and *The Water Babies* by heart. They got on well with all the Kingsley children and with their pet kinkajou; a sleepy, comfortable animal – though they thought that Mary Kingsley, one of Charles' daughters, was its mother. Mary became a novelist, calling herself 'Lucas Malet'. She died in 1931.

Maurice Kingsley, the Canon's eldest son, was a pupil at Wellington. He was a high-spirited boy with a dark complexion and hair. Grenfell, the second son, had similar looks and disposition. 'He is going to be a Civil Engineer,' Mrs Kingsley told Minnie. 'He knows a good deal about engineering already, but not much about civility!' Actually it was Maurice who became the Engineer. He stayed at Wellington until he was 18, then went to America, and eventually became Chief Engineer to New York's Harbour Works. Grenfell did not go to Wellington but to Harrow where he failed his exams, then attended a crammer's in Chertsey which was run by the grandson of Samuel Taylor Coleridge and where he met Goldsworthy Lowes Dickinson.

Friendship with the Kingsleys also gave Minnie satisfaction and delight. Their monthly visits to Eversley for dinner or for tea on the lawn under one of the great cedars provided the stimulus, fun, and the sparkling conversation that she missed dreadfully in the Master's Lodge. For a few hours she was free from reproof and speechifying. She could laugh freely, tease her friends, and become for a time the young girl she was not allowed to be at home. She observed the Kingsleys together – equal in loving, equal in reverence and gentleness, equal in intellectual banter, and she could not help regretting that her relationship with Edward was so different; then she hastily rid her mind of any criticism of her husband's saintliness.

Children were born to the Bensons with inevitable regularity. Martin White, the eldest, was born in 1860, Arthur Christopher in 1862, Mary Eleanor (Nellie) in 1863 and Margaret (Maggie) in 1865. After Edward Frederic's arrival in 1867 came Robert Hugh in 1971, after a more decent interval of four years.

Minnie had a major nervous breakdown after Hugh's birth and that forced Edward to face the fact that there must be no more babies if Minnie was ever to recover from her faints, depressions and fits of crying. She spent a year convalescing, first in Scotland, then in Lincoln with their friends the Wordsworths, and finally with her brother-in-law Christopher Benson and his wife in Wiesbaden. While there she met a Lucy Hall, fell in love with her, and enjoyed many romantic walks and talks, to the annoyance of Christopher's wife, who felt herself neglected. During Minnie's long absences Edward grew increasingly unsympathetic towards her condition, and complained that she was neglecting her duty to him and the school. Once or twice Minnie dragged herself back to Wellington for an official function, but had the courage to decide that her health was more important than standing beside her husband on Speech Day.

Sympathy for Edward cannot be entirely ruled out. His career had reached a crisis. If he failed at Wellington there would be no further advancement for him, and his task there was almost insuperable. Often at loggerheads with the Governors on some very fundamental questions, his autocratic nature would only rarely allow him to give way. In his blacker moods he could not see any way forward. He felt that the boys had no interest in learning, and he decided that everyone was on the lookout for signs of failure in his administration. His insistence on being responsible for every aspect of life in the school meant that he could not relax for a second. On one occasion, annoyed by what he thought was irreverence, and dissatisfied with the way the younger boys responded in Chapel, he ordered them all into the Great School and rehearsed them, not humorously, but strictly, in responding out of the Latin syntax. So he missed Minnie dreadfully and felt abandoned.

He did not mix with the boys to any great extent, though he would invite two sixth form boys to breakfast every day, and a few favourites were allowed to make free of the house. The Benson children were not encouraged to make friends with the schoolboys, and therefore naturally speculated wildly about them, observed them with the remorseless gaze of children and gave them absurd names.

Masters were often invited to the Lodge. They were on the whole sensible and kindly men, but their individual qualities were submerged by Edward's dominant temperament. The only Master who was immune to his criticism was the red-bearded Mr Tebbs, irascible and unbalanced, his sarcastic tongue dreaded by the boys even more than they dreaded Edward's. Edward realised that he had met his match and left the young man alone, glad that he was, bad temper apart, one of the ablest members of the staff. Another man who stood out was Mr Freer, small, quaint-looking and quietly humorous, who left Wellington in 1875 to become the Archdeacon of Derby. Mr Eve was the most intellectual member of the staff and was the only one who would argue questions of general interest with Edward.

Mr Penny, one of the most outstanding teachers the College had known, joined the staff in 1861 (and stayed there for 30 years). He arrived at the local railway station, which consisted of two platforms and a box which did duty as a ticket-office, and saw two young men awaiting him; future colleagues, he assumed. The younger took the lead and introduced himself and his companion. 'This is Fisher and I am Benson.' The new Master was dumbfounded. Benson looked so young – but a closer glance showed that he was older than he looked. He was actually 32. His hair was flaxen, his flashing eyes were light blue and rather prominent, and he was clean-shaven. His legs were short in proportion to his long body and though he was above average height, it seemed that he should have been taller still. His manner was affable but there was steel behind the friendly overture, and as the three men reached the College Mr Penny noticed how much the boys were in awe of him, and with what scrupulous care each one touched his cap.

Mr Penny became the closest friend that Edward had among the Masters. He was tender-hearted and demure, with delicate features half obscured by full dark side-whiskers. He became Edward's Secretary in 1867 and saw him in his moods of depression, usually firmly hidden from his colleagues, and once caught him in tears because he was feeling so baffled. His work did not prosper, he declared, the Governors were hostile, the boys were so heavy and unintellectual, the sixth form was a dead weight. 'I cannot think,' he said, 'what makes my teaching here so ineffectual.' Mr Penny tried to restore him to his usual buoyancy and pointed out that in all parts of every school there was sometimes a time of dryness when apparently all labour seemed to be thrown away. His good and brilliant teaching must tell in the end ... and so it did. Before six months had passed four of the sixth form boys had obtained scholarships, two at Oxford and two at Cambridge.

When Wellington College first opened there were nine Masters during the first two years, six of them clergymen. They were all very young men, but they made up in enthusiasm what they lacked in experience. They quickly learned to become self-sacrificing, to give time, money, thought and ability to every aspect of the College's development, and they were encouraged to pay unwearied and minute attention to every detail – from dormitory regulations to the laying out of the playing fields; though all plans and suggestions had to be subservient to those of Edward's. He would spend hours arranging timetables for the different departments of the school, seeking a right proportion to be observed among a variety of subjects, fair adjustment of labour among many workers, and infinite pains to avoid clashing. In general the Masters loved and admired him for his enthusiasm, generosity and accessibility and (when he was not in a rage) his great personal courtesy. And when Edward was gracious, there was none more so, and the wisdom of his counsel was eagerly sought.

In 1862 Edward thought of applying for the Headmastership of King Edward's School, Birmingham, where he had been a pupil, and he wrote to his friend Lightfoot, who had been elected Hulsean Professor of Divinity at Cambridge the year before, asking for advice. But before Lightfoot could reply Edward wrote again, saying that his work at Wellington was too important, 'in spite of some pangs, some angers and some disgusts.' So he laboured on at Wellington, cherishing the place for the boys he loved, his babies' birthplace, the Masters he had chosen, and the work there was still to do. In 1863 he was chosen 'Select Preacher' at Cambridge and had to be prepared to preach to his peers without a congregation, and in 1864 he preached on Good Friday, Easter Sunday and twice in April. He asked Lightfoot for counsel both as to what he should say and how he should say it, 'for fear of those holy walls which doubtless will change like opals at the sound of poisonous doctrine.' Edward's letters show a picturesque turn of phrase and a touch of irony that he did not always use in conversation, which was inclined towards heaviness and dogmatism. In later years he had mellowed sufficiently to regret that he had thought it necessary to be so stern a ruler and explained that he had tried to struggle against the explosions of violent temper, but at the time he had not realised it was possible to rule by sweet reasonableness. He would say that he thought anger hardly ever justifiable, but had fallen back on it as a disagreeable but easy method of achieving his aims.

The dichotomy between his temper and his natural generosity was a tug-of-war between duty, religion and natural goodness. He was not a sadist. He was extraordinarily sensitive to the sight of suffering, especially in animals, and did not even like to see plants struck with a stick; yet it was an awful sight to see him fold his gown around him and cane a malefactor before the whole school.

On his own children he exercised a powerful effect, and their feeling for him comprised as much awe as love. He was unpredictable – he did not always remember the rules he had laid down, so there was an element of uncertainty about his justice and the children were always on tenterhooks. He never hit them, but his displeasure was worse than any amount of physical punishment and it was a great relief to see him don a cap and gown and leave the house at the beginning of the day.

Basically he was a shy man who nursed a feeling of deep inadequacy, wanting to be loved but bound by the strictness of his faith to punish all who offended against law and order and against any suggestion of laxness in religious observances. He could give comfort and reassurance to the timid and inexperienced, making them feel braced and exhilarated, and yet he could be terrible in his rages and accuse the person he was reproaching with a lack of honour and loyalty, telling him that he was unfit for any position of responsibility. Then the tempest would subside when the recipient had burst into tears, as many a Master did on such an occasion, and the blue skies would appear again; an apology for having gone too far and an outstretched manly hand soon put everything right.

In 1866 there occurred what might have become a serious incident in which the Prefects were involved. Edward was only peripherally caught up in it and for once showed restraint and commonsense. The Prefects had decided to keep the whole school in on a half holiday writing lines because they could not discover who had let off some fireworks. Giles, the Head Boy, appealed to Edward to authorise this decision. Edward was not happy about it but reluctantly consented. He had always urged the Prefects to exercise their authority, and he realised that if he overturned their proposal they would in the future be entirely discredited.

On the appointed afternoon 'Calling Over' took place without incident. The Prefects did not then disperse, as they usually did, but led each form below the sixth to a different classroom, where enough of them stayed to keep order and exact the lines. The most troublesome forms were collected in the Great Hall in charge of three large, tough Prefects who patrolled the room and looked menacingly at anyone who showed signs of rebellious behaviour. In the meantime Edward and the Masters remained near at hand in case of trouble. 'I think this is the most critical day in the history of the College,' he remarked. He was very agitated and nervous until a messenger arrived with the news that the school had submitted to the inevitable and were busy writing lines. Edward knew that when detention was over the boys would be very angry and inclined to let off steam in some way or other. So when they rushed out of College in the short interval between detention and the final 'Calling Over' at 5.45 p.m., Edward and the staff took off their caps and gowns and walked casually about the grounds, chatting to each other as if nothing unusual had happened. The boys swarmed about like angry bees and there was a lot of shouting and horseplay, and for a time it looked as though there might be some ugly moves against the Prefects. But the sight of the Masters strolling about, talking and laughing, brought them to their senses, and presently they dispersed to their dormitories. Then followed tea and it was clear that the boys had nothing more in their minds than food. The excitement was over, the incipient rebellion stillborn.

On another occasion Edward again practised his belief that vicarious suffering not only represents, but *is* justice. The sinfulness of society, he alleged, breaks out in the sins of individuals, and if society punished itself instead of making examples there would soon be no examples to make. Three boys had lied flagrantly and two were expelled. As a consequence the school lost its half holiday – notice had been given some months before that if any boy lied they would all suffer. So for two hours the boys wrote lines, seething inwardly at the injustice being done to them. At a Masters' meeting Edward had been urged to punish the wrongdoers before the whole school rather than to expel them. Normally he would have relished the job but for once he refused. The many must suffer for the few. He told the Masters that he valued their comments above everything, but he could not consent to act on the opinion of the majority if it was opposed to his own. That anti-democratic attitude summed up Edward completely.

Edward devoted a great deal of time and effort to his sixth form and expected an almost excessive thoroughness in return, and as high a standard as each boy was capable of. The cleverer boys were stimulated by the pressure, but those of lesser intelligence were crushed and depressed by never being able to attain the perfection that was Edward's ideal. One overtaxed pupil wrote a parody of the weekly questions that Edward set on the history of civilisation in Europe and pinned it to the noticeboard in the sixth form room. A friend of the joker was reading it with great amusement when he heard a rapid step coming along the passage. He quickly tore down the paper and pocketed it, just in time to save his friend from retribution.

Chapel was a nerve-wracking ordeal for the boys. Punctuality was the strictest of rules. As the Master strode along the long cloister that led from the courts to the Chapel no boy could pass him. To be behind was to be late, a serious offence. Even to be a few steps in front was frowned on because his minute of silence was disturbed, and it was almost as serious as being late. The sixth form boys sat near Edward's own stall, and if anybody sat, stood or rose awkwardly, he would note it and later reprove the miscreant gravely and publicly.

On other occasions Edward was equally successful in dominating the scene; even on Speech Day, when so many powerful and high-ranking personages were present, he took the lead by the forcefulness of his personality. The only man over whom Edward could not tower was Lord Derby, the Prime Minister; only he could act up to Edward's level, though he was unconscious of doing so.

CHAPTER SIX

WELLINGTON College consisted of two courts, made of brick with stone facings, flanked by two towers with lead roofs. The Master's Lodge was in the north front of the College, over and on either side of the principal entrance. In 1865 a new Lodge was built, and this was the home that the Benson children remembered. Edward had been given a free hand in planning the new Lodge, and had it built in a nondescript sort of Gothic made fashionable by Ruskin. The windows were choked by solid stone mullions which had no real function. All the wood in the interior was pitchpine and the walls were painted with a lilac-coloured distemper which retained all the children's sticky fingerprints. The drawing-room had an elaborate chimney-piece, the wallpaper was either a sullen green or grey, the curtains were of maroon rep. On the whole the furniture was good, and the nursery was warm and comfortable. Edward himself covered the walls with pictures which he varnished after the children had cut them from illustrated papers. They were all of an improving nature, of course, nothing violent or crude. One of Edward's successors obliterated the varnished cuttings on sanitary grounds.

Visitors entered the Lodge through a gabled path into a broad passage, on one side of which was Edward's study. Glass doors separated this from the hall, with Minnie's sitting-room, the drawing-room and the dining-room opening out of it. The stairs started in the centre and after one flight separated into two, each of them leading up into a gallery out of which the bedrooms and the day and night nurseries opened.

The grounds were laid out with great care, the garden melted into heathland and rabbits gambolled on the lawn in the twilight. Edward and Minnie would dine in the garden during the summer, shaded by birch trees; round them grew old-fashioned flowers like hollyhocks and Sweet Williams.

When the children had grown up enough to be able to keep up with Edward's determined stride he took them for nature rambles, helping them to observe and name the flowers, trees and animals they encountered. He played with them too, hiding among the ferns or behind a giant beech tree, leaping out after a suspenseful few minutes during which fear and excitement struggled in young breasts.

When the new Master's Lodge was built, Martin, the oldest child, was five years old, Arthur three, Nellie two, and Maggie still a baby. Fred and Hugh had yet to arrive on the scene. As the children grew and could toddle and chatter Edward delighted in their society. They talked to him as he shaved before breakfast and in the evening he showed them pictures in the *Penny Magazine*; and they always sat at table during dinner, helping their parents to finish their dessert.

In the holidays Edward's greatest interest was sketching. He was particularly interested in architectural subjects, which he drew on a small octavo block of tinted paper with a reed pen or crowquill. He was not very good at trees or foliage and would leave them out of the picture, so the foreground would be oddly bare. He never travelled without a notebook to jot down anything that took his fancy, especially architectural features that were out of the ordinary.

The children grew up with a love of the open air, of heath and woodland, streams and pools, of forest depths and rolling views; and were never happier than when they were walking or playing in the pine woods and among the heather, exploring the water meadows and penetrating deep into the mysterious hearts of clumps of pine. But the garden of the Lodge, with its rhododendrons and sweet-smelling summer flowers, was the centre of their outdoor life. There was safety and peace, with secret haunts and familiar hiding-places; and there was Miles, the mild-eyed gardener, to chatter to and plague with endless questions. He once gave Arthur a silver penny of Edward I which he had dug up. When Arthur showed it to his father his feelings were dreadfully hurt when Edward accused him of asking for it, disturbed lest the little boy should develop acquisitive ways. Arthur's protest that the coin was given freely was brushed aside. He had earned a black mark.

Life in the Master's Lodge was in some ways as uncomfortable for the Benson children as it was for the boys in the school. Young as they were they felt they were continuously poised on a knife edge. Their father loved them dearly and would join in their activities as any loving parent would, but he could never refrain from trying to mould each child into his own conception of what a true Christian should be. He never resisted the temptation to turn a moment of fun into a sermon on good conduct, as though he feared that too much laughter would rot moral fibre. Slouching in a chair, shouting too loudly in the garden, leaving a crust on a breakfast plate, failing to roll up an umbrella properly, were all signs that salvation was in danger of slipping away.

On family walks he devised games to test their intellectual ingenuity, the results of which would be earnestly discussed and criticised. He gave the children little old-fashioned books of an improving kind to read, such as *Philosophy in Sport,* in which a poor boy could not even throw a stone without having the principles of the parabola explained to him, plus diagrams.

Edward's hurt expression and sad words were a form of emotional bullying that the children instinctively resented. A straightforward beating would have been preferable. So there were many reservations in the love that the children were expected to feel for their father, and sometimes did; but fear was the ruling emotion.

In Arthur's partly autobiographical novel called *Memoirs of Arthur Hamilton* his little boy character wrote, 'I hate Papa' on a piece of paper and buried it in the garden. Whether this incident actually happened or not, it was symptomatic of what one young Benson at least felt about his father.

Minnie Benson's relationship with her children was very different from her husband's but in some ways equally difficult. They had a devoted admiration for her and thought her the liveliest, most amusing and inventive person in the whole world. Her love for them was eager but indiscriminate. Minnie, still in her twenties, had not the experience of dealing firmly with childish tantrums and would show her unhappiness too obviously, making the children feel suffocated by her emotions. They needed steady affection rather than over-solicitude, and Minnie, with her easy tears, could not, at that time of her life, provide it. Later she gained confidence and became an indispensable support to Edward in his black moods and her attitude to the children was less smothering. Arthur wrote of her: 'She opened, one by one, the doors of life to me ... she knew by instinct what we were thinking and caring about.'

It was to their nurse, Elizabeth Cooper, known affectionately as Beth, rather than to their mother, that the children turned for comfort. She was a little, wiry Yorkshire woman with a strong constitution, born in 1818. She had had simple teaching at a Dame's school, where she learned to spell a little and did exquisite sewing, and little else. When she was 16 she went as nursemaid to the family of Minnie's father, William Sidgwick, Headmaster of Skipton Grammar School. He died young, leaving his wife with four children. Two others had died in infancy. Beth brought them up: William, who became Tutor of Merton, Henry, Professor at Cambridge, Arthur, tutor of Corpus Christi College, Oxford, and Minnie. When Edward married Minnie in 1859 Beth joined the family at the Master's Lodge the following year and remained with them as nurse or housekeeper until her death in 1911, aged 93.

She was wholly and devoted to the Benson children, as they were to her. Her face bore a touch of severity, but her expression could quickly turn into one of sweetness and tranquillity. She was full of shrewd repartee and homely epigrams and her stories were usually about illness and death, but the children hung on to every word and knew them by heart. She was a stern judge of character, but for those she loved she had an uncritical affection. She never scolded, never interfered; her displeasure was slow in coming, and silent and sorrowful when it did. She was the first human being of whose love the children were directly conscious, and she remained a dear friend of them all, claiming nothing, giving everything.

The children were affectionate to one another and lived together happily in spite of an occasional clash of wills. Martin was remote from Hugh as there was an 11-year difference between them. Martin was a precocious boy. By the age of seven he was writing grammatically correct, though stilted letters. 'I love you till my heart stands still,' he told his mother when he was six. In 1870, at ten, he went to Temple Grove, an old-established private school at East Sheen, near Richmond, which catered for about 100 boys and had an excellent reputation. Two years later Arthur joined his brother there, and after they had both left Fred became a pupil. Arthur and Nellie were a close couple, as were Maggie and Fred. Hugh tended to be spoilt, and to Beth, because he had taken most rearing, he was her 'Darlingest child'. During Minnie's breakdown and absence abroad after his birth, Beth was, in all but name, mother to the temporary orphans. Edward was far too preoccupied to give them any extra attention.

When Minnie had returned to be a proper mother she taught the children herself. She was a brisk and clear teacher, though her French was insecure, and she could never interest the children in her history and geography lessons. Her greatest gift was her ability to inspire them to love reading. She herself was a dramatic reader – she read *Ivanhoe* and George Macdonald's *Phantastes* to them, and made the characters and events glow with life. By themselves they read Grimm, Hans Andersen and *Alice in Wonderland*, and began to act out little stories which sprouted from their lively imaginations.

When Francis Martin came to stay the children did not know whether to be pleased or terrified. They saw a formidable old man, gruff-voiced, with a shock of white hair. His high collar scraped his chin, and his loud, peremptory questions tended to paralyse them. But they soon became aware of the kindness underneath the gruffness, and they noticed how deferential their father was to him. Edward, however, gradually began to find his benefactor a little tiresome, a little over-affectionate. Minnie noticed it in her diary, when the three of them were on holiday in northern France; but she hoped that Mr Martin would never find out. At his death in 1868 Edward felt both sorrow and relief; and guilt at his relief because his old friend had left him part of his fortune.

Other visitors to the Lodge included Henry and Arthur Sidgwick, the children's uncles, their Aunt Ada, Edward's sister, a forceful lady who tended to argue with Edward and generally did not stay long; Aunt Etty, Minnie's aunt, majestic in pale silk, and Dr. Lightfoot, always recognisable by his loud laugh. Then there were members of the governing body, the most memorable of which was Lord Derby. He was a handsome man who wore a sprigged waistcoat under his frock coat, and tight, light trousers. He had a mass of curling hair and bushy side-whiskers, and was remembered as a very cheerful man. The most notable, however, was Queen Victoria, who again descended on the College in 1864 and afterwards looked over the Lodge. Arthur saw the dumpy figure, dressed in deep mourning, but was too young to realise that she had to be treated with special respect. She asked Martin how old he was, and he said he was four. Immediately Arthur, aged two, thrust himself forward and said, 'And I'm going on five,' whereupon the Queen took him on her lap and kissed him. She chatted too with Beth, the two women on equal terms, except that Beth called her 'My Majesty'.

Broadmoor Asylum was not far away from Wellington, just beyond Crowthorne. Dr. Meyer, the Superintendent, was a great friend of Edward's, an interesting talker with a quiet manner and kindly expression, and very good to the children. Beth used to take them to see him and his family, which consisted of Mrs Meyer, two handsome daughters, a son, Robert, who was a day boy at Wellington, and an assortment of nieces and nephews. They had to go through the woods and past the grim high walls of the Asylum with its barrack-like buildings, tall towers and chimneys before reaching Dr. Meyer's house. They watched the patients who were visible from the garden with great interest, showing no fear because they did not know what madness was. Once or twice they were spoken to and offered flowers, which Beth let them accept, but when a bag of sweets was proffered she took it and later disposed of it in case the sweets had been poisoned. When it was time to return home the children felt a sense of flatness at having to go back to the nursery routine after a lively and stimulating afternoon, wondering what their father might say or do to spoil the rest of the day.

The later he came in the better they were pleased. They chatted eagerly to their mother but were mostly silent in Edward's presence, expecting every moment that he would rebuke them for some very minor breach of etiquette, even the arrangement of food on a plate. Woe betide anyone who made a little hill of potato in order to dam up the gravy.

When Nellie was a very little girl she went for a walk with Arthur and her father and, as usual, full of talk, began to tell him some harmless parodies of Bible stories that her grandmother, who was staying with them, had told her. Arthur knew that his father would not approve and nudged her, winking violently at the same time. 'What is the matter?' she asked. 'Granny told us the stories.' Edward said severely that he did not like the stories, they were making fun of sacred things. Not only were the children rebuked, but Mrs Sidgwick also got into trouble later on.

The first intimation that all was not well between Edward and Wellington came in July, 1868, when he wrote a confused letter to his friend Canon Wickenden: 'I am 39 today. And full of grumps. I feel I ought to congratulate my friends on their having had another year over me, and really life is so full of mere work, with a constant sense of dissatisfaction brooding over the hours, and so little time for enjoyment that the very power of enjoyment goes away fast, and I constantly go off from pleasant things to work which is not pressing simply because I can't enjoy pleasant things. My mood all day is to be glad that elasticity does not act as once it did, and repair all that was bent at a bound, and I own I mourn less for what time takes away than for what it leaves behind. One has no business to say all this even to one's oldest friends, however I must say it to someone, and to whom so well as to you?'

In 1868 the Benson family joined Dr. Westcott, Dr. Lightfoot and Canon Wickenden for a holiday in Langland Bay, near Swansea, where they took two adjacent houses. One visitor was John Wordsworth, Bishop of Salisbury, who had been an Assistant Master at Wellington for a few months in 1866, and through him Edward was later introduced to Christopher Wordsworth, John's father, then Archdeacon of Westminster. It was a momentous meeting though neither of them realised it at the time. Dr. Wordsworth was appointed Bishop of Lincoln later that year and perhaps Edward felt the stirrings of change blowing through him, for in December he wrote again to Canon Wickenden: 'You have no idea what life is becoming to me – a humming-top is the only thing that resembles it. Perpetual motion, very dizzy, hollow within, keeping up a continuous angry buzz. Oh, if you could only know all my bitterness of self-reproach, called to a work of which I am not worthy, and not often sensible of its importance...'

Two days later he was offered and accepted the Chaplaincy to the Bishop of Lincoln. But the humming-top was not to come to rest for another four years.

Bishop Wordsworth was enthroned in March 1869, and Edward went to Lincoln for the ceremony and stayed in Riseholme Palace. From there he wrote to Minnie a long letter describing the ceremony in great detail. He and John Wordsworth, as Chaplains, followed the Bishop as the procession went right up to the High Altar. The Bishop sat upon his throne and read the Lord's Prayer. Then there were versicles and responses and the Collect.

The Chapter went to their stalls and Edward and John Wordsworth sat on either side of the throne. The service was very beautiful, the boys sang carefully and precisely. Edward criticised the Dean and Chapter for their mismanagement of the arrangements because the Mayor of Lincoln was not present and the laity woefully under-represented. The letter ended with another diatribe against the Dean and Chapter who, he said, 'stand on precedent as some people on etiquette. It may be questioned whether the Dean would think it correct to put out the Bishop's robes if they caught fire – unless some Dean could be proved to have done it before. They would not allow a Canon's baby to be baptised in the Cathedral though there is a font there – on that same ground.'

Edward's appointment, which involved no residence but only two sermons a year, was an immense pleasure to him. He was so glad to get back into the ambience of religion. The Cathedral delighted him, and he tackled Cathedral problems with relish. He became so involved with his Lincoln post that he wrote a long article called *The Cathedral: its necessary place in the Life and Work of the Church*, which was published by John Murray in 1878. He wrote to his friends Westcott and Lightfoot, asking them what were the duties of an unendowed Prebendary. 'I have to preach twice a year and to recite daily two Psalms. Is that all?' But his friends replied in a light-hearted vein and he was left to puzzle things out on his own. If he had a private fortune, he wrote to Westcott, he would certainly go and live at Lincoln and see if he could be allowed to do something.

Two years later he felt somewhat differently and wrote to his friends again: 'It seems to me that a Prebendal Stall has ceased to be a shadow even, or to contain a hope.' The reason for his disillusionment was that at Lincoln a fourth Residential Canon was added to the three already existing, and the Prebends were converted into Honorary posts, their income being merged into the Commissioners' Common Fund. So the holder of a Stall had become simply a person allowed to wear a surplice and preach twice in the Minster. Edward was bitterly disappointed – he had hoped to do so much more to infuse a new spirit into ancient forms. In a prayer he had written the night before his installation he had asked: '...O Lord, restore to Thine house Thine old armies of priests and companies of preachers, but let them be the people's priests – not lovers of wealth nor courtiers of power...' Edward had been desperate to help the Bishop to achieve a return to simpler, more Christian ways of work and prayer. Now his office meant nothing more than a name, and Edward, who had wanted to feed the Lord's sheep better than he had fed His lambs, felt useless. He thought of writing to the Bishop to resign his Stall but, because the traditions of Lincoln were already very dear to him, he destroyed his half-written letter.

CHAPTER SEVEN

A CLOSE relationship sprang up between the Bensons and the Wordsworths, which was a source of great happiness to them all. Christopher Wordsworth was benign, unworldly, and a man of vast learning. Mrs Wordsworth showed the Bensons a deep affection. The family consisted of Elizabeth, who had an uncommon facility in literature and art, and who eventually became Head of Lady Margaret Hall, Oxford, Mary and Priscilla, who married clergymen, also Susan, Dora and John. Christopher, the youngest, was at that time a student at Cambridge.

Elizabeth Wordsworth was a year older than Minnie, and much more assertive. At first Minnie was attracted to her and wished Elizabeth would reciprocate her feelings, but later decided that her mind was too noble to have time for romance, and she turned to her attentions to Susan instead.

Edward's life became revitalised. With so many like-minded friends to stimulate and broaden his outlook on life, the school became less of a burden, and he recovered his vigour of body and mind. Much of the improvement was due to the particular relationship that sprang up between him and Elizabeth Wordsworth. The two families spent holidays together; at Whitby in 1869 and Ambleside in 1870.

Many years later, after Edward's death, Elizabeth's recollections of him were enthusiastic. She recalled every detail of his appearance, his distinction, quickness of observation, magnetism, his artistry and ability as a draughtsman. 'His look of youth lasted quite into middle age; this was partly due to his abundant hair, light brown and for a long while hardly touched with grey, his clean-shaven face and active eager looks and movements. He had the hands, too, of an enthusiast, every finger full of character and vigour. No photograph could ever produce what is seldom seen in a grown man to the extent it was in him, the rapid changes of colour in his face. I have often seen him blush with pleasure like a schoolboy. He was a very quick observer, with a most delicate eye for minutiae. Things like the tooling of a well-bound book, or some slight architectural detail, or the different forms of letters in early MSS were dear to his very soul. Such things as the tone of a bell, or even some detail in dress or jewellery or furniture were all matters to which he was keenly alive.' If there was a slight dimness in his halo it was because he never quite did himself justice in his literary style. 'Certain it is,' said Miss Wordsworth, 'that while (even in his private letters) there are many most felicitous phrases, as a whole his style was more nervous than easy and attractive. However, it was his own; a voice and not an echo.' Then the halo brightened. 'He possessed in an unusual degree that kind of magnetism which makes those who are in company with its owner always conscious of what he is doing, and instinctively disposed to follow his lead.'

When Edward wrote to her he began with 'My dear Elizabeth' and ended his letters 'Your most affectionate...' There was no doubt that Edward was greatly taken with the spirited, intelligent and high-minded young lady. She was equally attracted by him. They struck sparks off each other, dazzling each other with the brilliance of their conversation. Edward had never felt so relaxed, and this showed itself in his renewed zest for life and ability to push school troubles more into the background. There was a spring in his step and a light in his eye that Minnie, rolypoly tremulous Minnie, had not been able to bring about since the early days of their marriage, which now was not going well. Edward had always taken Minnie too much for granted and had failed to appreciate the toll that frequent child-bearing had taken of her. Like most husbands of his class and period he was kind but domineering, well-meaning but selfish. Minnie, still feeling guilty because of her failure to love her husband enough, and confused by her inexplicable tendency to feel romantic yearnings for women, was unable to cope with her own emotions and her husband's demands and criticisms. Elizabeth would never have been so incompetent at doing the household accounts as she was, nor would she have bought too many candles, but would have sailed through the problems of house, children and servants with ease, and still found time for the higher things of life. She would have been the ideal companion for Edward; they lived on the same plane and shared the same beliefs and opinions. But if Edward ever thought on those lines guilt at comparing wife with friend would have frozen such wicked thoughts in a moment. Minnie, in spite of her household deficiencies, her inexperience with sick or fractious children, her easy tears when rebuked, was his wife, till death did them part, and that was that. But he and Elizabeth continued to write to one another in the warmest terms: 'The expectation of letters from you has changed my views with regard to the post and the wondering Porter ... well, he wonders to behold me about post time advancing to meet him, instead of disappearing round the Chapel at his approach.' In another letter he wrote: 'I have often wished for you by the half hour together.' And there were meetings at Wellington or at Lincoln, walks on holidays and a communion of like spirits in the frequent letters that passed between them.

In 1869 Dr. Temple, Headmaster of Rugby, who had been so helpful when Wellington College had opened, was appointed to Exeter, an appointment that was fiercely opposed by many High Churchmen, who regarded him as a dangerous heretic. Bishop Wordsworth was the leader of the anti-Temple brigade, and this put Edward in a difficult position, since he was a great admirer of Temple and knew him to be a saintly man and unreservedly loyal to the Church. But, never one to shirk a duty, he wrote to friends and to the newspapers, firmly denying the charges of heresy brought by Dr. Pusey against Dr. Temple, one of them being hostility to the Creeds and another holding the Bible story to be but 'a stimulant to the conscience'. In his letter Edward described Temple's patience, courage and manliness; his power of inspiration, his sympathetic charity and the might of his Christian faith, and put up such a good case for his saintly friend that within a month or so the virulent criticism had died down. He had sent copies of his letters to the Bishop of Lincoln, together with a letter of resignation of his Chaplaincy which he was sure the Bishop would have requested anyway; but the Bishop only smiled and threw the letter into the fire.

When Dr. Temple was finally installed at Exeter he asked Edward to be his Examining Chaplain. With Dr. Wordsworth's blessing he agreed; and for a few months he was Chaplain to two Sees. Edward was also exercised about Rugby and its vacant Headship. He consulted various friends, and their answers almost persuaded him to apply for the post. 'But,' as he wrote to the Bishop, 'my heart falls back on my younger and poorer bride here. I don't think I could give her a writing of divorcement.' It was his convoluted way of talking about Wellington.

In a later letter to Elizabeth he admitted that the Rugby business was well and happily over and that he now walked about Wellington ('this beautiful place') with a tenderness he had not felt for ten years. The letter ended with a delightful picture of what the Wellington boys were doing on a beautifully warm November day. 'The boys are all out in Blackwater Meadows running or watching Kingsley's Steeplechase – for which he gives them a prize every November – painting themselves red in our iron streams or black in our peat, and with such a blaze of warm clouds in the most glorious sky over the heathery ridges and fir woods. The lanes were full of flies and gnats. Never was such a November, and yesterday the cows were standing winking in the sun all afternoon, and lazily lashing their sides with their tail-tassels.' A month later he wrote again: 'Your delicious journal has come and it breaks out – in the few pages I have read of it – on my present sadness as the sun is just rolling out his gold through black falling rains.'

Edward had visited Dr. Westcott, Canon of the Cathedral at Peterborough, and had afterwards gone on to London where Dr. Temple was to be consecrated as Bishop of Exeter. He and Westcott had sat up late the night before talking about their situations, and Westcott had advised Edward that he should, at the first opportunity, give up school work for Cathedral work, and Edward agreed that that is what he would do. 'I am hopeful that my call will come with His direction,' he wrote to Elizabeth, 'and I hope that I am not presumptuous. Westcott was stronger than I am that I ought not to go in for ten more years of school work without some most distinct voice.'

Edward took nine-year-old Martin with him to the consecration ceremony and noted the child's pale face and wide open eyes fixed on his godfather's face as he struggled to take in the significance of the service. God had wonderfully upheld Martin in his sincerity and goodness, he thought. Martin was the most docile of his children, the one least likely to offend by wilfulness or tantrums, or to depart from the truth. Edward tried not to have favourites, but he doted on his eldest, seeing in him a future servant of the Lord, even more steadfast than he was himself.

Edward's old Headmaster, James Prince Lee, Bishop of Manchester, died in 1869. He received the news from his friend Wickenden and was shocked. But the day of dying struck his imagination and he wrote: 'To die on Xmas Eve – to pass into Paradise on Xmas Eve – and perhaps catch whispers of angels or prophets telling what Heaven was like when first *He* was gone from among them to be a child.'

When Edward was at Wellington he could best be described as a High Churchman; he had no leanings to Puseyism and its reaction towards primitive Catholicism, nor had he any sympathy with Broad Churchmanship, in spite of his friendship with Charles Kingsley. He was an ardent Anglican and he believed in the principles of the Reformation and that the Anglican Communion was by descent and inheritance a branch of the Catholic Church. The Church of Rome had corrupted the true Catholic doctrine. He never had a high opinion of Newman's intellect or logical faculty, neither did he think much of *Tracts for the Times*, 90 of which had been published at Oxford between 1833 and 1841. He liked the solemnity and dignity of ritual and was conversant with its smallest details. He showed this in the Wellington Chapel services which were in the Catholic tradition, but not overwhelmingly so. His liturgical observances included Matins and Vespers every day, with three services on Sunday; yet in his early days he even had evening Communions. His sermons were simple and practical, but so long that their effect was somewhat lessened. He never disguised what he believed, but tried not to give offence by showing any denominational bias. His High Churchmanship was deliberately moderated, both in ritual and doctrinal statement, so that no Master, parent or Governor had cause to complain of extremism or an attempt to influence the boys towards any particular doctrine.

In worldly matters Edward was a complete Puritan. His anxious imagination held that the world, which he scarcely knew, was hard and wicked, dangerously attractive but full of temptations of every kind. Theatre, fashion, sport, racing – all appeared to him to be lying in wait to entice godly young men into cynicism and abandonment of religion. Though he grew more tolerant in later years, at Wellington he preached that enjoyment without a serious background would relax the moral fibre.

There was an occasion when Arthur, during his university years, was invited by an acquaintance of the family to a supper party at a club at which Henry Irving and other theatrical personages were to be present. Edward did not forbid the young man to go, but wrote him a long and affectionate letter which Arthur thought rather pathetic. Edward spoke as though the outing might lead to a parting of the ways between them and that such an apparently innocent and interesting evening might mask dubious standards, even immorality. He also mentioned, in careful and delicate phrases, that acquaintanceship with prominent people (unless they were Bishops, of course) would be a vulgar conception of success. Arthur could not bear the implied reproach that would follow his acceptance, so he declined the invitation. But he could not help reflecting that his father did not allow for the buoyancy of youth and youth's clear-eyed resilience against things that could harm him; although on that particular occasion it is not likely that Arthur would have been sucked into much debauchery. Edward was delighted that his blackmail had worked.

Minnie was very different in her outlook on life, religion and morals. She saw things in truer proportions, though never ceasing to care deeply about great issues. If life was to be understood, she realised, one must sometimes just be content to sit down, watch it, and reflect upon what one saw. Edward would have thought that to be almost a dereliction of duty. He had a mistrust of tantalising by-ways. The difficult path was preferable to the easy one; the prospect of Heaven was so much nearer if one had to struggle. His principles and practices were hard to live up to.

CHAPTER EIGHT

I N 1870 a serious outburst of illness occurred in the school, possibly due to faulty drainage. On March 19th the first boy died, and in all three boys died that year: William Blackett-Ord, Stanley Marriott and George Alban, and a gloom descended on the school. By Speech Day it had lifted somewhat. The Duke of Wellington presented a colossal head of his father, the Iron Duke. At first it was placed in the centre of the front quadrangle where, however, it was found to be 'inconvenient' and consequently moved to above Great School.

At the beginning of 1871 Edward joined Westcott and Lightfoot at the Borrowdale Hotel, Derwentwater, for a ten days' holiday. They walked over the frozen lake, up Borrowdale, from Honiston Crag to Buttermere and from Lodore to Barrow Falls. During their time there the three friends talked mainly of the Revelation of God through Christ and in the evenings Edward worked at his book on the life of St. Cyprian for many hours.

Before they left the Lake District the frozen falls were beginning to move, the bracken was clothing the slopes of the hills, which were laced by a fine fretwork of ice and snow, with the highest summits in a milky mist. A sharp hailstorm filled the valley with rolling curtains as they descended their last hill. Then there was deep snow and the sky was dark with what had still to come down.

On December 9, 1872, Edward received a letter from the Bishop of Lincoln, offering him the Chancellorship of Lincoln Cathedral, made vacant by the death of Chancellor Massingbird, who had held the office for ten years. The offer was solemnly made; the Bishop had prayed to discharge his duty so as best to promote the Glory of God, and Salvation of Souls; for the good of the Cathedral, the City and Diocese of Lincoln, the Church of England and the Church Universal – a heavy burden for one man to have to bear.

The Bishop attached certain conditions to his offer. Edward would have to devote himself wholly to his Office, the study of theology and the training of theological students, and to the work of Christian Education in the City of Lincoln; he would also have to promise not to take any preferment either in or out of Lincoln without resigning his Chancellorship. Although Edward was more than willing to oblige he refused to pledge himself unconditionally, and he was eventually appointed on his own terms. Before accepting he asked for time to consult Westcott, Lightfoot, and Minnie – 'though my third and best counsellor is not in England, she has always and eagerly loved the thought of a Cathedral home.' Minnie was still convalescing in Wiesbaden and her letter of approval had not arrived by the time Edward had to write his formal letter to the Bishop, so she actually had no part in his decision, though Edward promised to telegraph the Bishop if her advice was contrary to that of his friends.

On Christmas Day he wrote to Minnie again, telling her that the deed was done, and that they would have to live on £1,000 a year, half the salary he had received at Wellington, though expenses would be less, and, in any case, 'holy poverty' was their chosen portion. By the time he was ready to leave the school he was proud of its eminence, the quality of the staff and the responsible attitude of most of the boys. Every time the reality struck that the end was near, 'about every quarter of an hour, a shower of little sparks seem to shoot through one's chest.' Preparing to leave the dear place, in spite of the heartache it had often caused him, was dreadful.

The most dreadful thing, however, was an incident that occurred just before he left. One of the Masters had discovered a 'grave moral delinquency' (the details of which were never made public) concerning three of the boys. Whatever it was had taken place during the holidays. Edward asked the parents of the boys to remove them immediately, and this was done. But the parents of two of them, on the ground that the offence had not taken place on the school premises, objected to the request and brought the matter before the Governors. After a long discussion the anti-Bensonites persuaded the others to ask the Master to reinstate the boys. Edward consulted the Headmasters of some of the other leading public schools, and they all agreed that he had acted correctly; and a Memorandum, with the letters from these Headmasters attached and sent to the Governors, concluded by saying firmly that he would not reconsider his decision. If the Governors persisted in their demand then he would resign, and there would be a great and damaging scandal in the educational world. In the event the Governors reversed their previous decision, and the boys were not expelled, but discreetly removed from the school. Mr Penny was the first person to be told that Edward would be leaving after the next Michaelmas term. 'It was a bolt from the blue,' he wrote, 'and I was stunned. I could not restrain my tears and as I sat weeping before him, he rose from his chair and kissed me on the forehead.' The rest of the Masters, assembled in the sixth form classroom, heard the news in silence. The Senior Assistant Master tried to say something, but choked and fell silent; the rest rose up, shook hands with their Master and left the room.

When the last Speech Day came round Edward proposed the toast of his Governors, and the Duke of Wellington responded with 'the health of Dr. Benson'. Then the Duke outdid himself in incoherence, hesitancy and bathos. Edward returned thanks and proposed the health of his successor, the Rev. E.C. Wickham (who married the daughter of Mr Gladstone, the Liberal Prime Minister, and stayed at Wellington for 20 years). Afterwards, on their way to the Master's Lodge, the Duke linked his arm in Edward's and said, 'Made a hash of it – knew I should. But I really did try to say something this time. You have made the College what it is – not a mere charity school, but one of the finest public schools in England – and I and my family are more than content with the result.' Then he dug Edward in the ribs with his elbow. 'That's what I meant to say, but, Lord, when I stood up to speak it all ran out at my heels.'

On his last Sunday at Wellington in the summer of 1873 Edward preached a sermon, the text of which was: 'Esteeming the reproach of Christ greater riches than the treasures of Egypt.' It was a moving and solemn farewell in which he took no credit to himself for all the wonderful things that had happened during the last 15 years, though everybody knew that almost everything was a testimonial to his vitality and religious passion.

He began the sermon by describing gifts from God which may justly be called Treasures. 'The first is the wise *comparison* of our own treasure, worldly with spiritual, earthly with lasting. The second is the *recognition* of them all as treasures. The third is the *hallowing* of our treasures – the *consecration* of them to highest ends.' Then he went on to say what the Treasures are: The Method of Study, Tradition, Opportunity and Association: all, it seemed, to be found at Wellington in their highest manifestation.

Then, for once, he became simple and his words were moving. 'And now farewell. It has been given to me to watch for 15 years God's wonderful work, and I thank Him and praise Him for all I have seen. You will pray for me too that the years may in no sense be lost to me; for I have seen a new growth in England, organic, spiritual, healthful, abiding. Far above all material enrichment, I have seen the touching sight of youth and childhood gathering round us, partly conscious of ignorance, ready to learn, tremulously anxious to do right, to please the parents who surrendered them to us, or to honour a dead father's name. And how can I thank God for His works of grace, for the unfolding of high principle and the kindling of Christian fire? for such a power there has been in our prefectual order – the Lord increase it evermore. And I speak with diffidence, and I speak with reverence, of the nearer counsel and goodness that has been by my side; no-one has ever come to help me without some true touch of devotion to the high cause.

'Thus for 15 years I have laboured, often in most salutary trouble, yet with ever-increasing happiness. The trouble is gone like a shadow. The happiness cannot be taken away. I have seen you all come here; everyone who labours or is laboured for has been welcomed by me. I have seen near a thousand men go away to labour in their turn where and as duty summoned and God ordained. And now I go myself. I came to the newest educational and spiritual work in England, bidden to shape it. I go away to the most ancient. Here I have made rules for others; I go to strive to conform myself to rule.

'So let your hearts beat strong with energy, yet be cool through self-restraint: and your work be wrought with diligence and rendered with cheerfulness; and your faces bright with modesty, yet bold with frankness; and the grasp of your hands be firm and generous. For you will be men. You will seek Purity … Truth … Love… But that these things may be, you must fix eye and heart unflinchingly on Christ and His Reproach; you must adore it, you must achieve it, for there is no treasure like the Reproach of Christ, understood and loved and liked.'

Minnie and the family went to Chapel again the following Tuesday evening, and afterwards the Masters waited for Edward in the antechapel. He shook hands with them silently, then they walked through the corridor into the cloistered court. There the boys were assembled. They began by cheering him, and Edward raised his cap. His lips began to tremble, and tears started in his eyes. The boys crowded round to shake his hand; his imperfections, his rages, the rules that they resented, the weary hours of work, the absolute discipline, all were forgotten. At the door by the Masters' Library leading out towards the Lodge a number of Prefects pressed forward. 'Goodbye, my dear, dear fellows,' he said falteringly, then he and his family went out into the summer dusk, followed by another roar of cheers.

'If any one man made Wellington, it was Edward White Benson,' wrote the author of *A Victorian School*, ' he made a great public school – made it out of nothing. He was eager the school should not become a purely military institution, or a mere ante-room to the Cadet College, and, by every means, he strove to create a link with the universities and to enlarge the future of the boys who came to Wellington.'

CHAPTER NINE

T HE Chancery at Lincoln, which faced the east front of the Cathedral, was built in the 14th century. The front was of Tudor brick, had a large oriel window and a great double door of oak in which Commonwealth bullets were embedded. Inside there was a long low hall from which a staircase led to a stately lobby opening on to a beautiful panelled drawing-room overlooking the Close. In the corner of the drawing-room was a winding staircase with pentacles on the steps to ward off devils. There were vaulted cellars, a wall of ancient masonry pierced by 14th century arrows, servants' quarters, sitting-rooms, an oratory, a study, nurseries, schoolroom, bedrooms and many passages. With its dark corners and huge empty cupboards the house was a marvellous place for games of hide-and-seek, and a floor of attics full of gurgling water cisterns was the haunt of ghosts and corpses, which Fred was to describe graphically in *David Blaize* more than forty years later.

Martin and Arthur were given a sitting-room of their own, called Bec, after Anthony de Bec, a former Chancellor. The wall of the schoolroom contained part of a 15th century oak screen; when the wallpaper was removed an aumbry was discovered. The garden, which lay at the back of the stables, was an acre in extent, and was bounded by a high wall fringed with golden wallflowers, against which grew apricot and peach trees; and there was a pear tree that might have been designed specially as a climbing frame for small children. In the north-west and north-east corners were two ivy-covered towers belonging to the old medieval city wall. One of them was in a dangerous state of decay, but the other was solid and an ideal place for adventurous outlaws and sheriff's men. A grassy space was given over to lawn tennis, which Edward, Martin and Arthur played enthusiastically but inexpertly. The 'racquets' were wooden bats and the court was marked with tape fastened down with hairpins. If a foot got entangled in the tape the whole construction came to pieces... In the garden there was a large Roman sarcophagus which had been dug up in a nearby gravel pit, and which Edward had bought for a few shillings from the workmen. To the ghoulish delight of the young Bensons it contained the bones of two children. A lot of Roman and medieval pottery, coins and tokens came to light when the gardener had been busy.

Under Edward's direction the interior of the house was greatly improved. Two bedrooms were turned into a large study, the lobby windows were filled with stained armorial glass, and a tiny chapel was created from a room above the porch, and beautified by stained glass windows given by Canon Wickenden. Prayers were said there morning and evening, and on Wednesdays and Fridays a Litany which Edward had translated from the Greek was used, and in the evenings a simple form of Compline.

In spite of the grandeur of the house and the wonders of the garden the Bensons lived very economically. They had neither horse nor carriage, and only maid-servants. A previous Chancellor called Pretyman had lived in such state that a footman stood behind the chair of every guest at dinner.

Minnie was still in Germany at the time of the move from Wellington, and this was partly why Edward suffered from the worst depression he had ever experienced. Allied to his unhappiness at her absence was a reaction against the move itself. He felt that the new surroundings would never suit him; nor did he relish the fact that his salary had been halved. He sent a postcard to Minnie in September, 1873, in which he tried to be gay and insouciant and, surprisingly for him, succeeded. 'All going well,' he wrote. 'Boys very industrious and happy. Arrangements are very complete at the Chancery; there is a man to make dust, and a man to burn paint off doors, and a man to make a noise with a hammer, and a man to throw soot at the books, and a man to dig for tobacco pipes in the garden, and a boy not to fetch or carry, and rods and rings not to fit, and carpets not to fit also, and women to wet floors … and I fell down yesterday and scratched a shilling's worth of skin off my elbow, and today made a two shilling hole in my trouser knee. Baby is splendid and so dirty and happy … and Beth seems to like everything.'

But to Wickenden he later wrote: 'I am beginning to look on the months hitherto as a sort of illness. So many anxieties, so many uncertainties, so many wonders whether one had done rightly or quixotically. Now as one gets into work the clouds drift away.' 'We have been through a bad time,' he wrote to another friend. 'My dear wife mends so slowly.'

When Minnie eventually returned from Wiesbaden she had obviously improved physically, and was able to take up the household reins with a fresh determination to surmount them, and show a new efficiency that was all part of her resolve not to be made miserable by Edward's sulks. Although still fond of her difficult husband, she was much more clear-eyed about the situation. Her native intelligence, formerly repressed, now charmed all who came into contact with her. She realised that she had a first-class mind, untrained though it might be. From then on there was a more equal relationship between man and wife.

At first Minnie did not take to Cathedral life. The society was not stimulating and she missed the Kingsleys, Mrs Meyer and other friends. Elizabeth Wordsworth was too much in evidence for her liking, but it was impossible for Minnie to be jealous, such a thing was not in her nature. Besides, her own heart had melted into love once again and Lincoln became the source of a new happiness. Caroline Charlotte Mylne, known as 'Tan', was the wife of a theological student who was taking Orders after a career in business. Many years later he became Vicar of Addington. She was a middle-aged woman of charm and unaffected dignity, with strong evangelical leanings. Minnie, passing through a religious crisis, was convinced that Tan was a gift to her from God, and for the first time God became real to her. No longer was he a mysterious, unknowable Being hidden behind rites and rules, but a personal Father in whom she could confide. Tan's Christianity was simple but fierce; it appealed to Minnie's uncomplicated mind and helped her not to become sceptical or impatient. She did not confide in Edward, who would not have understood her born-again rapture. He was left to struggle with dogma, ritual, the Trinity and Jesuitism. Minnie's crisis was resolved in a mystical awareness of the message of religion. For the remainder of her time at Lincoln she was deeply attached to Mrs Mylne, whom she considered to have been an anchor to her troubled spirit when she was full of doubt and mental turmoil; and when circumstances parted them the friendship endured. Edward was puzzled but never imagined that there was anything but a spiritual bond between the two women.

Seven-year-old Fred fell in love too – with one of the Cathedral choristers. Once Cathedral services had been purgatory for the lively boy, but now Sunday was a day of joy – for as long as the passion lasted. During the Lincoln years the young Bensons were encouraged to take up numerous hobbies, all of which stimulated their interest in the world around them. They drew pictures, wrote poems and stories, acted home-made plays, collected wildflowers, shells and birds' eggs and set up a museum in a room their father provided. Fred and Maggie were allies because they were nearest in age, and thus there was a special closeness between them. Martin was now away at school; Nellie and Arthur formed their own team, and Hugh was too babyish to participate in their activities. Fred was the most imaginative of the children and the most extrovert; he endeared himself to everybody. The other siblings were of a more serious turn of mind and Hugh could be petulant and stubborn, playing on the fact he was special to Beth.

When Edward's depression had lifted he flung himself into the work at Lincoln with great enthusiasm. He had thought he might have more time for literary work, but instead found himself busier than he had ever been. He started a Theological College for young men studying for Orders where he lectured twice a week. He had a Chapel in the Cathedral restored for holding a daily early Matins. He began a Bible Class for the mechanics from Clayton and Shuttleworth's, and Robey's Works. He gave Lenten Lectures on Church history and, with many misgivings, opened a Night School in the city for working men and boys, and presided over a band of voluntary teachers. Many of the students were rough and tough, but Edward's personality carried them all with him. In his first speech to the school Edward began: 'Gentlemen – no, – Men and boys' 'And Nippers!' called out a boy of about 15. 'Men, boys and nippers!' Edward began again. When the Night School opened in the Central School in Silver Street it had 400 students. Simple test papers in writing and arithmetic were set, then classes formed, and without any fuss good order was established throughout the school.

The men of the Bible Class were delighted with Edward's outspokenness and lack of condescension, and he was equally pleased with their vigour and refusal to touch their forelocks. When he left Lincoln they made him a set of dessert dishes out of bronzed metal from the Coleby mines. He loved this service, even though, in terms of artistry, it was not especially beautiful; and it appeared on the Benson dinner table for the rest of his life.

The qualities that endeared Edward to the working class of Lincoln were almost too intangible to describe. It was not because he was a clergyman. If he had been a working man he would have been just as trusted as a leader. When he was with his men he seemed to be one of them, not because he consciously tried to be, but because he could not help it.

He became the first warden of the Society for Mission Priests, which was formed in 1875, and he was the life and soul of a general mission which was held throughout the city in February, 1876. He was also the leading Missioner in the Church of Saint Peter-at-Arches, and his sermons, earnest and practical, were like no other sermons preached at a mission, dwelling as they did chiefly upon the duty of loving God and loving one another.

Edward and Minnie, she with her new-found confidence and natural gaiety at last being able to express itself, blew like a spring wind through the autumnal Close. Minnie started a musical society which met weekly to sing Victorian glees and Bach Chorales, she singing alto and beating time with a paper knife. She was also prominent in the Essay and Discussion Society and was considered rather daring for openly advocating George Eliot's novels to the wives of Canons, telling them not to mind the shocking parts. She read *The Mill on the Floss* to the children, and no-one was corrupted. Sex education was, of course, confined to birds and bees, and when Fred asked her what was the difference between a bull and an ox, her immediate reply, uttered without hesitation, was that the bull was the father and the ox the uncle.

In Lincoln, as in most Cathedral cities, society tended to break up into cliques, and there was a physical line of demarcation in the steep hill (one of the steepest in the country) which divided those below from those above. Edward and Minnie set themselves to break down barriers and to bring all together, and in that aim they largely succeeded, so that 'above hill' and 'below hill' gradually lost all meaning. Their popularity with all classes was very marked, so that Edward could say, 'dearest Lincoln, its angels and its men!'

Edward especially delighted in movements which brought him into contact with the city's Labour leaders and though he was a natural Tory, he often advocated reading a red-hot Socialist paper to counterbalance the opinions given by one on the Right wing. 'The reception awarded me by the working man was ridiculously and divertingly affectionate,' he wrote after a meeting, 'you can't think what funny things they said. But their looks, behaviour and tone and evident upward progress were all most striking. There was no playing ladies and gentlemen though they were very well dressed. I gleaned some capital hints worth a clergyman's knowing.'

Edward's unbending was such that he even developed a sense of humour. 'I've had a Colonial Bishop lately,' he wrote to Wickenden, 'who has utterly sickened me. I vow and declare that if any friend of mine is made a Colonial Bishop and doesn't eschew – buckles – tights – and Aprons – I won't speak to him – it's the buckles that ruin the Colonial Church – and the loops of the hats. Think of it. Men taking Shepherdships, for Buckles and Loops. But true as I sit here.'

Edward nearly became a Colonial Bishop himself, for in May, 1876, he received a letter from John Wordsworth who had been asked by Lord Salisbury, the Secretary of State for India, to sound him out about accepting the Bishopric of Calcutta, a post perhaps next in importance to the Throne of Canterbury. Edward was tempted, for it was several rungs up the ladder; yet again he sought advice from Westcott and Lightfoot, then drew up a paper with reasons for and against accepting. 'Pro' included 'Receive it as a call from God'; 'You could introduce Cathedral life in Calcutta' and 'The forsaking of a family for the Gospel's sake is recognised as a distinct necessity and has a special promise of blessing.' 'Con' included, 'In the present state of Society and thought, Anti-Christian temptations beset boys of 14 and 16. Personal influence is needed';

'Cathedral life in England is a spiritual function for which I have surrendered more visibly useful work and larger means.' The last 'Con', however, seems to have settled the matter – 'Wife suffers under hot temperatures.' And he declined to let his name go forward. So the young family of six children, ranging from the age of 16 to five, were not put at the disadvantage of spending their formative years in England without their parents.

Edward was not long without another decision to make for in December, 1876, Lord Beaconsfield, at the suggestion of Queen Victoria, and with her expressed wish that he would accept, offered him the newly-created See of Truro, which was to be detached from the unwieldy diocese of Exeter. Disraeli knew of Edward's essential Tory principles, his capacity for hard work and his devotion to the Church. He would receive £3,000 a year, though out of it he would have to provide a house and pay the travelling expenses in largely railwayless Cornwall, thus having to buy carriage and horses. Edward had few doubts or ritual hesitations, and appeals for guidance that had accompanied previous invitations were neglected; though he did ask Westcott, 'Had I better say Yes or No?' After an interview with the Prime Minister he accepted the lofty post, excited by the new challenge, the chance to inaugurate, administer, order. Instead of being a subordinate in a great tradition, which had always irked him, he would be pre-eminent and supreme, as he had been at Wellington, but this time not answerable to a Board of Governors.

The news of the Chancellor's approaching departure was received with real regret, both in the diocese and in the city. His zeal and tenderness had been greatly appreciated, and the gifts he received showed what the feelings of the people of Lincoln were. The Tutors and students of the Theological College presented him with a pastoral staff of ivory and ebony, filled with silver and set with carbuncles. (In his will Edward bequeathed the staff to the Cathedral at Truro). The City gave him a magnificent present of silver plate, which was presented at a public meeting presided over by the Mayor, at which Edward heard the story of the man who had suggested arranging the forks, spoons and fish knives to spell out the words 'Farewell, Beloved Chancellor'. But the present that he valued most was the set of dessert dishes made by the men from his Bible Class.

For the children the move was welcome; the future promised change and excitement. Martin was now at Winchester and Arthur at Eton: the rest were growing up innocent and artless, their days spent doing delightful things, their mother and Beth loving and caring. Their father's constant scrutiny and occasional displeasure were irritations that were borne with increasing resignation. Nothing tragic, even serious, had happened during the three-and-a-half years at Lincoln; there had been nothing to battle against. The time had been a placid idyll, a pleasant diversion rather than a time of discovery. On the morning that the news had been broken to them Fred and Maggie went for a walk. Instead of telling each other stories, as they usually did, they whispered, 'The Lord Bishop of Truro! The Lord Bishop of Truro!' And the sedate walking pace turned into a little dance, and the words were blown away by the breeze so that everything around them shared the news.

Edward was consecrated to the Bishopric of Truro on April 25, 1877, in St. Paul's Cathedral by Dr. Tait, the Archbishop of Canterbury, assisted by the Bishops of London, Winchester, Hereford, Lincoln, Salisbury, Exeter and Ely; and the Suffragan Bishops of Nottingham and Dover. The occasion was one of the utmost solemnity. The Church of England had made a fresh start and restored one of its waste places and it was touching to see the newly-consecrated Bishop kneel at the altar with his wife and children. Canon Lightfoot preached the sermon, bidding the friend of his boyhood and youth a heart-felt God-speed, taking as his text for the sermon the words of the Apostle from 1 Corinthians: 'I am made all things to all men that I might by all means save some.' Canon Lightfoot reminded his congregation that of all the counties in England Cornwall was unique – in the occupation of its labouring classes, its fishermen and its miners; unique in its religious condition – the wide influence of the Wesleyan body; unique in its nationality – in the tenacity of the British character and the pride of British ancestry, who held the land long before it was overrun by foreign invaders, just as much as it was unique in its vegetation; and unique also in the physical conformation of its coast, its rugged piles of granite and its rigid masses of serpentine; and in the Apostle's spirit the new Bishop must strive to be all things to all men so that he might bring all together in Christ. And he would take with him the prayers of many hearts – of the friends who had grown up with him from boyhood, the prayers of the pupils whom he had sent forth armed for the battle of life; the prayers of his own dear people of Lincoln; the prayers of the fathers in God who were assembled that day; the prayers of the congregation, of the Diocese. and of the whole English Church.

CHAPTER TEN

The movement for the resuscitation of the ancient Cornish bishopric dates back to the Reformation. In the reign of Henry VIII, on the suppression of the monastic houses, Cranmer proposed that a part of the revenues should be set aside for the foundation of new bishoprics. The funds, however, were put to purposes which can hardly be described as ecclesiastical, and the scheme was not revived until 1847, when Henry Phillpotts held the See of Exeter. In that year a Bill was introduced into the House of Commons by Lord John Russell, the Prime Minister, for the foundation of four new Episcopal Sees, of which Bodmin was named as one. This second attempt failed, and a subsequent proposal in 1854 to establish a Cornish See at St. Columb also came to nothing. But when Bishop Phillpotts died in 1869 the long-pending question was reopened. The Diocese of Exeter was far too unwieldy, and when Dr. Temple went there he was, from the first, an advocate of its partition. It was not, however, until 1876 that the Home Secretary presented and carried the Bill for the formation of the See of Truro.

Edward was installed and enthroned as Bishop of Truro on May 1, 1877, in St. Mary's Church, that church having been chosen to have the Cathedral Church of the Diocese built around it, and Truro was raised to the style and dignity of a City. Letters patent were signed to that effect on August 17, 1877.

The new Bishop's remarkable energy was shown almost immediately. Once more he was called upon to create. He had to set in order a diocese: to plan and to inaugurate the various institutions which constitute the necessary machinery of such an ecclesiastical district; to build a Cathedral; to select a Chapter: and to visit and infuse Church life into every parish within his jurisdiction, which included the whole of Cornwall and five parishes in Devonshire, with a combined population of about 330,000. Few men would have had the courage to face such a prospect, but Edward's goals included the surmounting of obstacles.

The Ecclesiastical Commissioners did not provide a house so the Bishop had to find his own, and he chose a large Queen Anne house about a mile out of Truro on a hill overlooking the town and the tidal estuary. It had been the vicarage of Kenwyn with an extensive glebe and a large garden, and was more like a country house than a vicarage. The Vicar of Kenwyn, who became one of the first Canons of Truro, wanted to take a long holiday and then move into a smaller house, and was very willing for the new Bishop to take over. With the aid of a fund raised to provide a suitable residence the house was enlarged; stables were converted into kitchens, two new wings and a library were added, and a kitchen became a chapel. New stables and a drive were built and the house was renamed *Lis Escop* (Bishop's Court in Cornish). There were plans for further enlargements but the money ran out.

Lis Escop was simple and comfortable, much smaller than the Chancery at Lincoln, but large enough. There was a good schoolroom, various bedrooms and nurseries, half a dozen attics, but not until Edward had planned and overseen the alterations were there any rooms for guests. The house was set in 15 acres of copses, valleys and streams, and near it were beehives, haystacks and a summerhouse. The mild climate encouraged trees and shrubs to grow with great luxuriance. Camellias flourished and hydrangeas grew richly out of doors, and with fuchsias and magnolias there were flowers blooming all the year round. A gardener and a boy assistant kept it all in fair order, though the weeds grew profusely and no-one could call it a smart garden. From the windows of the house there was a wide view down the green valley and the spire of St. Mary's rose from a muddle of grey slate roofs. The high viaduct of the Great Western Railway crowned the valley and below it lay the wide tidal creek with its great mud-flats among the steep hills. It was a view of great beauty, full of mystery and peace. The ancient church of Kenwyn, with its four imposing pinnacles, and schoolroom built over the lych-gate, stood behind the house. There was a flight of fern-fringed steps by the main door leading to a spring which had once been a holy baptismal well.

The Bensons soon owned a barouche and a brougham with a pair of strong horses which could be ridden if desired. The railway station was only two miles away at the other end of the town and when the boys were going back to school they walked to the station and the town bus fetched their luggage.

The first time the barouche was used was when it was sent to the station to meet Edward's train. Fred begged that he might go to meet his father on his own, and was seen by other members of the family, who were shopping in the town, sitting upright in the middle of the back seat, his hands clasped, his eyes cast down, and a look of bishopric importance on his young face. Edward was not told how nearly his position had been usurped – making fun of the cloth was not to be encouraged.

Edward had hardly set foot in Cornwall when he began to raise funds to
build a Cathedral, which would be the first that had been built in England
since the Reformation. St. Mary's, the nucleus of his vision, had practically
no congregation for much of Cornwall was a stronghold of Methodism. At
the first Diocesan Conference, held in October, 1877, he made his views on
Dissent and on the work of the Church open and unequivocal. 'We
withhold not our sympathy from every company which loves the Lord
Jesus Christ in sincerity and truth; and we are bounden to tenderness for
our own people who have lived and laboured for higher and more delicate,
as against ruder, less articulated forms of faith, remote, unknown, all but
despondent. I shall lay it down as an axiom that, irrespective of every other
work of our own, and of every work done by every other body in Christ's
name, it is the final and ultimate duty of this Church to provide Church
worship and Church instruction wherever there is a group of people out of
reach of them. And it is futile to bid us acquiesce in teachings which we
know doctrinally to be unevangelical, philosophically to be mere food for
modern critics, historically to be incapable of permanent independence,
marked for either wider errancy in the future, or for gradual return.
Spiritual submission to Scripture, philosophical consistency with all the
explored truth, historical adaptability to circumstances, may make us
confident as we again and again review this Church's title-deeds and
transactions in our studies; but, if confidence has begotten indolence
abroad, then right humbly we may learn the very elements of Christian
duty from those who have dotted, nay crowded, our land with tabernacles
of Christian assemblies.'

At the same Conference a Committee was appointed to consider the
necessary steps to be taken to provide a suitable building, but nothing
further was done until April, 1878, when there was a county meeting in
Bishop Phillpott's Library, under the presidency of Lord Mount-
Edgecumbe, the Lord Lieutenant. The Rector of St. Mary's generously
placed £4,000 in the hands of the Bishop, money which had been collected
towards the restoration of the church. No less than £15,000 was contributed
in the room during the meeting. This was remarkable because Cornwall,
with the decline of its tin-mining industry, was a very poor county. Edward
himself contributed £2,000. To make his heart even fuller, the elderly Lady
Rolle of Bicton, whose father had been a Cornish clergyman, sent him a
cheque for £40,000, letting it be known that she had lost her heart to him
– she was about 85 at the time. Her very infirm husband, Lord Rolle, had
attended Queen Victoria's Coronation, had tripped over his robes as he
ascended the dais where the young Queen sat, and rolled down to the
bottom of the steps. So the Queen got up and went down the steps to
receive his salutation while he was still spread-eagled on the carpet.

The site of the proposed building, and some adjacent property, was bought for £10,000, and J.L. Pearson R.A. was appointed architect, though he did not submit a design as the other applicants had done. His attitude towards a religious building was that it was successful, not because it was beautiful, but if it made the visitor fall to his knees with awe; and that was apparently enough for the committee. The building operations began and it was estimated that £100,000 would have to be found to cover all the expenses. All the money was found before Edward left Truro.

Edward took Arthur Mason and G.H. Whitaker with him to Truro, both of whom had been Assistant Masters at Wellington. Mason had gone on to be Assistant Tutor at Trinity College and Vicar of St. Michael's, Cambridge; he became Diocesan Missioner at Truro. Whitaker, a Fellow of St. John's College, Cambridge, was made Chancellor of the Cathedral, with a view to founding a Theological College as Edward had done at Lincoln. The effect of the College, in the increased spirituality and efficiency of the clergy who eventually passed through the course there, was widely felt throughout the Diocese.

The Rev. John Andrewes Reeve, subsequently the Rector of Lambeth, after a period at Addington, was the curate at Kenwyn, an undergraduate friend of Arthur Mason, and an intimate friend of the Bensons. He adored children, continually tossed back his mane of yellow hair and burst into peals of laughter in a rich high tenor at the slightest suggestion of a joke. Fred gave him his sloppy heart, transferred eventually from Mrs Carter, the organist, and every Sunday evening after tea the two would retire to a spare bedroom where, with the curate's arm around Fred's neck, he would read him the sermon he was about to preach. Hugh, however, did not respond to the curate's advances. He would survey him with disdain, and disagree with his rapturous enthusiasms.

The Truro Bishopric Act of 1876 gave power to the Bishop to appoint 24 honorary Canons. Edward, with his reverence for antiquity, and his strong desire to show the continuity of the Church, was anxious to link the newly-found See with ancient memories, and attached to each Stall the name of some early missionary Bishop or renowned Saint from the old Celtic calendars, or from those who, in early ages, gave their names to the numerous villages in the county.

The laying of the Foundation Stones of the new Cathedral took place on May 20, 1880, in the presence of a great multitude. Truro put on its brightest colours, and triumphant arches spanned the streets. The Prince and Princess of Wales, accompanied by their sons, Prince Albert Victor and Prince George, were guests for the occasion of Viscount Falmouth of Tregothuan, and from his home they drove to the city and were received in state by the civic authorities. The stones were laid by the Prince of Wales as Duke of Cornwall – one at the north-east corner of the exterior of the choir, and the other in the nave – with full masonic as well as ecclesiastical ceremonies. The Grand Officers of England and the Provincial Officers of Cornwall assisted the Prince, though doubts had been expressed at the fitness of Freemasonry to be present. But the Prince's address attempted, though somewhat superficially, to show that everything was above board: 'Be it known unto you we being lawful Masons, true and faithful to the laws of our country, although not ourselves operative masons, have been from time to time immemorial associated with the erection of buildings raised for the benefit of mankind and the glory of the great architect of the universe. We have among us secrets concealed from those who are not Masons, but they are lawful and honourable, and are not opposed to the laws either of God or of man. They were entrusted to Masons in ancient times, and it is our duty to convey them down to our posterity. We are assembled here in the presence of you all to erect a house for the worship and praise of the Most High, which I pray that God may prosper as it seems good to Him, and as the first duty of Masons is to invoke His blessing, I call upon you to join our Grand Chaplain in an address to the Throne of Grace.'

The most solemn part of the service was the benediction of the stones by Edward, followed by hymns and psalms sung and chanted by a choir gathered from various parts of the Diocese. The Bishops of Exeter and Madagascar were there, and a great body of the Diocesan clergy. Among the laity who attended were the Lord Lieutenant, the Lord Mayor of London, originally from Cornwall, whom Edward had specially invited because Londoners had given him substantial support, the Mayor and Corporation of Truro and the municipal authorities of various boroughs in Cornwall and Devonshire. Archbishop Tait of Canterbury was not able to be present owing to a family bereavement. 'The weather was gorgeous,' Edward wrote later in his diary. 'When the ceremony was at its height, the sky was more beautiful than I ever beheld it. One deepest lustrous blue over the whole heaven above the great enclosure, and right above us and in view the tiniest, most delicate white clouds flecked it all over in the most symmetrical way. I must not write what it suggests.'

Edward plunged into the work of his new Diocese with his usual enthusiasm, and the welcome he received from most warm Cornish hearts made him feel very affectionate towards them. Communications were very difficult in the Cornish peninsula. Many places were quite out of reach of the railway, the hills were steep and the roads bad. Edward's first task was to get to know personally every parish and every incumbent in the Diocese, so he went on long driving tours, staying at remote vicarages and old country houses in out-of-the-way places; and he returned with many curious stories of the doings of 'Christian' people in those secluded places; and in his diary he made some acid comments about the lack of generosity he sometimes found.

He looked over the plans for a church at Mount Hawke where the vicar, in three years, and helped by Nonconformists, had raised £800 for a church and £100 for a parsonage. 'Lord Falmouth and Mr Basset, its two great landowners, have given £10 each and refused further help,' he wrote, 'though each receives £500 or £600 a year from the district. Sir E. Williams expresses himself as ready to subscribe if the rest will. The rest will not.' On the same day he added, 'Today Mr Brougham, the small, deformed, but fine-faced Parson of Colan, came. His church is dangerous. The whole roof of the nave has inclined eastward 30 from the perpendicular, parting from the tower. The woodwork is rotten. The great landowner, Sir R. Vivian, has from £700 to £800 a year from the parish; and he will not answer Mr Brougham's letters. At Probus the principal resident farmer is a Noncomformist who says he would rather see people come out of a public house than a church.'

At the conclusion of his first tour Edward felt that he had never met such eccentric men and women in his life, and he was saddened by the animosity that many Nonconformists showed to him.

In one village the Vicar's sister read the lessons in church in a deep bass voice – the only example of a woman taking part in a service that Edward had come across. In another village he heard the story of a curate who had to be chained to the altar rails while he read the service because he would rush out of church if his own activities were interrupted by, for instance, the congregation's responses. The churchwarden unlocked the padlock and freed the curate when the service was over. Edward noticed a curious phenomenon about the many Nonconformists in his Diocese, after reading widely in their lives and writings in order to understand the hold they had established over the religious Celtic mind. Whenever he gave a sermon or address in the remotest parts of Cornwall where Methodism was especially dominant, he was surprised to find that his congregations included a large number of them who apparently were edified by his oratory in spite of themselves. He frankly recognised that Nonconformity had kept religion alive in Cornwall when the Church had lost its sacred flame and Church teaching was at a very low ebb; and he was ready to be an enthusiastic friend, willing to be drawn into the fuller truth of Christianity, and not an envious foe. Many Methodists accepted his proffered hand, but there were unfriendly sectarians who resented his powers of persuasion, and some of them, like the farmer, delivered fierce invectives against those who forsook the Chapel for Church. One of them stood in the main street of Truro shouting abuse at his recalcitrant congregation; another, standing in the church porch to hear Edward's sermon, loudly exclaimed, when he heard it was to be about baptism, 'Here's the Bishop and that damned Regeneration again!'

'The Cornish Methodists are far narrower than the fine Lincoln strength and eager to find fault,' he wrote to Canon Crowfoot. 'But the land is theirs at present, and they strain every nerve. Middle-class education is in their hands; at Redruth two enormous over-crowded meetings, two moderately empty churches. Much the same elsewhere. But the Church people very good, very quiet, most beautiful, and all hearts very warm – Are we too late to recover ourselves? It's a question I really can't answer. All I know is I've dived, and it's very dark so deep down, and the stream runs very fast. Shall I get to the surface? that matters little – but I am sure it matters very much to morals as well as principles of faith, whether or no Church thought prevails at last.' And to Arthur Mason: 'Human nature and Cornish nature don't mean the same – at least Cornish nature has a big slice overlapping and flapping loose. Missionising here must be a totally different thing from any previous conception of mine. The confusion of sensual excitement with religious passion is awful. The Immoralities of Revivals simply appalling...' Here he was referring to the large number of illegitimate babies he had heard about, especially those born to farm girls and boys; the incest that was common, and the actual orgies that took place in the darkened chapels after particularly hectic revivalist meetings.

Edward took Arthur with him on some of his expeditions. In a bare and windswept miners' hamlet some miles from Truro they came across a modern church of brown stone. At the nearby vicarage they found an old clergyman with a long grey beard digging in the garden. He was dressed in shabby, mud-stained clothes, his coat green with age. The house he asked them into was coldly and barely furnished, and he, having changed into an ill-fitting coat of broadcloth, complained loudly and passionately about his sorry lot. He was 80 years old; his wife had died and there were no children. He had been in the hamlet for 40 years but his congregation had dwindled to three or four families. The Dissenters, whom he had offended, had taken the rest of the people from him. He had no neighbours and spoke to no-one, and filled his time with gardening and turning the Second Book of Chronicles into rhymed verse. He had paid for the printing himself but had not sold a single copy, and he was left with a huge pile of unbound sheets. The old man was not an attractive figure, being tactless and vindictive, but he was pathetic, too, and Edward felt sorry for him – until, not long afterwards, he heard that the clergyman had become engaged to the schoolmistress, a girl of 18 who played the organ in church. Edward could not help writing to him, expressing disapproval of the obviously unsuitable match. He did not expect that the old man would read his letter aloud in church, but he did, and announced to the sparse congregation that, in obedience to his Bishop's wishes, he would abandon the proposed marriage and release his fiancée from the engagement. The girl, who had not been told of her fate, fainted dead away at the organ.

In the direction of Newquay they came upon a ruined church with a churchyard full of tumbled headstones. The interior of the church was green with mould, the books were mildewed and the broken windows let in the winds from the sea. The vicarage, though, was modern and set in a large bare field. Only one downstairs room was furnished, otherwise there were neither carpets, curtains nor furniture anywhere. The room held a deal table, some hard chairs and a few books. On the table was a bowl of porridge and a jug of milk. As Edward and Arthur were looking about in amazement the clergyman returned. He had walked to Newquay, several miles away, to buy a newspaper, as he did every day. He was a dull and depressed man in charge of a church that nobody attended; all the parish were Dissenters. He had simply nothing to do, no enthusiasms and no message to deliver. Though a man of education, he had been defeated by grinding poverty – his living worth less than £100 a year. The vicarage had been built by former wealthy vicars. At the end of the visit he burst into tears and confessed to Edward that he was so lonely and miserable in the evenings that he rented a pew in the Wesleyan chapel and went there to get a little warmth and light, to see human beings and hear them speak. 'I know it is wrong,' he said, 'but I can't bear the perpetual solitude.' Edward tried to comfort him, but there was little he could say.

While on tour in north Cornwall Edward wrote to Minnie: 'Yesterday an old woman sent me her best roses from her cottage and an old blind woman blessed me, and a baby was held for me to kiss at a cottage door. And here where the dissent is something outrageous, the butcher has killed his best bullock, the fishermen went out specially.' The following month, in a letter to Canon Crowfoot, he was in one of his depressed moods: 'Work here is bewildering – the people religious but religion having no more controlling power than if they were studying theology. The principal Church doctrines, except the Atonement, considered as mere superstition – the Atonement not much dwelt on – the Last Judgement supposed to be intended for England, but not for Cornwall. Worship consists in singing hymns. Calvinism has pervaded nearly every place. Now in all such places Sacraments are simply abhorred.'

To another friend he was equally despairing. 'You would scarcely believe what has to be done. Some of our clergy are excellent but crushed with despondency. Some of our laymen are excellent, but their attitude is simply one of pity. Others of both orders are glad enough that nothing is done.'

But Edward laboured on, in spite of the uncooperative attitude of some clergy and laymen, and the fierce enmity of some Dissenters. He continued his county-wide tours, giving Confirmations, taking encouragement and spiritual refreshment to every part of the diocese; and he took the greatest pains with sermons and addresses delivered to the smallest hamlet or the largest town. Sometimes he would himself write an account for the newspapers of a restored church or mission chapel, making the people feel that they were not forgotten, but were valuable and valued.

His institution of the 'Festival of Nine Lessons and Carols' at Truro, now a world-wide Christmas service, would ensure that Edward's name would never be forgotten whatever else he had contributed to the Church.

CHAPTER ELEVEN

T HE climate of Cornwall did not suit Edward's brisk and fiery temperament. There was a dreamy languor and a steamy humidity about the county that fretted him strangely. When he was depressed little things weighed on his mind with fierce acuteness. He was unhappy that his beloved books lost their gilding and that the pages grew mildewed. Engravings became foxed and written papers blurred. He frequently lost control of his feelings and once said gravely to Arthur, his voice full of meaning, that the behaviour of one of his clergy was killing him and that he would have to leave Cornwall.

However, when the cloud lifted, as it always did eventually, to everybody's relief, his attitude to his work was characterised by a remarkable brightness and buoyancy. He relished the freedom to make his own decisions (much more democratically arrived at than when he was at Wellington); he discovered a flair for ecclesiastical organisation, and he was able to ignore politics and outside influences and concentrate entirely on the problems of his Diocese. In spite of the climate he grew to love Cornwall, its romantic past and its romantic people. He found refreshment in the scenery, the hills, wild moorlands, rich valleys and gigantic cliffs. He used to say that Cornwall was the only place where a conversation with anyone he met, in any part of the county, was always stimulating. He was happy because he was able to indulge his devotion to all things venerable and traditional, and felt that his religious life had developed a new freshness and vitality.

That happiness was shattered completely and a fierce trial of faith and patience was to test the bedrock of his faith when, in February, 1878, during his second year as Bishop of Truro, Martin, his eldest and best loved son, died suddenly at Winchester of meningitis. He was nearly 18, a scholar of most singular gifts, having only just failed to secure the school's highest honour, the Goddard Scholarship.

'On Saturday night, 9 February, 1878, about 10 p.m., our sweet eldest son breathed out his soul. It was the hour he was born into both worlds, and he was aged xvii years v months xxi days all sweet and without reproach. His Saviour knew his secret soul not only because he knows all things, but because Martin laid it open to Him.' These are the opening words in the account, covering 34 pages of an octavo-sized diary, that Edward wrote a week after Martin had died. When he wrote it life seemed no longer to have any meaning and he thought he would never understand the mystery of God's purpose. 'It has changed all my views of God's work as it is to be done both in this world and the next, to be compelled to believe that God's plan for him really has run on sweetly, and rightly for him and for all – and yet O he is dead.'

Martin had been having tea with one of the Masters at Winchester when, with flushed face, he suddenly got up, unable to speak. He made signs that he wanted a piece of paper and tried to write the word 'paralysis' on it. He was taken to the sanatorium and a doctor was summoned.

In response to an urgent telegram, Edward arrived on the same evening and found the boy somewhat better. The next day he seemed to be quite himself again – 'his digestive and internal action was returning to normal.' He asked for books, prayed with his father and looked at some pictures. The doctor had not anticipated such a rapid improvement and was sorry to have called Edward, who left for Truro on the Wednesday evening after reading some psalms with his son.

But on Sunday Martin suffered a relapse and became delirious. Edward returned and Minnie arrived on Tuesday. He recognised her with pleasure. Before she came, however, he had uttered what were to be his last words, according to the nurse, while gazing at a part of the room where nothing visible stood. 'How lovely...' he exclaimed. The aphasia returned and he spent the next few days in deep sleep. He clasped his fingers together with the palms joined, just at the top of his breast, as though he were in contant prayer. On Saturday he had difficulty breathing and could not take nourishment. Minnie said, 'Do not be afraid, darling, you are in the Valley of the Shadow of Death; but do not be afraid; God is with you.'

Martin looked at his parents affectionately, sometimes taking their hands for a moment or folding his own together, thus keeping them praying aloud almost continuously. Then he grew tearful, his breathing becoming even more laboured. Minnie said, 'He will wipe away all tears from our eyes...' He formed the letter B with his fingers and Edward said, 'Bread and wine,' and the boy looked happy. Some bread was brought and the three received it after Edward had consecrated it; the Matron put a little wine in a spoon but he could not take it. Instead he grasped the wine-glass with a drop of wine in it with both hands and managed to take it to his mouth. A few minutes before ten o'clock the heavy breathing stopped and they heard a few gentle sobs. Then these ceased. 'Our Martin was quite gone to God,' Edward wrote.

Later Minnie wrote to Beth, a letter eloquent of her courage and faith. 'Be comforted for Martin. He is in perfect peace, in wonderful joy, far happier than ever we could have made him. And what did we desire in our hearts but to make him happy? And now he will help us out of his perfect happiness. He died without a struggle – his pure and gentle spirit passed straight to God his Father, and now he is ours and with us more than ever. Ours now, in a way that nothing can take away... My heart aches for the dear ones at home ... keep before them that God is Love, and that He is loving us in this thing also. And I want them to think of Martin in perfect peace for ever, free from fear, free from pain ... and to think how he will rejoice to see us walking more and more in love for his dear sake. We cannot grudge him his happiness...' Minnie afterwards affirmed that she had experienced a couple of hours of the most wonderful happiness on the day that Martin died, when she realised that though God had taken, yet she could give. But when Edward returned to Truro and stepped from the carriage into the lamplight, his face was, Fred remembered, the face of a most loving man stricken with the death of the boy he had loved best and was knit into his very soul.

Martin was buried in the cloisters of Winchester College, his coffin carried by eight of his Prefect friends. Every year Edward and Minnie returned to Winchester on the anniversary of his death to see the brass, showing him in his scholar's gown, which Edward had caused to be put above the grave.

Edward never fully understood why Martin had been taken from them; it remained the great and inexplicable grief of his life. His faith was unshaken but he could not adapt himself to his loss. And he wrote a poem, found among his papers after his death:

The Martin

The Martins are back to cornice and eaves
  Fresh from the glassy sea.
The Martin of Martins my soul bereaves
  Flying no more to me.

One of them clung to the window-side,
  And twittered a note to me.
'There's a Martin beyond or wind or tide
  Whom you know better than we.

'His nest is hid in clustered rose
  On the Prince's own roof-tree,

When the Prince incomes, when the Prince outgoes,
  The Prince looks up to see.

'Calls him hither or sends him there,
  To the friends of the Holy Three,
With a word of love, or a touch of care.
  Why was he sent to thee?'

Martin I know. And when he went home
  He carried my heart from me.
Half I remain. Ere Martinmas come
  Go with this message from me.

Say 'Thou Prince, he is wholly Thine!
  Sent once on a message to me.
Yet suffer me soon, at morning shine,
  To see him on Thy roof-tree.'

Martin's masters and friends had been amazed at the extraordinary depths of the knowledge he had acquired, the perfection of his taste, the maturity of his thoughts and his devotion to religious matters. There was little wonder that his parents' deepest hopes were bound up in him. 'So much skill, beauty, power and love were wrapped up in his growth and constant progress,' Edward wrote in his diary, 'such admirable preparation for good work, with such persuasive gentleness; such thoughtfulness and such reverence.' To Dean Goulburn of Norwich he wrote: 'Our boy was spiritually of a higher sweeter promise than he was intellectually. And of his intellectual promise and even performance I have seen indeed but one or two his equal.'

But in spite of what Edward wrote in his diary and to friends such as Crowfoot, Wickenden and Westcott, and in spite of the touching deathbed scene, Martin had not been a Saint and would not have relished being called one. It was only during his last two years at Winchester that the striking advances in his intellectual development took place. At the beginning of his time at Temple Grove he disappointed his father terribly, and the letters that the boy received were full of complaints about his laziness, his poor reports, and peremptory demands that he must never let his father receive further reports that mentioned lack of concentration. 'What is the use of sending our boy to be taught if he is so silly as not to give attention to the teaching...' At home the relationship between father and son helped to give him an adult perception of religion and literature, and when he was there his father could only see his exceptional ability and his serious attitude to the things that mattered in life. But at school he was a boy – not working particularly hard nor exhibiting conspicuous piety. He could be quick-tempered, combative, inclined to law-breaking, lively, quick-witted – in fact, a normal boy with normal instincts, faults and prejudices. The first onset of maturity came when he was 12, still at Temple Grove, but beginning to be a more accurate and attentive scholar; and in 1873 he was top of the school, beating the boy beneath him by 23 marks. However, he still received nagging homilies about attention and accuracy from his anxious father.

Then the family moved to Lincoln and Martin was old enough to try for a top scholarship. He had been awarded an Eton scholarship but Edward preferred Winchester, though Martin would have to work really hard. 'Your fault intellectually is to be rather dreamy,' Edward wrote to him, 'and let the grass grow while you are turning round. Novel-reading is a great cause of dreaminess as it is as tiring to the head as any other reading, and so you come with tired powers to your work. I wish you would make a resolution to open no more novels and dream no more until the holidays.'

At Winchester, where he went in 1874, he blossomed mightily and usually received excellent marks, though at times his enthusiasm flagged and he became introspective and, his father's favourite adjective, 'dreamy'; and the letters from home arrived, full of anxiety that he might fail to realise his full potential. 'Do not flag with the goal just in sight.' 'The low place, the Euclid, the want of attentiveness are all blows. You must recover yourself. I shall be displeased more than I remember being with you, if you do not...' 'I hope you are playing hard as well as reading hard or you'll turn out a dull boy after all.' If Martin ever uttered a sigh and muttered, 'Oh, please, leave me alone,' such a reaction has not been recorded.

In 1876, the year in which he was confirmed, there was another change in his work and his attainments. He became much more distinguished – in natural science, Italian, literature, history and the Classics. He joined the Debating Society. In 1877 he won the Sixth Form Prize, became a Prefect, and runner-up for the prestigious Goddard Scholarship, and won the Duncan History Prize. In the two holidays he spent at *Lis Escop* he and his father rode together, prayed on horseback and had discussions such as 'Did an advance of scientific knowledge help poetry?' To his sister Nellie, who had consulted him about ways of curing herself of various faults he wrote, hoping that she would be confirmed before long, and telling her, 'I feel that I can never do anything at all myself except through this: "The Blood of Jesus Christ His Son cleanseth from all sin."' Dr. Rodding, his Headmaster, said that Martin's great charm was the enthusiasm which made him always the centre of a group of boys ... so much life and so much merriment.'

The last walk that Martin, Arthur, their father and John Wordsworth had together was on the Piran sands. They had driven there and then walked to the buried church. As they returned, keeping near the rocks, Martin was very silent and, as Wordsworth said afterwards, there was something prophetic in the way he walked alone, in the fading light, along the margin of the waves. 'Yes,' Edward wrote, 'you were already, dearest boy, on the edge of an ocean greater than the Atlantic. You have crossed it alone, and our light fades while we strain after you.'

CHAPTER TWELVE

A T TRURO Edward and Minnie led a much more social life than they had at Lincoln or Wellington, with a great deal of entertaining of county magnates and diocesan notabilities. In turn they were entertained at country houses and remote vicarages. Lady Rolle was always welcoming at Bicton; she was still very proud of 'her Bishop'. The children, however, found that immediate neighbours of their own age were few and intimate companions seldom found, and they were content to be a close little community of their own with their family interests, a little timid where the outside world was concerned. Maggie and Nellie attended the Truro High School for Girls, which Edward had helped to found and Nellie in particular distinguished herself there. She took many prizes, had a good contralto voice and was a devastating underarm bowler. Maggie took the prizes that Nellie didn't and painted in watercolours and oils. They naturally made friends at school but not being gregarious by nature, Maggie being the shyer of the two, they were always glad to rejoin the bosom of the family. Martin and Arthur were, of course, caught up in the activities of Winchester and Eton and Fred was happy at Temple Grove; but when it was a question of home against school they all winged their way back to the warm welcome of *Lis Escop* without a backward glance. After Martin's death, Arthur became more of a companion to his father than he had ever been. They would go off on expeditions to see cathedrals and they rode round the diocese on horseback to visit outlying parishes; and Arthur became aware of the darkness and bewilderment into which his father's spirit had sunk. He found his relationship with his father easier now that he had become more of a confidant, but there was a reserve between them that never completely went away. Arthur never wholly broke through his childish awe and felt that he had to be earnest and adult; he never found it easy to prattle, as Fred could, though Fred had his own difficulties. Hugh was a pert, almost cheeky child, but Edward, in his tenderness towards him, rarely checked the boy. Minnie was his official teacher, but Edward found time to take him for half an hour each day, part of which would be spent on digging up dandelions from the lawn – Hugh had his own special spud – while the boy listened to a detailed account of the story of the Good Samaritan.

In summertime the young Bensons lived chiefly in the garden and held meetings of their secret society in the summer house; even the 17-year-old Martin and the 15-year-old Arthur were not above participating in such childish games when they were at home. The secret society was something of a flop, however, because there never seemed to be any business to transact and after the members had been sworn to secrecy, the badges had been given out, subscriptions collected and titles allocated there was a yawning silence and then it was decided that it was time for tea.

Maggie and Fred in particular became passionately interested in natural history, and there were summer evening expeditions to raid wasps' nests and go tree-sugaring for moths. Plants and flowers were dug up and carried back to be re-planted in the little gardens at home, but Edward would never allow a plant to be taken from a hedgerow if it were conspicuous, only if it were found in a secluded place, and no patch of ground could be despoiled of its most attractive specimens. Watch, the family collie, would accompany the straggling party and Maggie's goat trotted along behind them, Watch making sure that she did not stray too far away. Then there was the neighbourhood to be explored, the bare uplands and scrubby moorlands to be crossed, and there were gaunt skeletons of mines with roofless engine-houses and tumbledown sheds to give a frisson of terror to imaginative minds. The steeply-cut valleys, full of trees and streams and exotic plants, were almost tropical in their luxuriance, as big a contrast to the windswept hills as could be imagined, and rambles could lead to little stone-built hamlets surrounded by tall trees, or great barrows on the high rides; and there was a huge circular British encampment in the centre of an oak-copse known as Bishop's Wood, below which was a swamp full of bulrushes.

It was in that wood that the Bishop once met his match. One windy day the family had driven out to the wood in a pony carriage for a picnic. They came upon a locked shed in the wood and in its shelter Edward lit a fire and put the kettle on to boil. Suddenly an excited little man rushed at them from the bushes, picked up the kettle, poured its contents over the burning twigs, and trod out the embers. It was all over in a minute, during which time the picnic party sat stupefied. Then Edward began to remonstrate, his temper rising, but the man cut him short. 'The next time you light a fire don't do it under a powder magazine!' Then he explained that gunpowder was made from the charcoal burned in the wood and stored in the shed that had sheltered their fire. When normal relations had been restored the man gave his name as Spargo and said that he had been a Class Leader among the Wesleyans. Edward was interested, became friendly with Mr Spargo, and he and Minnie later went to tea with him to hear more of his experiences.

Edward had no resident Chaplain and was his own secretary, though Minnie helped as often as she could. He rose early, worked till Matins, which he held at 8 o'clock in Kenwyn Church. He was accompanied by Watch, who had a place in a pew and another under a window in the Chapel, and his own special rug. Breakfast followed, then family prayers in the schoolroom or a short service in the Chapel. The children who were at home were subjected to a daily Bible reading, then Edward worked at letters or sermons or went down to Truro to the Bishop's Library, a relic of Bishop Phillpott's industry. In the afternoon he took exercise, walking or riding, and during the school holidays there were picnics and nature rambles; and the summer months passed like some fugue built on all the delightful things that had happened, coloured and decorated and fused into one delicious whole. Edward once put up a prize for botany. It was won by Nellie, who afterwards confessed to Fred that she had stolen some of his pressed specimens. They decided to keep the matter secret in order that Edward should not condemn her to everlasting fire and brimstone. A collection of birds' eggs, started with one addled swan's egg, grew to very satisfactory proportions, especially after the family groom had presented Fred with his own collection. It contained a wood-pigeon's egg which they had never been able to find, since Edward's rule was that no egg should be taken from a nest that contained less than four, and then only one. An aquarium was set up and stocked with caddis-worms, water snails and a stickleback. Photography briefly took precedence over other activities, but was abandoned when only once did a smudgy image of a yew tree appear on a plate.

When the weather prevented outdoor excursions the young Bensons joined together to produce a literary effort called the *Saturday Magazine*, though it might just as well appear on a Tuesday; and a flood of dialogues, satirical sketches, adventure stories, essays and poems would pour out. Each member of the family had to contribute at least four pages of prose or one page of verse, and the finished magazine consisted of the most varied contents – from Fred's poem on the Devil to Maggie's conversation between two of her guinea-pigs. The parents were mocked, but only gently in the case of Edward who was likely not to find anything too sharp-edged entertaining.

Whole afternoons were spent in the garden playing 'Pirates', a game which had evolved almost by accident and which they considered the best invention of modern times. It contained tension, cunning and heart-stopping excitement, and the rules were complicated. Two pirates, chosen in rotation, were given five minutes in which to hide in a maze of trees, hedges, paths, beehives, kitchen gardens and orchard. The rest, usually three, occasionally four when Minnie could be persuaded to play and (only once) five when the incongruous figure of the Bishop of Truro joined the line-up, were non-pirates. They chose a captain who had to decide what trophy each of them should take back to the home base (or Plymouth Sound, which was the summer-house) without being caught by a pirate. The trophy might be a croquet hoop, an apple, ivy leaf or other ordinary object. The main rule was that no-one should be caught unless he or she was carrying the chosen trophy, and the cunning lay in the psychological trap into which the pirates could fall by supposing that what the player was carrying was the actual trophy when the real one could be a leaf behind a lapel or an apple hidden in a pocket. Then it was a case of bluff and double-bluff, misunderstandings, abortive chases and desperate sprints to reach the summer-house. It was a very strenuous game and Minnie would collapse in breathless laughter, black bombazine quivering and white lace cap askew.

Chapter Thirteen

EDWARD and Minnie had been in close contact with Archbishop Tait and his family for a number of years, and an affectionate and intimate relationship had existed between them. The Archbishop had given Edward a set of rooms in the Lollard's Tower at Lambeth Palace which he shared with the Bishops of Durham and Chichester, and it was there that he stayed on his frequent visits to London for meetings and services. The Archbishop had left a deep impression of majesty and dignity when he once paid a visit to Kenwyn. He had a voice of resonance and depth and his movements were slow and deliberate, as though he were far removed from the fret of human life. But behind the dignity was a sweetness that endeared him to everybody who met him.

Edward's first intimation that all was not well with the Archbishop was at the beginning of June, 1882, when he went to see him at Addington Park, his country house near Croydon. After 20 minutes or so Edward realised that the Archbishop was becoming exhausted, so he made his farewells and left. On August 30 he received a letter telling him that the Archbishop was improving after months of gradually decreasing strength, but the situation changed when he began to hear daily from one or other of the Tait family, letters that filled him with apprehension, and in his diary he wrote, 'I cannot conceive what will become of us in the next few years if God takes him from us. That "gracious life" with its hold on the laity of England seems our sheet anchor in the shifting storms of the present.'

By the end of September the Archbishop had taken to his bed again and looked like staying there for many weeks. Edward saw him and noticed how large and bright his eyes were, and how low and husky his voice. He read to him part of Kempe's abstract of the work of the Ecclesiastical Courts Commission. It was evident that the Archbishop was at death's door but still refusing to pass through. Two days later there was again a slight recovery and Edward read to him again.

But Edward's joy at the improvement in the Archbishop's condition was turned to sorrow when a telegram from Bedford informed him of the death of his sister Ada on October 11, a week after her second child, a boy, was born. 'Little Ada – upright, devout, conscientious, laborious, able Ada gone – just after "never so well',' he wrote. And he began to remember all the good things about his relationship with his sister; and the arguments, compressed lips, heaving breasts, silences and periods of barely suppressed dislike slipped into oblivion. She was ten years old when she confided to Edward that she was determined to work hard and become a governess, and earn money in order to restore a certain decrepit pinnacle on Lichfield Cathedral. After being brought up with Minnie and her family at Rugby, she went for a year to Germany, then to France, and finally offered herself to the High Schools' Committee in Norwich who were looking for a Headmistress for the High School. Soon she had 150 girls of the middle- and upper-middle classes thoroughly organised and at work. But the East Anglian climate disagreed with her and she moved to Oxford to open a similar school. There she achieved an even greater success. At Oxford she married Andrew MacDowall, a science teacher, who became the most devoted of husbands, and they had their first child, a daughter, in 1881. Edward was not pleased when she wrote to tell him that she had decided to leave Oxford, again for health reasons, and open her third school at Bedford, which she confidently asserted would become the most prestigious girls' school of its kind in the country. Both her husband and Edward trembled for her health, and Andrew insisted on keeping on their London house until she was sure that she would be strong enough to cope. But she did, her health improved, she found the organisation well within her capabilities, and she was enjoying her work. They gave up the London house a few weeks before the baby arrived, and her sudden collapse brought her bright, strong, bossy and holy life to an end.

Her funeral was most affecting. All the girls stood in rows, each holding a wreath. There were mourners from Norwich and Oxford, the school governors, parents, and all Bedford, it seemed. There was a flower-heaped grave and near it stood the lonely husband, the small girl and the baby. In the sky there seemed to Edward to be grand figures sitting in long lines on either side of a saffron rift in the clouds, the throned forms paling away as the flush deepened towards one central figure. 'What will God do for those bereaved souls?' he asked himself, and the answer that came into his head was: 'He woundeth and His hands make whole.'

At Addington another death was near. The Archbishop grew daily weaker and could rally no more. On November 23, Sir William Gull, his doctor, gave him no longer than a fortnight. Edward had a long talk with him about all the Church matters that were near to his heart. He spoke movingly of his early life and his fellow scholars at Balliol. He laid his hand on Edward's head and blessed him, and Edward left. The Archbishop died on Sunday, December 3. 'I am so glad it has come,' he said. 'Doctor, are you sure it has come?' Just before he died he insisted on writing an answer to the Queen who had sent flowers and a message. Only the signature was legible.

It was generally supposed that Dr. Harold Browne, the venerable Bishop of Winchester, would be chosen to succeed Archbishop Tait, and he himself had half expected to receive the call. Edward's friend, Joseph Barber Lightfoot, Bishop of Durham, was another possibility. But Dr. Magee, Archbishop of York, wrote: 'Truro would perhaps, all things considered, prove the best for the Church. He would certainly unite and lead the Episcopate better than Durham. As regards the future, I do not envy the man who will be seated in the Chair of Augustine in these times. The winds blow keen round it, and the rains fall heavy on it just now, and he may be a thankful man if, when his occupancy draws to a close, he can say, "I have done nothing to hasten the fall thereof."'

Dr. Browne said of Edward: 'He is vigorous, able, modest, warm-hearted, a strong Churchman, but with huge sympathies. Gladstone was quite right to pass by an antiquity like myself for the youth and vigour of Benson.' Bishop Thorold called Edward 'a delightful man, how fond I am of him. He is strong, large-hearted, very learned, wth a grand ideal of his office, and withal young.' And Dean Church was strongly of the opinion that Edward was really the best choice that could have been made. One consideration that may have prevailed in his appointment was the fact that Dr. Tait, when near death, had spoken of him as his possible successor. 'The Bishop of Truro,' he said, 'will come forward and do a great work. I am worn out...' So Edward's visits and readings had borne fruit, though no-one suggested that any thought of working his passage had entered his mind.

Edward received the offer of Canterbury just before Christmas, 1882. He opened Mr Gladstone's letter at breakfast, read it, then thoughtfully put it on one side. Later in the morning he sent for the children to see him in the library and, pale with emotion, told them the news. They were awestruck and little was said before they dispersed. The interruption of Christmas preparations by serious business from the outside world was not entirely welcome; so the news was pushed temporarily into the background for future discussion.

Soon a letter from Queen Victoria arrived, hoping that her favourite Bishop would accept the Prime Minister's offer, and a second letter from Mr Gladstone hinted that an early reply would oblige. Westcott, Lightfoot and other friends were naturally consulted and, after much praying by all concerned they urged him to accept. So he did, partly out of personal loyalty to the Queen and also out of regard for Gladstone, even though he disapproved of his politics. Nor was the love of ruling, nor the satisfaction

of organisation far from the forefront of his thinking, though he hoped
that personal ambition was the least of his considerations. He thought it
natural to want to expand his gifts, and to move onward and upward into
the realms of institutional religion, which occupied so much of his
thoughts and plans. He had administered a public school very successfully,
then had followed a time of reflection and training at Lincoln. At Truro he
had created a new Bishopric, with all the problems that that entailed, and
had started it off on new and vigorous lines. He had penetrated to the
heart of Cornish mysteries and won the affection of the Cornish people,
but he had not consolidated his position nor fully revealed his own special
conception of religion. In Cornwall his mental and physical powers were at
their strongest; personal pioneering work was most appropriate to his
genius. In future he would have to concentrate on dealing with a
conventional organisation and un-Celtic stolidity. He would have to toil at
Clergy Discipline Acts and patronage difficulties; he would have to try to
unite and centralise the Anglican Communion, settle ritual controversies
and dabble in social questions. He could no longer be an enthusiastic
creator. Caution and compromise were not really his ideals; he was going
to a post clogged by rigid conventions. His acquaintance with the practical
affairs of Church and State was slight, and he knew he would quickly have
to master all the administrative problems that would surround him.
Everything poetical and romantic, the very essence of his view of life,
would be left behind in Cornwall. He had been about to develop an
entirely new conception of episcopacy at Truro and his departure meant
that it would never flower in the way that his genius would have
encouraged it to. When he thought of the years ahead regret was as strong
an emotion as a terrified excitement.

Edward was overwhelmed by more than a thousand letters of
congratulation (not a single one containing a sour note), and he replied by
sending back illuminated cards, rather like Christmas cards, but with a text
and a few words of thanks scribbled on each, asking for prayers that he
might be worthy to bear the heavy responsibility. To the Church in
Cornwall he wrote a heartfelt letter, full of gratitude and humility. For his
successor (not known at the time, though it turned out to be Canon
Wilkinson) he would pray. 'I scarce think you can have one who will love
Cornwall better than I – her primeval church and warm-hearted children
and her vestiges of old story, her shores and shrines and the Fair House of
God which is rising in the midst. For her prosperity, both temporal and
spiritual, I and mine shall never cease to pray; for her enrichment in every
grace, in hope, and love, and generosity, in purity of faith, in perfect truth
and perfect peace.' Edward's long apprenticeship had made him the most
able word-spinner of his generation.

It was Professor Hort of Cambridge who issued a warning of dangers ahead. He wrote, not a letter of congratulation, but one of heartfelt sympathy, reminding Edward that the convulsions of the English Church, grievous as they were, seemed as nothing beside the danger of its calm and unobtrusive alienation in thought and spirit from the great silent multitude of Englishmen. But no-one who knew him could be otherwise than eagerly hopeful as well as eagerly wistful. Edward replied by saying, 'Yours was the most historical and real letter I have had. That is why I am concerned...'

To the Benson children the change from Truro to Lambeth was full of excitement. Their father had been a credit to them, they patronisingly admitted, and they looked forward to taking full advantage of the expanding horizons that lay enticingly ahead. The splendour of his office, the dignity of Lambeth Palace, the interesting people they would be sure to meet, the opportunities to participate in the glittering life of London, state dinner parties and summer garden parties – the prospect was entrancing. They would be at the centre of a busy universe instead of seeing it from a distance. What was there to regret? Only Arthur, a solemn Cambridge undergraduate of 20, had a sense that they were leaving a rare and precious experience behind them.

Fred was in his second year at Marlborough when his father was called to greatness. Soon after his appointment Edward went down to the school in order to conduct a confirmation. Fred was among the boys to be received, and Minnie and Maggie went along to witness the ceremony. The new Archbishop was impressed by the boys' behaviour and the religious atmosphere in the Chapel, but Fred was more excited by the fact that the school was given a day's holiday in honour of the visit, and he basked in reflected glory quite shamelessly, especially when his friends urged him to be confirmed again.

On January 9, 1883, Edward went to Osborne to have an audience with Queen Victoria who sent her yacht to Southampton for him. They had an interesting and stimulating conversation for about an hour, and Edward was impressed by her ability to read people and their motives and weaknesses, and her quiet amusement at their foibles. She left him much wiser about a good many men. 'The Queen is wonderful,' he wrote to Canon Mason.

Edward remained at Truro for the first two months of 1883 to put in order the various organisations that depended on him so that his successor could take up the threads without a break, and also to make a start on the routine business which had begun to accumulate. The 'confirmation' of the Archbishop was held in the church of St. Mary-le-Bow on March 3, in the presence of the Bishop of London, Dr. Dean and Dr. Tristram, and the quaint and ancient proceedings were duly observed. The Apparitor-

General advanced to the barrier in the centre of the church and cried in a loud voice: 'Oyez, oyez, oyez, all manner of persons who shall or will object to the confirmation of the election of the Right Reverend Father in God, Dr. Edward White Benson, Lord Bishop of Truro, to be Archbishop of the Archiepiscopal See of Canterbury, come forward and make your objections in due form of law, and they shall be heard.' The challenge was repeated – nobody objected – after which the Bishop of London pronounced and decreed that the Archbishop or his lawful proxy should be inducted into the real, actual and corporal possession of the said Archbishopric of Canterbury, and be instituted and enthroned. A large number of people were present, and on leaving the church the Archbishop was loudly cheered. A rush was made to the table at which Edward had sat and someone made off with the blotting paper on which appeared the reverse of the first signature of *Edw. Cantuar.*.

He gave his last sermon in Kenwyn Church on February 25. The subject was 'simplicity', and once again his words, coming from the heart, struck to the heart of every member of the subdued congregation which filled the small church, giving final expression to a principle which had characterised his Episcopate and made him the recipient of so much regard and trust. 'So let us know each other, and love, and be together in mutual intercession; pray you for me, if you will be so kind, and I for you, I steadfastly promise you. We may not see each other's faces, but God will see us both, and we are one in Him.'

Before his official enthronement in Canterbury Cathedral on March 29, Edward was granted a personal happiness which meant as much to him as his new and glittering office. Maggie, 18 years old and studying at Lady Margaret Hall, Oxford, had taken up political economy and moral science, and had come out equal first in all England in the senior examination of women for political economy. Edward was delighted and proud of his introverted but brilliant daughter.

The enthronement was both a magnificent pageant and an occasion of religious solemnity. Everybody wore a lily-of-the-valley, the supposed emblem of Thomas À Beckett. The day before the ceremony Edward, his family and friends were received in state at the South-Eastern Railway Station in Canterbury by the Mayor, Councillors, and Dean, and a large number of clergy and ordinary citizens. A guard of honour, provided by the local Yeomanry, was drawn up outside. Edward removed his hat in recognition of the cheers that greeted him and stepped into the midst of the group which represented the ecclesiastical and the civil parts of national life. There was a procession to the Guildhall where he was greeted by loud blasts upon the wardmote horn, which provoked some irreverent laughter, and an address was presented. On the following day he was enthroned, in the presence of the Duke of Edinburgh. Also present were the Municipal Corporation of Canterbury, the clergy of the Diocese, the rural Deans, members of the Convocation of the Province, the Cathedral body and most of the Bishops of Great Britain. The Archdeacon of Canterbury, Bishop Parry, preceded the new Primate who walked between the Dean and the Vice-Dean and was attended by his Chaplains and officials. The honour of carrying his train was shared by Hugh, then a boy of ten, and a King's Scholar of Canterbury, both wearing surplice and purple cassock. At the altar the Archdeacon addressed Edward, requiring him to maintain the rights and liberties of the Church and observe the approved customs thereof. Edward affirmed his intention to obey the injunctions. There were hymns, psalms and the Hallelujah Chorus. The Archbishop was first seated on his throne just below the sanctuary steps, then as Metropolitan he moved to the ancient marble chair of Saint Augustine, and lastly to the Dean's stall, as a sign of having taken real and actual possession of the See.

At the luncheon held at the Chapter Library in the Deanery afterwards Edward replied to a toast to his health with a carefully prepared speech which took half an hour to deliver. He dwelt upon the qualities of his predecessor but his main theme was the essential concord of the Church of England. 'She need never be afraid of education, never afraid of research, or anything that science or philosophy may find out, because science and philosophy have their fountains in the Throne above,' he finished up. It was not a speech of eloquence or rhetoric; there were no jokes, no show of egotism, no effusiveness. It was delivered with humility, dignity and gravity, in choice and rich language, and the listeners were riveted. There was no-one like Edward when it was a question of saying the right thing in the right place and with the utmost sincerity. His sarcasm, dark looks and capacity for destroying innocent enjoyment were all reserved for behind the doors of the Master's Lodge at Wellington, the Chancery at Lincoln, *Lis Escop*, and soon, Lambeth Palace and Addington. In public there was only charm, wisdom, loving concern, and holiness.

When Edward had finished Bishop Thorold said to Minnie, 'Are you satisfied? You are hard to satisfy, I know.' She said, simply and happily, 'Yes, I am.'

Edward was 53 when he ascended the throne of Canterbury. He was full of life and energy and, to all appearances, a long and vigorous Primacy lay before him.

Immediately after his enthronement and even before the family was settled into Lambeth Palace, Edward entered enthusiastically upon the multifarious duties which crowded upon him. Easter was imminent, and for the next three months, with attendance in Parliament, the round of

May meetings, sermons and constant engagements of all kinds, the strain, both mental and physical, was severe. His determination to keep up to date answering the enormous number of letters received daily at Lambeth Palace was never relaxed. From the beginning he laid down the rule that every reply drafted by his Chaplain should be submitted to him. During the busy summer months there were occasions when replies had to be drafted when he and his Chaplain were driving from one meeting to another, and the Chaplain, trying to make notes, found his hand made unsteady by the swaying of the carriage; and when they arrived at their destination the often-important reply was illegible. The infinite variety of the letters was remarkable. Edward was asked to give guidance on many vital matters of policy affecting the Colonial Church. The Japanese, for instance, wrote to record their wish for a native Church, in communion with, but distinct from, the Church of England. The Church in South Africa had many difficulties. The Churches in India, Canada and Australia each claimed Edward's attention, and each received courteous and helpful guidance. The many Church Societies wrote to him, so did members of the laity from all walks of life. The Diocese of Canterbury had its own problems and Edward was especially concerned for his parish, where he loved to go whenever he could spare the time. In fact, he bore the burden of diocesan work with special eagerness; the spiritual work that uplifted him at Canterbury made the administrative organisation he was normally swallowed up in much more bearable. Among his letters were many from eccentrics or madmen, but when a secretary suggested they should end up in the waste-paper basket Edward shook his head. 'It seems nonsense to you,' he said, 'but perhaps it means a great deal to the writer. Send him a kind reply.'

The weeks during which Convocation was in session always put him under great pressure. It was his function, together with the Registrar, to prepare the agenda paper, each subject requiring careful preparation, and for four consecutive days he had to preside over the meetings, and his concentration could not waver for a moment. There were important measures in the House of Lords to take charge of and great debates to participate in; and when he returned to the Palace, utterly fatigued, he still had to work far into the night dealing with routine business. Meetings of Church Societies came thick and fast throughout May and June, and in the height of the summer the following year's engagements were fixed, long before the date was formally published. Many evenings were taken up with big meetings or public dinners, and Edward's listeners were not aware that he had composed his address, given in confident, ringing tones, relieved by flashes of wit, in the time occupied in driving from Lambeth to the conference or dining hall.

Edward spoke in the House of Lords for the first time on the Cathedral Statutes Bill, sponsored by the Bishop of Carlisle, and was obviously nervous. Bishop Magee of Peterborough spoke strongly against the Bill, though it was eventually passed, only to be withdrawn by the Commons later in the year. Edward was not seen at his best in Parliament. He was not a ready debater and did not command as much attention as had his predecessor. Archbishop Tait had been more of a statesman and found himself at home in the House of Lords. Edward often showed signs of nervousness when addressing the Peers, but his speeches always had one great merit; they were short and to the point. He often used to say that taking part in a Lords debate was one of the duties from which he would most gladly have escaped. He would comment on the lack of enthusiasm that characterised the Peers when they were assembled for business, their willingness to slide off when dinner-time approached, the poor acoustics of the Chamber; and the technical character of most of the legislation seemed to inhibit the readiness of speech which usually never failed him. The atmosphere of chilly criticism that emanated from their Lordships he found most alien, so that the liveliness and humour of his extempore speaking deserted him, and because he felt he had to be weighty his speeches became too concentrated. He was apt to become irritated when the argument went against him, and be either sharp or sulky in reply. But he could be forceful when the subject interested him, such as the Deceased Wife's Sister Bill, the Cruelty to Animals Amendment Act, and the Franchise Bill of 1884; and then his carefully considered opinions created a great impression.

Edward and his family were at first overawed by life in Lambeth Palace; it was so different from their other houses, lacking charm and cosiness, although it was a dignified well-planned building, cool in summer and warm in winter. The gardens were spacious and contained a bowling green, thickets and winding walks made shady by sumachs and elms. Even though the roar of London came as a monotonous undertone of subdued sound and the adjoining fields were full of shrieking children it was a peaceful enough place, though sooty marks were left on fingers and white clothes turned grey.

Adjoining the Palace was a large field belonging to the See. This was given over to the use and recreation of the people of Lambeth. Nearly 60 cricket clubs were allowed to play there every week in the summer, and football clubs in the winter. Besides this, thousands of family tickets were issued every spring and mothers could constantly be seen taking their children to 'the Bishop's' and leaving them to play in the field during the day while they were at work, and returning to collect them in the evening. There was a good sized pond in the north-west corner where young fishermen played their rods. Other activities included rounders, battledore and shuttlecock and kite-flying: and sometimes a local band added to the gaiety. Occasionally Edward and Minnie paid a surprise visit to the lowly members of his large family and were greeted with noisy enthusiasm.

Edward, who had the soul of an antiquary and historian, soon knew every nook and cranny of the Palace and grew to prize its smoke-begrimed and weather-beaten walls. On Saturday afternoons he would turn himself into a local guide and conduct parties of working men over the place, rehearsing for them the chief incidents in its 600-year history. He greatly transformed the interior of the Palace. He searched through cupboards and garrets and found numerous old chairs, chests and sofas which had been hidden away for decades, and he furnished the long corridors with them. A rusty bunch of pikes was cleaned and displayed in a fan in the main entrance hall. The great gallery, dusty and neglected, held a great number of interesting pictures and these he had cleaned and placed in more favourable positions in the central corridor. Other full-length portraits, hanging on a seldom used staircase, were brought out and given greater prominence. One of them was of Sir Robert Walpole, whom Edward despised because he had used Church revenues as bribes for political services. The portrait was hung in a conspicuous place as a warning that it was possible for the Church to be corrupted.

In spite of its grandeur Lambeth Palace was not a particularly large house; the rooms were big enough but there were not many of them; and the number of guests had to be limited. On the right of the great entrance were three rooms for secretaries; adjoining them was Edward's library, with a private staircase into the garden. A door hidden by bookbacks led to a dressing-room, which Edward preferred to the library for there he could get down to work which needed a lot of concentration without interruption. This communicated with his and Minnie's bedroom, and that with her sitting-room and the family rooms. The guardroom, used as a dining-room, had a high-vaulted timber roof and the walls were hung with portraits of former Archbishops. From the guardroom a picture gallery led to Lollard's Tower and descended to the Great Library. Drawing-rooms communicated with a vestry, at the base of which stood Cranmer's Tower, leading to a Chapel, an exquisitely painted building with stained glass windows. Edward had the organ specially built and loved the Chapel very much. Agnes, Edith and Lucy Tait, daughters of the late Archbishop, presented it with two altar-frontals, the American Bishops gave an altar-cross, and the Duchess Adeline of Bedford and some of her friends gave a great eagle lectern.

Edward's tasks would have been infinitely more difficult had it not been for the help of the Rev. Randall Davidson, who had married Edith Tait and had been domestic Chaplain to Dr. Tait. He agreed to stay on as Chaplain to the new Primate and remained so until his appointment as Dean of Windsor later in the year; and his practical wisdom was constantly at Edward's service. The two men, already friends, became devoted intimates, even though their natures were very dissimilar. Davidson had been influenced in the direction of statesmanship. He had a wide knowledge of the world, of politics and politicians, and the whole intricate business of Church legislation was at his finger-tips. He knew what people were thinking, who was conniving with whom and how matters were likely to turn out. Edward consulted him on almost every difficult decision and in every crisis, and had the greatest respect for his Chaplain's power of foreseeing events and dealing with contingencies.

Minnie wrote an affectionate account of Edward's appearance during the early years of his Primacy. He had always looked impressive, she said, his face expressing eagerness and vivacity, but the development of its beauty was remarkable. His richly curved mouth grew more Italian-looking, the sharp and delicate cut of his nostrils got even more pronounced. Large bumps grew over the arches of his eyes and the length of his hair and its whiteness increased his likeness to John Wesley. On public occasions he showed dignity combined with the humility necessitated by his post; when ceremonious behaviour was required nobody could give a bow like Edward. He could appear both remote and paternal. He could play on the emotions of his hearers as though drawing tunes from a violin and could bring tears to the eyes of the most sceptical. He could give an effect of shyness but when he was annoyed and preparing to deliver a rebuke he would shake his head slightly with his eyes cast down, rather like a horse deciding to bolt or a bull to charge, and then the stinging words unfailingly hit the target. When he was in a genial mood his strong sense of humour would show itself in the telling of an abundance of amusing stories, and his loud laugh would drown all other conversations. He enjoyed telling stories in dialect, which he rendered with dramatic energy; unfortunately all his dialects, from Cornish to Yorkshire, sounded the same. Familiar stories acquired imaginative details with each telling and he often put himself into the situation described with such relish when he had not actually been present. At social gatherings Edward was generally mild and affable, but they were superficial qualities; on official occasions he demanded an unquestioning obedience and deference to his opinions.

Minnie did not realise that she was describing an actor *manqué*; and, in fact, Edward had enormous talent. He would have been able to bestride a stage like a Colossus, roar like a lion or whisper like a turtle-dove. The stage had missed a star when Edward decided that acting was the work of the Devil, but his performances in pulpit or conference hall gave him and his audiences all the satisfaction that the stage and limelights would have provided.

In spite of the fact that Edward was so popular and sought after, he was never an easy person to talk to on a one-to-one basis, or even as a member of a small group at a dinner party. He could not argue patiently and he put forward his own point of view at too great a length – and too prosily. He was impatient of abstract topics though he disliked gossip. All his conversations had an improving quality; he could not resist teaching or advising in even the most casual exchange. He would hold forth on any subject in which he was interested down to the most boring details, but would grow impatient with anyone who monopolised the conversation with *his* own interests.

It was dangerous to argue too fiercely with him because argument engendered heat. Never was he prepared to meet people halfway and he had so little in common with politicians of unorthodox views that he regarded them as dangerous enemies, not as rational opponents. In later life he did not make many men friends as he had done at Truro, but with women he was more successful. He needed to be looked up to, to be regarded with affection mixed with awe, then he could be gracious and expansive. But he froze into icy severity with people whose views differed from his own and who could express those views lucidly. A mind without religion, or one in which religion was not over-riding, was incomprehensible to him. Anyone who thought of religion as superstitious nonsense was utterly depraved; an assertion that liturgies were unnecessary and ceremonies tedious brought no spark of understanding. To him religion was the absorbing fact of life, belief was as necessary as breathing, and the Anglican Church, flawed in places though it may be, was the only rock on which the future of the world could be made steadfast.

There were two people in Edward: the stern moralist, devout religionist and saintly father in God; and the overbearing *paterfamilias*, seeking after love but not knowing how to give it. Minnie, Arthur, Fred and the girls had to recognise and deal with both. As the years went by they learned to do this with greater ease. Though they could still be shattered by Edward's moods, the effects did not last as long as they once had and it was easier for Minnie to coax him back into a more amenable frame of mind; and they could catch each other's eye and shrug a shoulder. The awe the children had felt was now mixed with pity and perhaps a little impatience. Edward could certainly be boring when neither he nor anyone else could do anything right, but being bored was better than being heart-broken.

CHAPTER FOURTEEN

ROM early autumn of each year to the following January, but also with other short breaks, the Bensons lived at Addington near Croydon. Until the beginning of the 19th century the Archbishops had a Palace at Croydon, not far from the parish church, but, owing to the site being considered damp, Archbishop Manners-Sutton had sold the Palace, and with the proceeds bought the estate of Addington Park. Though now swallowed up by Croydon, the country mansion then lay in the corner of a park of some 600 acres, and contained much varied scenery; a steep heathery valley, great tracts of woodland dotted with glades and open spaces, a home farm, landscaped gardens, and criss-cross grass rides in the park. The house had been built of stone in 1770, stately at the rear but rather plain and bleak in front. All over the park were traces of ancient British habitations, and the site of a hunting lodge of Henry VIII, marked by an avenue of elms.

Before he actually took up residence at Addington Edward was sure that no future Archbishop could live there; the house was too grand and the upkeep would be an enormous burden, in spite of his £15,000 stipend. Later, though, it became a beloved home; it was conveniently near to London and its seclusion gave him the rest from Lambeth that was essential. After a few months there he never again seriously thought about giving it up.

One entered by a large hall, to the left of which was an anteroom which Edward turned into a library; it also housed his large collection of photographs and prints. The drawing-room and Edward's study led from the library, and from the study a door opened into the Chapel. In the south-eastern corner of the house was a large sitting-room – designated the schoolroom – where nursery tea was served when the family were alone, and which was the meal that Edward most enjoyed, though he was not allowed to drink more than three cups of tea so that he would not 'spoil his dinner'. A hideous staircase led to the floor above, and the bedrooms. The railing of the gallery was insecure but Edward refused to have it strengthened. His reason, only partly joking, was that when the Church was disestablished – the great fear of its leaders at that time – Addington would be confiscated and the new owners – sacrilegious spoilers, he called them – would lean on the railing, which would collapse and plunge them into the hall below, killing them outright.

When Edward was in London he hankered after Addington and would steal away there for a day's rest whenever possible. He maintained that his health and spirits were better there than at Lambeth, but in fact the opposite was the case. He was too busy at Lambeth to have time to dwell on ill-health; at Addington his depressions were more severe and lasted longer.

The months spent at Addington were almost as busy as the first six months of the year at Lambeth Palace. There were still meetings of Church Societies, and those seeking interviews had to be accommodated; there were attendances at the House of Lords, sermons to be preached and visits made to other parts of the country. But Edward was able to give more uninterrupted attention to subjects requiring careful thought, and occasionally he was able to take up the threads of his work on Cyprian on which he had been engaged for many years. He was devoted to animals, particularly dogs and horses. Watch, his collie, had accompanied him from Cornwall, and had attained the position of faithful old friend. During prayers in Chapel he would lie at full length just outside the door, and one evening, when the lesson concluded with the words: 'What I say unto you, I say unto all, Watch!' the dog slowly rose and walked into the Chapel in a dignified manner and lay down at Edward's feet.

Edward was an enthusiastic horseman and almost every day, whether at Lambeth or Addington, would have the horses out and go for a canter, accompanied by his Chaplain or one of the family. On these occasions he was in the best of spirits. Though he was not a good horseman, he rode fearlessly and spoiled his horse by humouring its every whim and over-indulging it with lumps of sugar. He rode with a very slack rein which was dangerous for a man of his weight and he had several falls. A favourite horse called Quentin, on which he rode for several years, had a treacherous nature, but Edward always made excuses for its bad behaviour. Once the horse had a sore ear and was nervous of being touched, but Edward, refusing to acknowledge that he should not do so, slipped into the stall, only to be struck a severe blow on the chest. Although badly bruised he had not been nipped by Quentin's teeth. He was more upset by dropping a small wooden cross set in gold which the horse bit and crushed out of all recognition.

At Addington the Bensons were able to indulge themselves in almost every outdoor activity – shooting, riding, golf, croquet; and skating and tobogganning in winter. The evenings were taken up with painting (Maggie painted her family of Persian cats in oils), writing for *The Saturday Magazine*, making music (Arthur composed voluntaries for the organ and Nellie studied the violin), and Hugh built a marionette theatre. Once at least during the Christmas holidays they all jointly wrote a play. One year mediums were exposed in *The Spiritualist*; another year *The Rose and the Ring* was turned into an opera. Unfortunately only Nellie had a good singing voice, but the servants, lodge-keepers and neighbours all enjoyed the amateur thespians even when time and tune were far from perfect. When the family was gathered together during the holidays from school and university, life at Addington was an orgy of argument, discussion, criticism and laughter. But the most enthralling occupation was writing, and their contributions to *The Saturday Magazine* gradually began to give way to more professional efforts. The magazine was still enjoyed as a communal effort, but wings were being spread that took the budding authors into other realms. Nellie, who, to her dismay, was soon to be taken away from Lady Margaret Hall, Oxford, in order to help her mother with hostess duties, had published an article on George Crabbe in *Temple Bar*. Arthur had written his first novel, *Memoirs of Arthur Hamilton*, an uneasy mixture of autobiography and fantasy, under the pseudonym 'Christopher Carr', and Maggie and Fred were collaborating on a story which gave hints of what was, many years later, to become Fred's first and bestselling novel, *Dodo*. The venture was abandoned long before it was finished because the technique of trying to convey character by means of conversation rather than description and analysis defeated them. So Minnie, as Mrs Vivian, had to wait many years before her debut as a Fred character.

Sundays at Addington were dreaded by everybody but Edward. Even Minnie sighed when she woke up to realise what they would all have to go through. Edward revelled in every activity he could organise to set the day apart from the rest of the week, and would have completely failed to understand that his delight was not shared by his family. The pattern for Sunday devotions had been set many years before, even before some of the children had been born, and the routine was so much bound up with their pattern of living that it was inconceivable it could be criticised. Worshipping God on God's day – well, what else was there to do?

The day began with an early celebration in the Chapel if there was no midday celebration in Addington Church, otherwise there were prayers at which Edward used a Greek Litany which he had compiled and translated. The Wellington College hymn book, another compilation of Edward's, was used. Breakfast followed the service, then Edward retired to his study where he busied himself doing odd jobs and talking to whichever member of the family could be persuaded by the others to follow him there. Then it was time for church. He would have preferred everybody to walk slowly with him to church, but this seldom happened because Fred and Hugh had a habit of rushing down at the last moment, breathless and giggling, thus receiving black looks from their father. After lunch came the walk – exactly the same walk every Sunday, and a slow one. Although only about a mile and a half was covered it took two hours, and Edward liked all his children to accompany him so that he could read Keble's *Christian Year* and George Herbert to them as they sauntered. Usually it was either Maggie or Lucy Tait, a frequent and most welcome visitor, who walked with him; Minnie and Nellie had Bible classes to take and Arthur and Fred branched off halfway to take a longer route which they finished in half the time. Sunday conversation during the walk had to be conducted in a gentle, reverent atmosphere; secular subjects, though not forbidden, had to be carefully chosen. Before tea there was a Bible reading for the youngest Bensons; and after tea there was the evening service in Addington Church. But that was not the end of the day's religious observances, for after supper Edward read *Pilgrim's Progress*, immediately starting again at the beginning with Christian's first lament after finishing the book; so that the audience almost knew the book by heart. Edward's acting ability came out again in his reading, which was full of light and shade, fine and delicate inflections, and he knew how to bring forth tears, either of sadness or amusement.

Sunday was formally closed by Compline in Chapel, with psalms, canticle and hymn. To fill up the intervals between services and readings 'Sunday' books might be read, but there was no other kind of relaxation permitted. No games were played, not even those, such as lawn tennis or golf, which would not cause the servants any extra work. However much snow covered the ground there was no tobogganing, and however thick the ice on the pond there was no skating. For all except Edward the day of rest was a day of pitiless fatigue and crushing boredom. Edward himself felt so much spiritual refreshment that he could not think for a moment that the others did not share his happiness.

If the day was too hot for a walk they sat under the big cedar tree on the lawn and everybody in turn read from some saintly chronicle, and usually everyone except the reader drifted off into sleep, Edward among them. On one hot Sunday Fred was reading from *Lives of the Saints,* glancing occasionally at the unused tennis court and croquet lawn, and he noted that all his listeners had closed eyes and breasts that gently rose and fell. Edward's head was thrown back, his mouth was open and faint snores punctuated Fred's droning words. A wicked plan came to him... He continued to read, not forwards but back to a page that he had already read; then he turned over a hundred pages and read a paragraph about an entirely different saint. Then he flipped back to the book's introduction for a couple of minutes, gave them a little about Saint Catherine of Siena before returning to the end of the chapter on Saint Francis on which he had originally been engaged. He stopped and closed the book.

Nellie was the first to wake up. 'Oh, how interesting that was,' she said. Edward came to with a jerk. 'Wonderful!' he said. 'Is that the end, Fred?'

'Yes, that's all,' said Fred, looking virtuous and longing, but not daring, to confess his crime.

Edward had his own version of a Sunday afternoon at Addington, with Hugh reading the *Life of Paul the Hermit* aloud from Kingsley, 'and we concluded that if it was *right*, and necessary for the weal of Christianity, that such an awful centrepiece as the desert life should be entered on, in such an age of Sin and Delight as the Alexandrian life exhibited, then we had every right to expect birds to fetch us bread and lions to dig our grave. We terrified ourselves also by the memoirs of the Hermit Crab and the Sacculina, as exhibiting how frightfully we get punished, if we dare to love without working, in body and spirit, and that Degeneracy is an almost intolerable vengeance on Degeneration' (This was a reference to Drummond's *Natural Law in the Spiritual World*). 'Then Fred read Stanley's account of Jerusalem as it was and is, but alas by this time I fell asleep under a tree and did not hear all. Tea under the Cedar, and a strain or two of George Herbert – the London fatigue seems passing off in this sweet holiday.'

Minnie was now a very different person from what she had been as wife of a Headmaster, Chancellor and Bishop. Age – she was 40 when Edward became Archbishop – had brought composure and serenity. No longer was she frightened of her husband's benevolent tyranny. She was devoted to him, but in a more detached way and could look dispassionately at some of the things that once caused her to feel miserably crushed. She was sympathetic to his neuresthenia and heedful of his many needs and demands, but she had so much else to occupy her time and thoughts, and often Edward had to be put into the background while she busied herself with her responsibilities as mistress of two great houses. She dispensed hospitality with charm and dignity, presiding at table or in drawing-room so calmly that no-one would know how hard she had worked to make the hidden wheels of the machinery work smoothly. She loved entertaining and being entertained and she acquired a social gaiety that put all her guests at ease and ensured the success of whatever gathering she was presiding over. She enjoyed the debates and ceremonials at which Edward was a star; and meeting politicians, princes and prime ministers held no terror for her. Pomp and pageantry seemed to stimulate her, and she found it romantic to be in the middle of the important things that were happening to Church and State. Minnie Sidgwick, frightened child-bride, was light years away from Minnie Benson, gracious hostess and fluent conversationalist.

Edward looked upon her with love, pride and slight puzzlement. It seemed at times that she did not need him – that he was her consort, not she his. He could not criticise her housekeeping any more or censure what he considered were her frailties. To his regret he did not fully understand her, but she had a far deeper comprehension of him. She kept from him only two things – her personal relation to God and her personal relation to her children and friends. All else he could dominate, but upon those two secret places he could not intrude. When she had had a deep spiritual crisis during the Lincoln years she had not taken her difficulties to Edward, knowing that his attempts to shore up her tottering faith in Christianity would be alien ground to her. He had never questioned for a moment the validity of his religion and could not have summoned up the tolerance to sympathise with her questions. So it was to Tan, Mrs Mylne, she had fled for protection and enlightenment. God became a Father for her, not an omnipotent Being and the difference between her vision and Edward's remained permanent, but unacknowledged, for all their married life.

Minnie was no saint. She could be silly, flighty, secretive, self-indulgent where food was concerned, even occasionally untruthful, and on more than one occasion borrowed money from a member of the family which was not repaid, but her faults were negligible when weighed against her love, self-abandonment and hunger and thirst after righteousness. Her talents were widely recognised by many competent judges. Bishop Thorold wrote of her as one of the keenest and cleverest women he had ever known, and Gladstone called her 'the cleverest woman in Europe'.

All her children adored her. They trusted her and turned to her for everything. They were entirely at ease with her and found her the gayest and most perceptive of companions. Thus they obeyed her promptly and gladly. If only Edward had been less in evidence life at Addington would have been perfect. But as always its quiet and repose soon brought depression and melancholy reflections.

Edward had always kept a diary, though spasmodically, and there were often weeks or months between entries. It had been a confidential and outspoken work but, after becoming Archbishop, it became even more so, and it is difficult to imagine how, with his days crowded from morning to night, he found time to write such long accounts of his doings and his thoughts for it was written late at night, tired though he was, after the day's strenuous labours. The whole diary, a volume for every year of his episcopacy, is a remarkable historical document, frank in its criticism of himself and other people, full of personal details, irritations, struggles and fears, disappointments that so masterful a man had to endure when faced with so much opposition and indifference, and depressions when both the present and the future offered nothing but failure. He draws a picture of a man of deeply spiritual instincts who would have preferred study and seclusion to the organising, superintending and directing of practical enterprises. In letters and speeches his tone was more cheerful; the diary was a safety-valve; nobody saw it or was meant to see it during his lifetime, and he seldom allowed what he was feeling to appear in either voice or expression.

On Tuesday May 1, 1883, he spoke at the Church Missionary Society meeting ... 'to a vast (crowded actually) mass of people at Exeter Hall; urged them to consider that educated, cultivated men, Hindoos, etc., had souls not less dear to God than the souls of the ignorant' – which puts the poor Hindoos in their place. A few days later he and Minnie went to a private view at the Royal Academy. Normally Edward had no time for any art that was not based on religion, but on that occasion he was touched by a picture that he believed bore on the mysteries of animal life and feeling. 'The collie putting its paw on the knee of the dying child and looking – if it is looking – just as my Watch looks at a mystery which moves his feelings. Something or other, whatever it may be, passes out by a dog's eyes, not merely is taken into them; the human eye is not used thus because we have speech. And Rivière has seen this, and I have seen it.'

On May 10 he was entertained at a dinner in Birmingham given by old pupils of King Edward's School. 'It was a sort of resurrection. So few of them have I seen in the meantime though those few are my dearest friends.' During his speech Edward made an innocent but unfortunate observation which was to haunt him for over a year. He mentioned the stall in Lambeth Chapel, the very stall which Laud erected with the screen, and of Laud he said, 'In spite of his misjudgements and misunderstanding of what was good for Church and for State alike, he had set the great example of devotion to the English Church and had undoubtedly died for her.' *The Standard* reported him as having said 'having sate (both he and Arthur always wrote 'sate' for 'sat') in the Chair of the martyred Laud'. *The Spectator* and the *Pall Mall* assaulted him daily for ten days for his 'model Archbishop' and 'glorying to sit on the Throne of the martyred Laud'. Was this mistaken reporting a blunder or malice? *The Spectator*, particularly, had an antipathy towards the Archbishop (any Archbishop). Edward wrote to Bishop Lightfoot, asking what he should do to put the matter right – ignore the Press or strenuously deny their accusation. He decided on the former course and there the matter seemed to rest until, nearly a year later, a Mr Willis, moving a resolution in the Commons to remove the Bishops from the House of Lords, averred that 'when the present Primate was enthroned at Canterbury, he could find no comparison to describe his feelings in his speech on that occasion but to compare them with those of Laud.' After that the storm in the teacup gently subsided and Edward was allowed to forget his *faux pas*.

On the day after the Birmingham dinner he and Randall Davidson had an interview with the Queen, during which she said, 'As I get older I cannot understand the world. I cannot comprehend its littleness. When I look at the frivolities and littlenesses, it seems to me as though they were all a little mad. The wickedness of people's spite against one another is so great.'

A few days later he visited Lincoln, and the people crowded into the Minster at the evening service. He was also touched that the choirboys gave up their half holiday to sing at the service. He found that Bishop Wordsworth still read and wrote as much as ever; still quoted Church Fathers and Classics aptly and abundantly, and still reasoned as illogically and was as beautifully courteous as ever. On May 26 he went down to Tunbridge Wells and confirmed 400 people in Canon Hoare's church; the next day he laid hands on 339 boys in Tonbridge School Chapel, in the evening 138, and the next morning above 100 in St. Stephen's. Tunbridge Wells was the very heart of the Evangelicals and Edward stayed with the leading members in the town, and met their friends. 'They are all right,' he wrote, 'they hold nothing but the truth and they hold it strongly, consistently, sweetly, but with just a tinge of Torquemada. They are happy in the Court of Israel and of the Women. They have never seen the Court of the Priest. I keep nothing back from them in my address, yet they do not seem displeased. There is something in Evangelicalism, as it exists now, which is very concordant with wealth.'

He returned to Lambeth and had a terrible day of hurried and impatient work. Every morning he was convinced that the day would be serene and orderly, but every evening he felt dissatisfaction with every hour of it, and he knew it was his own fault. He did not get to bed before half past one in the morning, not physically tired but mentally worn out by the frictions that had accumulated during the day.

There was an unexpected but welcome diversion from the daily round in June when he and Minnie went to the Crystal Palace to a Handel Festival to hear 'Israel in Egypt'. Edward had no interest in music if it had no basis in religion, just as he had not in art; secular music tended to take people's minds away from the real priorities of life, he thought, and he was, if not antagonistic to, at least suspicious of, composers who were not God-orientated. But he had no qualms about attending the oratorio, and joined the other 22,000 people present, and marvelled at the 4,000 strong orchestra and choir. 'The truth of Handel's genius is in nothing more manifest than in the ever-increasing glory of his work, as it is, so to speak, more and more magnified.' The next sentence in his diary reveals the muddle that Edward could sometimes get into when he was not able to sit down and clarify his thoughts and express them lucidly. 'Other works reveal their thinness of tissue when they are committed to orchestras far beyond their author's possibility of even imagining...'

On June 24 he preached to a terrific congregation which crowded the transept of St. Paul's, down almost to the west end, and stood in the gangways. 'These scenes must come to an end, but I wonder that their curiosity last so long. When they find what few barley loaves and what very small fishes this poor soul, hungry itself, possesses, this five thousand must melt away. Or will Christ have compassion? Meanwhile let us make what running we can. The Church of England has to be made up again from the very bottom. It is the lower- and middle-classes who must be won. And it must be humility and intense devotion which must be laid at the disposal of the poor. There is little to be done yet with the rich.'

August saw the family at Addington, where Edward began to busy himself with alterations to the house and park. First he concentrated on the Chapel, which he thought was hideous, with stalls on both sides of the altar and all other seats facing eastward. He had Bishop Juxon's rails, which he had found in a lumber room at Lambeth, brought down, also some seat fronts which had been made in imitation of Juxon's work, and with these he constructed a screen which he said 'looked quite Belgian', a reredos and some side panelling, and had the seats turned chair-wise. Nellie and Maggie painted frescoes in red lines on the walls, and Canon Wickenden gave new glass for the windows. Edward hoped the effect would be quaint and grave, though perhaps not exquisite.

'Such a beauteous harvest,' he wrote in September, 'Gathered in such golden weather, and after it such deliberate soft rain that you can scarcely see it falling outside the windows, but only the whole land grey with it at a short distance. Beech trees and cedars standing as still as possible in it with such gentle slow waving as to make the most of it – like great creatures liking to be stroked and pressing up under your hand – and a bloom coming over the grand flat boughs even while one watches their lowering blackness.'

Then he made a note about Matthew Arnold, the poet son of Arnold of Rugby, who was going on a lecture tour of America. 'What discipline,' he commented obscurely, 'to grind for Phillistines after he has mocked them with his foxes and firebrands and all his riddles so long!' Edward had first met Matthew Arnold when he was teaching at Rugby and had sat next to him at dinner at Charles Arnold's house. There Matthew Arnold had uttered some humorous, semi-cynical statement to the effect that it was useless to attempt to enlighten the general public or to give them a sense of due proportion in the matter of truth. Edward strongly disagreed and quoted a few lines from the celebrated sermon of Dr. Thomas Arnold on Christian Education – which naturally he had remembered word for word

– and was somewhat nettled when Matthew smiled at him affectionately, drooped his head sideways in Edward's direction and patted his shoulder, saying, 'Very graceful and appropriate, my dear Benson, but we must not take for granted everything that dear Dr. Arnold said.' The patronising rebuke had rankled ever since.

Shortly after his work in the Chapel Edward became ill. He was troubled with an abscess which eventually needed an operation, and after it was successfully performed he was convalescent for some weeks, during which time he went north to visit his Sidgwick relations in Yorkshire, taking Minnie and Nellie with him. At Keighley he found a dear old cousin who, at 81, ruled her house, Riddlesden, with its gables, large low rooms and mullioned windows, and the parish too, as briskly as she had ever done. While there he walked up to Ilkley Manor and felt less fatigue that he had expected. In the afternoon the church bells rang and memories of his childhood flooded back. How odd, he thought, to look on oneself as a helpless little chap on top of the coach going to and from Leeds and Skipton, and chatting on the box seat to the coachman, 40 years ago.

They went from Keighley to Skipton. The castle was a great delight to Nellie. Edward pointed out the window of the room in which he used to read Newman's sermons to his stately old aunt, on condition that she allowed him to read Arnold's sermons to her, and the gateway out of which he used to patter to Church for the 7 a.m. service. And she went up the turret staircase to see his old bedroom. He met some of the servants, now very old, who still remembered him, and who were as forthright and unimpressed with greatness as ever. Willcock, the old parish clerk, came to see him. 'I heard His Grace wanted to see Willcock, and I said, "Then he shall see me," and so I comed.' And John Smith, almost blind but as shrewd as ever, said bluntly, 'I mind yer preaching last time you was here.'

'Ah, but, John, you've forgotten the sermon, I know,' said Edward.

'Well, I can't say,' the old man replied. Then he went on to tell how lucky he'd been in a dangerous accident.

'I hope you'll continue to be lucky,' Edward said, shaking his hand.

'Ah,' said he, 'I only want to be loocky now at t'last dee. That's the loock I want now.'

'There are no hearts like these Yorkshire hearts,' Edward wrote at the end of his visit. 'Blood is thicker than water.'

In December the black dog was again snapping at his heels and he found himself moody and self-pitying. The amount and the gravity of his work weighed on him heavily. 'Why has He put me in this place?' he asked. 'Thou hast done great things through souls becoming filled with humility as the grace of their childlikeness. But my humility, Lord, is not as theirs. My feeling is due to the knowledge of my mere emptiness. This is clear to

(Left) Captain White Benson (18th Royal Warwickshire Regiment).
(Right) Mary (Crofts). Mrs William Sidgwick. *From a sketch in water colours
by G. Richmond RA, 1830.*

(Left) Silhouettes of Edward White Benson and Harriet (Baker) Benson.
The father and mother of the Archbishop.
(Right) E.W. Benson (senior). The Archbishop's father.

(Top left) No. 72 Lombard Street, Birmingham.
The house where the Archbishop was born.
(Top right) Mary Benson at 20.
(Below) The Opening of the College, 1859.

Lord Derby

E.W. Benson.
Wellington College, 1869

Chapel at Wellington College.
From a photograph by Thomas Hunt.

Mary Benson (aged 30).

Charles Kingsley
Vicar of Eversley

Eversley House

Edward White Benson,
Chancellor of Lincoln, 1876.

Nellie, aged 13 (left) and
Maggie, aged 11 (rignt),

Christopher Wordsworth,
Bishop of Lincoln, 1883.

(Above) Canon Wilkinson,
1883. Bishop of Truro
after Benson.

(Left) Truro Cathedral,
East End.

(Below) The Garden Front,
Lambeth Palace.
From a drawing by
L. Beatrice Thompson.

(Top left) The three brothers: E.F. Benson at Marlborough, aged 15; A.C. Benson at Cambridge, aged 21; R.H. Benson at Mr Cornish's School at Clevedon, aged 11.
(Top right) Maggie, aged 28, 1893.
(Left) Archbishop Benson, 1892.
(Below) Addington Park, Croydon.

(Above) Addington Park, Croydon, from the Terrace.

(Right) The most recent portrait of the late Archbishop of Canterbury, taken September, 1896, with the Archbishops of Armagh and Dublin.

(Below) Hawarden Church.

me from the transitions to conceit which is another form of emptiness. I am so tremulous: so afraid of the face of men; so irritated by just carpings which are despicable only because they are carpings, not because they are untrue. I cannot conceive why Thou hast put me here. But I trust Thee to do something with me that shall be to Thine honour and not to my lasting shame.'

To continue his convalescence he went for a short tour in Dovedale in January, 1884, with his old friends Bishop Lightfoot and Westcott, Professor of Divinity at Cambridge. He seriously needed a good rest, which a bad cold seemed to provide, for he wrote to Minnie: 'I have not a single intellect, not pulse or stir. My cold has lulled all my faculties to rest, even to my taste and smell which are perfectly blank, and I feel sure the cogitative membrane of my brain is in exactly the same state. I have no ideas except what Westcott communicates, and they remain with me from 12 to 15 minutes, then sink into a copper-coloured glow and presently die out.'

The anniversary of his father's death on February 1, 1842, occurred during the tour and caused him further nostalgic regrets. 'He must have been a most remarkable person. His looks, talk, love of truth, energy, diligence, intensity about natural things, religiousness, delicacy of health, and enjoyment are as vivid and perfect to me as those of anyone I know, and my mother's force and beautiful profile and ruling power are equally clear, but I had many more years with her.' Edward could not have been the jolliest companion on the Dovedale tour, but his moods were not unknown to his two friends and they nobly put up with his silences and gloom.

Edward returned to Lambeth at least physically refreshed and immersed himself in Church affairs. He was cheered by the opportunity of offering the vacant living of All Hallows, Barking, in Trinity Square, to Arthur Mason, his friend and Chaplain at Truro. The church stands close to the Tower of London and contains the remains of Archbishop Laud. Edward thought hard about detaching Mason from Cornwall where he was doing such excellent work but, after making many enquiries, he thought it right to make the offer. Mason consented to the change. He took two houses in Trinity Square, fitted them up and formed a college of studious priests, on the same lines as the one in Truro he had been responsible for, to serve the Church and to take up missionary work. Edward was very fond of the young man, indeed thought of him more as a son than just a friend. Their natures, tastes, even their prejudices, were similar, and Edward expanded easily and naturally in his company, bringing out for him his store of knowledge of medievalism, and was charmed by the sympathy of his hearer. They remained in this loving relationship for the rest of Edward's life. Mason later became a Canon of Canterbury and then Lady Margaret Professor of Divinity at Cambridge.

The anniversary of Martin's death came around in February, too, and, as usual, he and Minnie went to Winchester to keep tryst with their son. They found that somebody had laid a beautiful cross of flowers on the grave before they placed their own wreath there. They prayed out of Martin's prayer book, went to Evensong in the Cathedral, and sat by William Wykeham's tomb as Martin had loved to do.

Edward had lost a lot of time since the previous July with 'poorliness, and feeling unequal to work, besides actual illness,' he wrote. 'But must not shrink from London and its harrying ways.'

He attracted some criticism from a group of High Churchmen in March because he had attended a banquet given at the Mansion House in honour of Lord Shaftesbury, who had just received the Freedom of the City of London. The event had taken place during Lent, and it was thought that Edward was being too secular and frivolous in his attitude to the solemn season. If his critcs had known how Edward, in his low-spirited state, intensely disliked such festivities they would surely not have maintained that the interests of the soul were being sacrificed to the pleasures of the body. His feelings of bodily prostration and mental depression continued. He became very pessimistic about the Church and its spiritual power. He wrote to Professor Westcott: 'The very streets of London, and the meanness of all, rich and poor, in them seems to negate the very consideration of such a thing. The Church seems to most men like any other business – well managed or ill managed – the managers to be envied or contemned or accepted, anything above 'nature' not to be named. Then comes Sunday and suddenly all is so changed. I know the fault is ours. But how are we to get out of it?' 'Can't recover vigour, voice or spirit,' he complained after a very large Confirmation in Croydon Parish Church, and afterwards, opening a school for 700 children which had cost £4,000, 'Was truly feeble.'

On April 23 he paid his first official visit to Oxford. By virtue of his office he was visitor of three colleges, Merton, All Souls and Keble. He was received with great formality at Keble, where he was met at the lodge by the Warden and Council, and conducted to the hall through a double line of undergraduates in surplices. During the ceremony to receive an honorary degree he had never looked more vigorous or stately than when he came in, very upright, in his Doctor's gown. Another recipient of a degree walked at his side, old and bent. Edward smiled good-humouredly at the remarks that greeted him, and turned with great courtesy and deference to help the older Doctor up the steps. It was the Eve of St. Mark, the college gaudy day. After dinner Edward's health was proposed by Lord

Beauchamp, in the presence of a large number of old members. In returning thanks Edward said, 'Keble has brought out a tone in the English Church, has struck a note that has been silent, but which now will never cease to vibrate.' He spoke of George Herbert as 'an earlier Keble', and he expressed the hope that all in that college 'might be men in earnest, laborious students, with all modesty and sweetness, looking forward to being teachers of future generations; that was what the prosperity of Keble College meant.'

He celebrated Choral Communion at Keble and afterwards High Matins. He could not help criticising the windows of the Chapel later in his diary. 'The Chapel is very stately as to its roof, and the bold division of wall spaces. But the dowdy ineffectiveness of its windows and prosaic colouring is sad. It is not brightness but glow which is so essential and so wanting here. Not height of colour but jewelled-ness. All the materials of those ancient effects were used, but there is no felicity in composing them.'

In June he was back in a depressed state. 'The first years of my Archiepiscopate when everything, within and without, crowded business details, talk, grind, meetings, interviews, letters without stop or stay, from early till past midnight, I thought I would acquiesce in it as God's will, and trust Him to feed me spiritually in the midst of this current. But He did not, and will not, and I thank Him. Little as I have got of separate moments, it is a great blessing, and it is clear that to get it is one's true work – and to refuse false work.'

On July 24 he held a reception, which Archbishop Tait had originated, for some of the poor and the sick from Lambeth Parish. It had become an annual engagement and one which gave him much pleasure. The gardens were thrown open and tea was provided. Afterwards there was a short service which Edward always took himself, choosing the hymns and giving a short and simple address. 'Had a party of 99 poor and halt and blind,' he wrote. 'Their manners and tone as they approach the grave became so sweet and considerate whatever their rank … we cannot be perfected except by suffering.' Minnie, of course, was present at the get-together, dispensing charm, understanding and helpful words.

Delighted as Edward was with the simple goodness of his elderly parishioners, he did not have the same feelings towards the villagers of Kent and Surrey. 'Except among the Addington villagers themselves, who are the simplest, friendliest people, there is no trace of kindly or respectful salutation among the Kent and Surrey villagers. Hardly will they give a growl if one wishes them "goodnight" first: most pass on mum and sulky. If this is not the result of the general upheaval against power above them, it must be due either to the general prevalence of "incomelings", uninterested in neighbourhood and neighbours and soon to depart for other settlements, or else to the increased touring about of unknown persons – so that the people forget to acknowledge any powers. But, whatever is the cause, you can be sure of a friendly greeting from no-one. It augurs ill if this is the early bud of the coming change, this contempt for authority.' Edward was not used to indifference, let alone antagonism, towards religion, and he became increasingly worried by it. At Wellington few people had dared to challenge his authority as Master: at Lincoln he had found only affection and a willing obedience; at Truro the opposition was mainly on religious grounds – Methodists versus Anglicans – and the struggle there had been more stimulating than not. But here in London and the surrounding counties there was a growing resentment against what was thought to be outmoded ways of thought and behaviour. Authority was there to be challenged – there were active anti-religionists, some politically activated by the ideals of early Socialism, and others who rejected the idea of God and believed that man was his own saviour. The movement, fragmented and unsure of itself, was only the beginning of a boil on the face of the conventionally religious establishment, and middle and upper classes with their usual arrogance ignored it. But far-seeing men, both in and out of the Church, could see how eventually the old order of things would be infiltrated and threatened by new ideas; and that when the Queen died, as soon she must, things would never be the same again. Edward was not the most percipient of men, but even he was forced to notice the coming of the change.

He was in a melancholy mood when Nellie celebrated her 21st birthday on October 10, and could not rejoice as the others were doing. All he could do was write in his diary: 'How can one help perplexing oneself in such a place as this? I find in myself no fitness for it. I could not resist, I had no right to resist. If calls exist, called I was; against my will. An unfit man, not unfit in his humility, subjective, but clearly seeing himself by God's help as he is – yet called. Follows from that, that there is something unknown in God's counsels for the Church and for His poor servant, whom He will not let fall to the ground for simply nothing, for His own love to the least – something He means to have done by one unfit for the thing He wants to have done. Then make him fit – and let, O God, whatever it be, be good for Thy Church. It is in Thy Hand.' The more sunk in gloom he was, the more incoherent Edward became.

In October Mrs Wordsworth, the wife of Edward's beloved Bishop of Lincoln, died, after a long illness, on her husband's birthday. The Bishop himself died the following March. He was buried on the Festival of the Annunciation, the Cathedral's great day. Edward was devastated. For once he wrote simply in his diary: his account of Christopher Wordsworth's funeral was dignified and moving. He had to write it, he said, for his own edification, remembrance and preparation. 'The completely-filled building, the sound of Great Tom in the air, the perfect stillness of such a throng, the quiet approach of two or three of the Chapter to meet me, the dearness of every stone of beauty, the vestry filled with well-known robed figures and faces, the Dean with suffering stamped on all his features, made a strange and trying dream seem to come over me. It was but the other day I followed him in a thin procession out of St. Hugh's Chapel for his enthronement, and now this great procession went to receive him.' Edward was followed by the Bishop's family and then by almost all the clergy of the diocese. 'They and the corporation and a few country gentlemen filled the whole of the glorious choir, while the coffin, with the Bishop's pastoral staff on it and wreaths of flowers, lay just above the grander choir, four chaplains standing beside it. The singing was of the quiet meditative and most sweet character which has long been peculiar to Lincoln. I read the Lesson. They gave me my dear old Chancellor's stall with my old prayer-book and its monogram... The Throne was hung with black where he used to kneel with that piercing force of devotion and his ejaculations of Amen, Amen, halfway through the next Collects. All has come and gone so naturally, and this is so natural itself, and the hope so perfect as to be not hope, and the thankfulness so intense that he is delivered from the terrible cloud and suffering of the months since Mrs Wordsworth's death.'

A few days later, back in London, he took Nellie and Maggie to the Royal Academy to see 'the most unlike pictures that ever were': Holman Hunt's *Triumph of Innocents* and Munkacsy's *Crucifixion*. 'The spiritual water in the former is a strange and unnatural conception. What can he mean by all those bubbles? – the largest of which shows in colour the history from the Dream of Jacob to the Adoration of the Lamb. He cannot have reflected that bubbles burst. This is beyond me. Perhaps spiritual bubbles do not. The *Crucifixion* finer. The merits of the great Dutchman are on this Hungarian. But the faces which should be finest are hidden like Agamemnon's. The awful being is Judas – it must be he – running for his life to death – in spite of the error of the date.'

On April 25 there was a great congregation in St. Paul's to see the consecration of Edward King as the new Bishop of Lincoln and E.H. Bickersteth as Bishop of Exeter. Canon Liddon preached a Manifesto concerning the power and authority of the Episcopate, condemning vehemently all 'Modernismus', not only the Courts and Public Worship Regulation Act, but also declaring the Education Act of 1870 to be the root of all evil, and Board Schools its evil fruit. 'Fewer persons than usual communicated,' Edward commented. 'This is owing to the growth of "Fasting Communion" as a necessity and not as a pious discipline only.

And this, which is in the Church a piece of Materialism that is in the world today, has taken great root among the followers of the holy and influential Canon King. It is strange that a great many years ago, when I was at Wellington, I remember Dean Wellesley's showing me some most strong letters to the Queen and Ministers against King's being made Professor at Oxford – on the grounds of intellectual inadequacy. The Dean gave me plenty of indication of the untruth of the allegation. I recommended him to persevere with the recommendation of King.' A few years later Edward had cause to ponder on those words and rue the day he had written them.

Soon afterwards Edward was presented with a magnificent Primatial Cross for the See of Canterbury, made of silver gilt set with splendid sapphires, a gift from the Church people of Truro. He said he accepted it as a remembrance that it was to be 'a standard of the King of Kings, the great sign of the Word of God which rode on conquering and to conquer'.

A more important event took place the following day when the Revised Version of the Scriptures was presented to the House of Convocation in the College Hall of Westminster School. 'That,' said Edward, on receiving it, 'is a far greater gift than the Archiepiscopal Cross with which the Metropolitan See has just been endowed.' Queen Victoria was delighted to receive a copy of the New Revised Version of the Bible. She congratulated those who had laboured so earnestly and promised to read the Sacred Volume with deep interest.

An entry in Edward's diary on June 23 gives an excellent example of the kind of day he spent. 'Work,' he comments bitterly, 'which is supposed to depend somewhat on thinking and studying. Up at 6.15, wrote until 8.30, chapel 9.15. 10, Adeney, Sir Ed. Hay Currie to explain Beaumont Trust. Grey, Hardwicke. Letters until 12.45, when Canon Hoare on Tunbridge Wells Cemetery. 1, luncheon, Hoare, Hutchinson; 1.30, drove to Charterhouse where we discussed the scheme for its alteration (Abp York, J. Talbot, Lords Devon, Clinton, Brownlow and Coleridge), and elected Elwyn Master of the Charterhouse. 3.30, Meeting for Beaumont Trust at Mansion House, Prince of Wales spoke, I seconded. 4.20, House of Lords, very full. Lord Granville sold all, in lieu of a 'statement', moving to adjourn to Thursday. 4.40, Assyrian Committee: decided on starting new move – not out till 6. 7.45, dined with the Cubitts at Prince's Gate – evening party after. Large conservative gathering – no-one in good spirits, but all bent to do their best. Now 12 midnight.' The chief event of the afternoon at the Lords was Lord Granville telling the peers that Lord Salisbury had accepted office (after the election defeat of the Liberals) and had undertaken to form a ministry. He was at that moment with the Queen at Windsor. Lord Granville then moved that the House adjourned until

Thursday when the Gas and Water Bill would be read a second time. 'Gas and Water,' Edward reflected, 'could anything be neater?'

At a Middle Temple dinner Edward sat opposite Lord Randolph Churchill, whom he had not previously met. The Ministry of Mr Gladstone had just been defeated and in the new government Churchill had been appointed Secretary of State for India. The company at the dinner was very conservative-minded and there was a great cheer when Churchill drank from the loving cup, almost as loud a cheer as when Sir Stafford Northcote, the new First Lord of the Treasury, drank in his turn. Lord Derby, the defeated Colonial Secretary, had to drink in absolute silence.

Lord Randolph Churchill had just returned from Paris where, he said, Bismarck was ruling everything. He was supreme with so many men among the political leaders that they were able to keep the Republican Party in power in spite of the feeling against it. Churchill added that the French had their revenge, for Socialist propaganda was leavening all Germany from its immensely strong headquarters in Paris.

Edward had always been interested in spreading social purity in the Church, and, with Lightfoot and Westcott, had been instrumental in setting up the Church of England Purity Society; and they spoke out for the formation of vigilance committees to fight prostitution in every town in the land.

In July certain articles had appeared in the *Pall Mall Gazette* which dealt with immoral traffic in young girls. The Editor, W.T. Stead, furnished his readers with a carefully-chosen political diet of Radicalism and sensationalism. He advocated passionately the widely-held view of 'fallen women', that they had descended from a state of maidenly innocence solely by reason of male depravity. He was horrified to learn how easy it was for a young girl to be inveigled into a brothel where she could be violated without any hope of redress because, if she had freely consented to enter the brothel, even though being ignorant of what happened there, she was held to have consented to her own 'ruin'. Stead decided to institute an investigation into juvenile prostitution in London and hoped that the disclosures, when published in the *Pall Mall Gazette*, would compel the government to make sure that the Criminal Law Amendment Bill reached the Statute Book. Edward approved of the idea but not of the method Stead had decided to use and gave him 'strenuous advice' against it, but 'The Maiden tribute of Modern Babylon' duly appeared and created an immense sensation, made even more so when Stead revealed that he himself had procured a 13-year-old girl by abduction, playing the part of a despoiler of virginity in every detail short of actually consummating the sexual act. The girl's mother had given her consent to the 'sale', but her father had not, and as a result Stead found himself at the Old Bailey, charged with criminal abduction, convicted and sent to prison for two months.

To find the truth behind the whole affair of child prostitution a commission of enquiry was set up. Edward agreed to be a member; others included the Bishop of London, Cardinal Manning, Mr Samuel Morley and R.T. Reid, Q.C.. After sifting all the evidence they published their decision that Stead's revelations were largely true. The Second Reading of the Bill making further provision for the protection of women and girls was rushed through and the measure became law on January 1, 1886, with the age of consent being raised to 16, though it was not high enough for the social-purity movement led by Mrs Ormiston Chant and General and Mrs Booth. Feminists and puritans such as Millicent Fawcett and Josephine Butler regarded the Act as a symbolic and substantial triumph. Edward was glad when it was all over.

CHAPTER FIFTEEN

PERHAPS because Edward felt the need to get away from London after the Stead affair and the knowledge of what lurked in alleys and behind the walls of Lambeth and elsewhere, he decided to go to Switzerland for a holiday, taking with him Arthur, Maggie, Nellie and Fred. Minnie had to stay at home to nurse Hugh who was suffering from scarlatina roseata and was feverish and liverish. They hoped to travel later. The passage from Dover to Calais was rough, but their first sight of Mont Blanc was thrilling. They stayed at Visp and Edward, trying to travel incognito, was annoyed when, in the hotel dining-room, a clergyman recognised him and shouted 'Your Grace' down the length of a long table. 18-year-old Fred cut a vein in his foot which bled horribly and for the next couple of days could only hobble. They drove to Zermatt where the Matterhorn provided another wonderful experience.

Edward's nature observations were always acute. At Zermatt he noticed that there were very few birds. 'Rooks have a melodious thin note, not at all like a caw. Nutcrackers are delightful round black balls as big as wood pigeons; a white line shows on their tails spread in flight. They are saucy little fellows and like to sit on the top sprays of the pines below us for a good stare. They make a chip-chip rather like a jay. We hear the marmots whistle in the lonelier places. The squirrels are black, with white chests. The despised field gentian lingers in warm corners – all other flowers but the harebells are gone – there are glorious scarlet patches everywhere of changed leaves, and the stonecrop lingers in flower near warm rills. The London Pride has died down since we came. In walking the glacier it is quite affecting to have a bee settle on one's bonnet or one's coat so often – they must feel the times are hard. There are a good many hawks – perhaps there would be small birds but for this.' Edward in happier mood could write simply and feelingly. The day before he had seen a priest and a peasant farmer kneeling to a Catholic Archbishop, and the sight provoked a tangled skein of confused questions about the Roman Catholic Church, the teaching of which had become more earthly, even whilst lives had become more pure. 'Where do they stand?' he asked. 'Is it a penance?

Is it a captivity? Is it a slope to still further decline and loss? A nothing? Is there to be a revival? Is there to be a better system of Christianity? And where do we stand? Is unchristianity and antichristianity to invade us yet more – or can we walk with the Cross and with the Truth of the Cross yet overcome? Not we. Will God use us and our sons?' And so on. Edward doubtless knew what important ideas he wanted to express, but in diary form they were often like a jigsaw puzzle with missing pieces.

At Zermatt Maggie fell slightly ill with a touch of scarlatina. When the hotel keeper was told he insisted that no-one else should know, saying that the other guests would be alarmed and would probably leave if they thought she was seriously ill. Fortunately Maggie's indisposition did not last long. At the next Sunday service Edward was horrified and his family amused when prayers were asked for 'Miss Pontifex' which Edward thought was a delicate way of concealing Maggie's identity. It turned out, of course, that Miss Pontifex was an English lady who was ill at another hotel.

A week later Fred went down with diarrhoea and kept to himself for a time. Minnie and Hugh arrived soon afterwards and the family was complete, slightly shaken still, but able to carry on with their expeditions. Edward ascended the Cima di Jazzi from the Riffel Alp Hotel with Canon Hutchinson, an old friend from King Edward's days, a Master at Rugby and afterwards Canon of Canterbury. The Canon was formerly a well-known Alpine climber, so it took Edward all his energy and determination to keep up with him. But in spite of his heavy build and the sedentary life he had lived for so long, he managed the ascent without disgracing himself.

Minnie and Maggie left for home on September 14, and three days later the rest of the family took the night train to Paris, thence to Boulogne where they crossed the Channel for home.

Fred arrived back at Marlborough on September 19 for the beginning of his fourth year there. At 18 he was a good-looking young man with very blue eyes and fair hair and was inordinately fond of sport, particularly cricket. Rugby, football and athletics ranked only slightly lower in his estimation, and racquets was a growing obsession. In that year he made the football XV. He was in the sixth form, had a study of his own and a fag to clean his boots and make his tea. He became head of his house and co-edited *The Marlburian*, the school magazine. The other editor was Eustace Miles, a friend throughout his life. A genial and energetic pagan, Fred filled his life with friendship, games and work, in that order; and the result was that he failed a series of scholarship examinations. He managed to persuade his Headmaster to write to his father, who – as he had in Martin's case – bombarded him with letters of complaint and disapproval, demanding that he put away childish things and bend all his energies to scholastic work, urging him to allow Fred to stay on another year before going to Cambridge. Edward agreed, but never found out Fred's real reason for wanting to stay at school. It was to help his house to win the racquets house cup, the fives cup, the gymnasium cup, the football cup and the singing cup: but most of all he wanted Eustace Miles, though 14 months younger, to catch up with him so that they could go to Cambridge together.

Fred did not love Miles in the way he had loved other boys as he progressed up the school, but regarded him with a steady and unsentimental affection. His predeliction was for boys who were strong and masculine, especially if they were musically inclined, and were younger than he was. His affections were violent but volatile; they lasted at most a year or two, and then another blue-eyed athlete would take his fancy, and a dip at the bathing-place or a game of squash would herald the beginning of another new friendship. He kept a diary from January, 1885, to July 1891, and the Marlborough section is full of rapturous references to the current attachment. Robert Nevill Dundas was one of them. They brewed together, walked, played and worked together and were inseparable – until John Shuckburgh Risley came on the scene. Dundas remained a friend but faded somewhat into the background. 'I am feeling hopeless about Risley. What on earth am I to do?' Fred wrote. 'There is none like him, none.' Then, a month later, he could write, 'The glamour has gone, I think, with respect to J.S.R. Perhaps it will come again?' It did, for Risley is mentioned in capital letters on several occasions later.

But at last the new sun rose over the horizon – Frederick Forbes Glennie, nearly three years younger than Fred; and the diary recorded equally fervent declarations of lasting affection. 'I have felt towards him as I have never felt towards anyone else,' 'F.F.G.,' he wrote later. 'I wonder who my biographer will be, and what he will make of those initials...' Fred was quite open about the passionate nature of his friendships in his autobiographical writings, but he insisted that they had only a healthy open-air quality about them, with no element of 'dingy sensualism', as he called it.

Most of the diary entries were laconic, but there were a few occasions when Fred let himself go and admitted us into the troubled mind of a young man full of self-doubts and sexual frustrations, revealing the turbulence of late adolescence. Most of the time, though, he was happy, as he had been since the first time he walked through the Marlborough gates – in spite of the Spartan conditions and strenuous days. He found everything bright and alluring, even the quarrels and reconciliations with his loved ones. Marlborough was a welcome escape from his problem parent; he could leave behind Edward's dark moods and crushing remarks, and the ghastly boredom of Sundays at Addington. Apart from that weekly purgatory Addington holidays were to Fred like the magic of a spring that lasted all year round. They gave him one of his greatest gifts, the habit of enjoyment. He found pleasure and interest in everything around him, everything he did and everybody he met. One of the pleasures he enjoyed was going to the theatre – in spite of Edward's disapproval. Sometimes his father got to know about the visits, but not about those of which he would have disapproved. For instance, in January, 1885, Fred went to see *The Pirates of Penzance* and *As You Like It*. In April he saw *The Silver King* as well as visiting the National Gallery, a concert at the Albert Hall, the Royal Academy and a Maskelyne and Cook show. In August he saw *The Mikado*, in January, 1886, *Aladdin* at Drury Lane. Eustace Miles, who lived in West Hampstead, was his companion on some of those occasions, Hugh on others.

Arthur and Fred were not particularly close and did not go out together much. There was a certain affection for each other, but little intimacy. Arthur was five years older and was critical of Fred's adolescent exuberance, and his eagerness to argue and criticise. He was by nature sober, detached, unwilling to get involved beyond a certain point in his many romantic friendships, a spectator rather than a participant, a placid and cosy philosopher, but also someone who could be trenchant, witty and provocative. His diaries, which he kept from 1897 until his death in 1925, consisted of 180 volumes, over four million words, and showed him to be fully at home in academic, church and literary circles.

Arthur wrote little about his career as an Eton schoolboy. He had been wretched at Temple Grove, so unlike Fred, but at Eton he was willing to observe all the rules and customs, petty though they might be, without getting involved emotionally. Discipline, administered by members of the sixth form, could be harsh, but Arthur developed the knack of fading into the background and he escaped the worst of what could be inflicted. His fagmaster, Reginald Smith, treated him with consideration, his Tutor was easy-going, and Arthur relished the indulgence shown to him. He was free to roam through Windsor Park and the surrounding countryside. Only one boy bullied him, and he was caned only once. His election to the First Hundred provided him with several friends who lasted for many years; the closest was Herbert Tatham, later a Master at Eton. They went on holiday together, and Arthur found him disrespectful, witty and unambitious – all qualities of which Arthur approved at the time. They both disliked sports and games in general, preferring to sketch old buildings and listen to church music; interests they shared with M.R. James (Monty) and Hugh Childers.

Only once at Eton did Arthur experience a whole-hearted attachment to one of his peers, whose name was hinted at but never identified. It broke the isolation in which he had hitherto lived and gave his thinking new freshness and vigour. The friendship is beautifully described in *Beside Still Waters*, a semi-autobiographical novel which was published in 1907, as one which brought both boys into a charmed circle of content, security and love, and it made Arthur's last two years at Eton a time of blissful enjoyment. He became President of the Literary Society, was elected to Pop and made more friends, some of whom he was to meet again at Cambridge in October, 1881, when he was 19.

Arthur took up residence in the old Chetwynd buildings of King's and found his new life highly congenial, though he read for the Classical Tripos with little enthusiasm and gained a modest place within the First Class of Part One. He found the academical system 'meagre', and felt starved intellectually. What honours he obtained were gained through his own wide reading and a familiarity with the Classics.

Among his friends was the Tutor J.E.C. Weldon, who later became Headmaster of Harrow and Bishop of Calcutta. Another was the eminent Brooke Foss Westcott, then Regius Professor of Divinity and Fellow of King's, an intense person of great modesty who was unable to relax and enjoy normal activities. He was, of course, one of Edward's dearest friends. They had been together at King Edward's School and had corresponded frequently and lovingly ever since. Occasionally Arthur would visit his uncle, Henry Sidgwick, who had resigned his Trinity Fellowship when he lost his religious faith. As the son of a famous father – Arthur had been at Cambridge for less than two years before Edward ascended the Canterbury throne – he found that many people wanted to meet him, even such a notability as Matthew Arnold, but his fame did not go to his head. He joined the Pitt Club and Chit-Chat Club (both of which societies had another Benson member when Fred was at King's), though he failed to gain *entrée* into the exclusive circles of the Apostles; it was thought that the free-thinking and largely homosexual members might endanger Arthur's prospects if he ever decided to take orders.

When the brilliant but perverse J.K. Stephen went down in 1882, Arthur took over his rooms on the ground floor of Gibbs's Building. Added to his list of friends was Goldsworthy Lowes Dickinson, Harry Cust, Lionel Ford, a future colleague at Eton, and Walter Headlam, the eminent Greek scholar. For Arthur this was a period of intellectual vitality, companionship and the promise of a bright future. There was honest enquiry and social responsibility among the undergraduates, due to a great extent to the influence of Henry Sidgwick. In Arthur's last year at King's he became active in the internal politics of the college, adopting a conservative attitude to any change to the Eton exclusiveness. Not an atom of Socialist enthusiasm was present in his makeup; he had no interest in reforming relations between rich and poor, being too introspective to spare thought for the less fortunate.

In 1882, a month before Edward received his letter from Mr Gladstone, Arthur suffered from the first crippling depression of his life, thus following his father, and being later followed by other members of his family. This terrifying experience was caused by two things, a crisis of religion and a crisis of emotion. They were only hinted at in his diary in the most oblique of terms, but their influence was lifelong, and they seem to have been connected: one with a Revivalist meeting that he attended, principally to give rein to his love of the absurd, but at which the preacher's words became so compulsive that Arthur felt full of self-hatred; the other, which also helped to scar him for life, was the collapse of a romance with a younger man, 'passion at white heat without taint,' Arthur called it, 'above all other loves, noble, refining, true.' The name of the object of his passion was never revealed, though it is possible that it was Harry Cust, a 'bright Apollo', who, as he grew older, became a tipsy, obscene and useless rake. For more than two years Arthur was intensely unhappy, and the end of his Cambridge days in 1884, when he got a First in Classics, signalled the end of a university career that had started off so brightly. Idleness and moody religion followed his depression. He read enough theology almost to wreck his religion, and in January, 1886, at the age of 22, he returned to Eton, this time as Assistant Master.

When Edward accepted Canterbury Maggie was 18, and in October, 1883, she took Nellie's place at Lady Margaret Hall, Oxford, when Nellie was wanted at home to help her mother with the intricate life of Lambeth and of Addington. Maggie in those days was enthusiastic, happy in her family relationships – she and Fred were especially close – and full of plans for the future. In her letters she used words like 'awfully nice', 'frightfully forbearing' and 'scrumptious'. She described going to a phrenologist's lecture, in which, among others, a diagram of Edward's head was to be exhibited and lectured on. 'Won't it be a joke! I will tell you what qualities good and bad he has got!' When she took up residence at the Hall she was a tall, slim, somewhat angular girl, diffident and with solitary interests, but with a mobile mouth, blue-grey eyes and a fresh laugh. At Oxford her artistic powers, encouraged by John Ruskin, blossomed and she matured rapidly. She took up political economy and moral science and found their intricacies absurdly easy. She found she could hold her own in talk and discussion with ease, she developed powers of gentle irony and her happiness overflowed into all she said and wrote. She loved and was loved, was deeply emotional but not sentimental, and, without seeking popularity, found herself at the centre of the little society that grew up around her. An example of her analytical habit of mind was her probing into her own reasons for enjoying things. 'I always want to know why I enjoy.' She tended to live on her nerves; her intense friendships used up her strength so that Minnie became health-conscious and sent her letters of advice about sleep, food and tonics, which Maggie dutifully observed; but she was still apt to get over-tired.

Maggie came to some interesting conclusions in her carefully considered opinions about religion, and made statements with which, if he had heard them, Edward would certainly not have agreed. 'In a world of atheists social needs would produce a moral code' was certainly not the sort of remark that the daughter of an Archbishop should have uttered. It would perhaps have been acceptable at Cambridge, which was rampant with agnosticism, but not at a ladies' college at Oxford. She also argued that the conception of a personal God was not necessary to the primitive idea of sin, and on another occasion she said that she felt no interest whatever in theology, it was only where philosophy came in that she was at all interested; and she expressed great sympathy with a mind that could only approach religion through thought. That was how she won her faith, not by a flash of lightning, or the attraction of bells, robes and ritual, but by argument, reason and philosophy. A Tutor of Keble College who coached her for the Honour School of Philosophy was astonished at the extraordinary keenness of her intellect and her incisive and unerring power of analysis. She could balance the arguments for and against her position with what he called 'absolute remorselessness'.

But Maggie was not completely cerebral. She played hockey and lacrosse and learned to swim in order to qualify for rowing in the College boat. She wrestled in the College gymnasium and enjoyed 'Blind Man's Buff' like a child. Her letters home were crammed with gossip, humorous comments on her tutors and contemporaries, girlish extravagances and quirky asides. In 1886, at the age of 21, she got her First in Women's Honour School of Philosophy. 'If only it had been Greats,' her tutor wrote. 'No-one will realise how brilliantly she has done.' No-one could ever regard her from then on a just a wonderful child with a wonderful future. That future had already begun.

Nellie Benson, born in 1863, thus two years older than Maggie, was very different in temperament, though they were the closest of companions. She was quick, active, resourceful and adventurous, and inclined to take the lead in the activities in which she was engaged. Her impulsive nature often led her to rush in where fools feared to tread. After Martin's death, she seemed to step into his shoes, being relatively at ease with Edward. She had no awe of him and gave him the sort of outspoken and open affection he longed for, and failed to receive from Arthur and the others. She was a constant support to Maggie. Her gaiety and freedom from shyness were just what were needed to counterbalance her sister's introspection and over-dependence on a sense of duty. Where Maggie delved into character and could be judgmental, Nellie could enter into the lives of others by imagination, and could accept and sympathise.

Nellie resembled her mother both physically and in character, being short and plump, plainer than Maggie but with a merry face. Very occasionally she suffered from a bout of the family curse. Emotionally she resembled Maggie with her preference for her own sex in matters of the heart. She had experienced a number of sentimental relationships at Lady Margaret Hall, and wrote and received many schoolgirl love letters. But later her deepest feelings were reserved for Ethel Smyth, a woman of formidable passions, a committed fighter for women's rights, and a composer whose talent was not then, and indeed is not even now, fully recognised.

Ethel Smyth was introduced into the Benson family in the autumn of 1885 by Edith Davidson, wife of the Dean of Windsor (her younger brother had married Ethel's sister). Ethel was immediately smitten by Minnie and for some years considered that, in a time of mental anguish, it was Minnie's friendship that had 'kept her head above water' and enabled her to regain courage, hope and the power to compose. But, as time went on, it became clear that there were fundamental differences between their natures. She expressed the difference by comparing the both of them to two trees, whose upper branches occasionally mingling, gave the illusion of one tree, whereas their roots were far, far apart. But one of Minnie's missions in life was the healing and directing of sick souls, and she pursued the cure relentlessly; and Ethel began to suspect that for Minnie she was less a human being in need of affection than a patient visiting the doctor; and she grew to resent the relationship. Then, too, Ethel had a horror of Low Church views and ways, to which Minnie leaned, and when her faith returned there was less harmony than before. But the final breaking of the bond was because Minnie did not have a single drop of artistic blood in her veins and had no idea what went on in an artist's soul; so the relationship languished and Ethel felt 'a long cold night of the spirit falling upon her'.

The intimacy of the friendship between Minnie and Ethel had alarmed Edward; he thought there was something unhealthy about the fervour of it all, and he took a great dislike to Ethel. Maggie, too, had little time for her, and it was left to Nellie to become Ethel's particular friend – a friendship that sprang up on the cricket field. Ethel, her sister and Nellie were all members of the White Heather Club, the premier women's cricket club of the time. It was Nellie's first adult relationship and she brought to it an intensity that touched Ethel deeply. Her letters were full of humour, profundity and high spirits, and their twin tastes in humour brought them even closer together. Though the affair was of comparatively short duration both women enjoyed and were stimulated by it. When Nellie died in 1890 Ethel was heartbroken.

Edward had a peculiar and touching affection for Hugh, his youngest, who was 12 at the time of his accession, and hoped that he would prove to be the beloved companion that Martin had been and which evidently Arthur and Fred would never become. Hugh was at school at Clevedon in Somerset, presided over by a Mr Cornish, and his father wrote to him frequently, rather beautiful, but at the same time pathetic, letters over-full of advice, criticism, suggestions and enquiries about work and religion, none of them relaxed or leisurely. Edward lived a life of strain and tension, but Hugh was completely different. Though he could work with fierce concentration and energy when necessary he preferred to enjoy rambling and inconsequential discussions, letting ideas and arguments bubble up out of nothing purposeful, a quality that had no counterpart in Edward. One of the most remarkable things about him was his independence of character, even as a child, and he completely disregarded other people's opinions. What was important to him was what he liked and felt, and if he could get his own way he was happy, caring neither for approval nor disapproval. People were to him channels through which he could follow his own plans, or obstacles to the attainment of his wishes. Whereas his siblings had their sensitive or shrinking sides, Hugh was without that kind of sentiment. He was quiet enough, and not in the least interfering in the affairs of others, but if his rights were menaced his growl was threatening.

The school in Clevedon, called Walton House, was well managed, the teaching was good, and there was little or no bullying, but to a boy like Hugh it was unbearable to have to account for himself at all times and be subject to the natural savagery of his companions. He made some friends but never really enjoyed Walton House. He was small and plain, with a rather goat-like face, and was not good at games. Fortunately, in 1885 he won a scholarship to Eton, and in September of that year he joined Arthur there, his big brother as Master, to Edward's great delight – all his children now at public school or college, and all, he was convinced, were going to bring much honour to the name of Benson. But Arthur did not see much of his insignificant sibling, and deliberately did not seek to find out much about him. Several of Hugh's friends were his private pupils and if it had been supposed that Arthur questioned Hugh about them or that Hugh told him tales about them, both boy and Master would have been branded as sneaks and distrusted from then on. So when they met they talked about work and home but not about school and its personalities. The boys in Hugh's set were quite clever, but very quarrelsome and extremely critical; cliques were always forming, breaking up and re-forming, and Hugh's difficult character was not helped by the spite and mischief-making that went on around him.

Only once did Hugh nearly get into serious trouble. A small boy was bullied in a most disgraceful way by some of Hugh's friends, and he was supposed to have been involved, in spite of his protestations of innocence, and when the victim supported Hugh's claims he was cleared without stain. Hugh was at Addington before the truth came out, and Edward, both indignant and heart-broken at Hugh's supposed involvement, confronted the boy with white-faced anger, which so paralysed Hugh that he was incapable of defending himself. Afterwards Edward clasped the boy in his arms and tearfully apologised for doubting him. In spite of his faults Hugh hated cruelty above all things. 'The existence of it,' he wrote later, 'is the only thing which reconciles my conscience to the necessity of hell.'

Hugh stayed at Eton for less than four years. He did very little work there in spite of his intellectual powers, and it became a matter of surprise to his family that he had won a scholarship in the first place. His determination to go his own way meant that he never became a typical Etonian, courageous, honourable, courteous and dutiful – also arrogant and superior; undervaluing enthusiasm, ideas and rebellion, and over-valuing sports and games. Nor was he a typical Colleger, one of the 70 boys who get scholarships and are boarded in College, a school within a school. Collegers had a sense of their own absolute rightness which did not need to be endorsed by the world, but Hugh was not interested in turning out like 69 others, only on being himself. He decided that he wished to compete for the Indian Civil Service, but there were no facilities for this at Eton, and Edward reluctantly allowed him to leave. Eton was exchanged for a coaching establishment in London. On his last night at school Hugh confessed in a note that his feelings on leaving ranged from excitement, sorrow, pleasure, a feeling of importance, a longing for India and plain, straight-forward homesickness.

CHAPTER SIXTEEN

O N OCTOBER 20, 1885, Edward opened his primary Visitation at Canterbury. 'In willing and affectionate duty,' he said, 'I come to this ancient and magnificent centre and fountain-head of sacred institutes, not for this diocese only, but for all.' In the afternoon he unveiled the cenotaph which had been erected in the north-east transept of the Cathedral to commemorate his predecessor, and gave a short address, speaking very feelingly of the purity, beauty and peace of the Archbishop's domestic life. 'The late Archbishop had wonderful political wisdom which never seemed to be political, and the power of reading the thoughts and feelings and impressions of the nation as if they were the thoughts passing through the mind of one man. He had the power, not of opposing or attacking, but just of throwing in matter which many times changed the minds of those who heard him. The same great characteristic came out in his daily life. Friends would not forget the gentleness of his own warm friendship, while equally impressed on their minds would be the sagacity with which he met their daily common difficulties.'

Edward's primary Visitation was published later the same year, together with other addresses, under the title *The Seven Gifts*, a book of 255 pages. His second Visitation, in 1889, resulted in *Christ and His Times*; and his third Visitation in 1893 became *Fishers of Men*.

On December 30 Edward delivered an address on 'Municipalities' in his capacity as president, for that year, of the Birmingham and Midland Institute. That, too, was published as a pamphlet. The speech showed that if Edward could have devoted more time to the study of history he might readily have achieved fame as an historian as well as a theologian. He showed great historical imagination as well as knowledge about the origin of municipality. 'It was the fruit of experience gathered alike in ages the most stirring and the most tranquil. It was an accumulation of powers, accommodations and usages possibly unsuspected, and apparently a specific character of the one great family of races and nations of which we were a very small part. They were the outcome of the Peace of Constance which ratified the liberties which the emperors had endeavoured to wrest from the people and which they in the first and noblest struggle of modern Europe had maintained. They secured the right to do that which more or less they had been doing all along – to have their own fortifications and their own armies, to exercise their own civil and criminal jurisdiction, and, above all, to elect their own chief magistrates by the voice of the people, and to have their rank on a level with the imperial vicars.' He went on to give a detailed picture of citizens, families and individuals of the Italian cities during the 300 years he was reviewing, living their lives and performing their duties with great spirit, virtue and mutual loyalty. 'But there was no patriotism, there was only citizenship, and the cities passed away because they had known nothing greater than themselves. Milan was not all the world, not Florence, nor Venice, and each of them behaved as if it were, and so at last succeeded to a tyranny of its own.' Edward went on to compare the cities of Italy with the cities of England, the village communities of India and those of old Germany. It was a scholarly, historically accurate, discourse, and how Edward found the time to evoke so complicated an historical survey is difficult to comprehend.

Edward's Parliamentary activities really began during 1883, and he never ceased to press forward Bills for the reform of patronage and for the provision of means by which the Church might rid herself of minorites who brought her into disrepute. He was worried about Mr Gladstone's attitude to Disestablishment. Though the Prime Minister insisted that it was far off, the question not ripe, and that when people should come, if ever they did come, to think that Establishment should be ended it would have to be done. There were no expressions of reluctance, rather an implication that he would execute the will of the people if it should happen to come (which it would not) in his time. This caused the greatest surprise to Edward, who had revered Gladstone as a Churchman, but his worries were lessened when the adroit Prime Minister announced that he had been misunderstood about a thing so distant and visionary. Then Lord Salisbury pointed out that Gladstone had once described the Disestablishment of the Irish Church as 'in the dim and distant future' and within two-and-a-half years he had passed the measure for it. It would always be a stain on the Liberals that they proclaimed everywhere that it was the Tories who had got up the alarm about the Church in danger when really they had been responsible.

Edward did not find Parliamentary work congenial. He was not a good speaker in the House of Lords and he had none of the Macchiavellian qualities of the lobbyist. His historical sensitiveness, love of antiquity and traditions were not valued in the Lords. His spirits were weighed down by the Peers' genial consciousness of position, their amiable toleration of religion and their well-bred contempt for enthusiasm, and he seldom spoke there with any pleasure. To Bishop Westcott he once wrote: 'I had to speak in the House of Lords last night. It is really a terrible place for the unaccustomed. Frigid impatience, combined with a thorough conviction of the infallibility of laymen (if not too religious) on all sacred subjects, are the tone, morale and reason of the House as a living being. My whole self-possession departs, and ejection from the House seems the best thing which could happen to one.'

The first piece of Parliamentary drafting that he did was in connection with Ecclesiastical Courts. He was the Chairman of a Royal Commission to enquire into their consitution and working. The report was presented in August, 1883, and excited a great deal of comment and criticism. Edward was in thorough harmony with the historical views on which the report was founded, and in the winter of 1884–85 he prepared a Bill to give effect to some of the Commission's recommendations. The Bishops, however, were not unanimous on the subject and Edward, following his policy of keeping Churchmen together, would do nothing that would disunite them; so, while he deeply regretted that there would be no legislation after the long, patient and laborious preparation for it, gave up the idea of introducing his Bill into the House of Lords.

Another piece of Church defence which this time Edward carried through with success was his action with regard to the Local Government Bill, which passed through Parliament during the autumn session of 1883–84. The Bill dealt seriously with existing parochial institutions. Under it the Churchwardens and Vestry were to lose their civil status and no longer discharge their civil duties. The Incumbent was to be similarly deprived of his old power, and parochial charities were to be moved from ecclesiastical control. The Bill had two dangers. One was that the clergy, especially in rural parishes in which the Bill operated, would rush into an unwise opposition and put themselves at odds with their people in their endeavour to preserve a worn-out régime, and to prevent the natural development of local institutions. The other danger was the loss of parish rooms and similar institutions through ignorance of the Bill's effect and a desire to support what was supposed to be the cause of the people. Edward was not the man to confound the interests of the Church with the civil functions of vestries and churchwardens, and he warmly supported the creation of parish councils and the transfer to them of powers hitherto exercised by vestries. But he insisted that parish rooms should not be confiscated. The Conservative Party in Parliament fought the Bill on his lines and after a prolonged struggle and a threatened collision between the two Houses, the Bill was passed into law with most of the modifications that Edward had asked for. The radical press protested that the Bishops were driving the parish council to the public-house as the village schoolroom, which belonged to the Church, could not now be used by the parish council when it was wanted for any of its primary purposes; and a further twist to the protest was an allegation that the Bishops had actually voted to hold parish meetings in public-houses.

No Archbishop had up to then identified himself so markedly and so persistently with attempts to obtain ecclesiastical reforms through Parliamentary action as did Edward. He never ceased working on Church Bills and Church reforms, adopting a policy of laying Church needs before successive Governments and claiming legislative help, a policy that dated from the Dissolution in 1885, when Gladstone resigned and Lord Salisbury took office, though in a minority in the House of Commons, and soon went to the country. The prospects of the Conservative Party were not very bright at that time; on the other hand the Liberals were still united, and most Liberal candidates were more or less pledged to support Disestablishment; a fresh element that caused Churchmen to rise up from one end of the country to the other and argue agitatedly against Gladstone's private views on the subject. However, there was no great Liberal victory, for though Gladstone resumed office, he was dependent for a working majority on Parnell's support.

Church matters had acquired a greatly quickened interest in the country. Not only was Disestablishment hotly debated, the public was acutely interested in the internal reforms of the Church. In December, 1885, a document promoted by the Bishop of Durham, and signed by most of the leading resident members of the Senate of Cambridge University, was presented to the Archbishops and Bishops, expressing dismay that the Church of England had long suffered serious injury from the postponement of necessary reforms, and urging immediate action as to Patronage, Redistribution of Clerical Revenues and Clergy Discipline, but insisting that the most urgently needed reform was the admission of laymen of all classes who were *bona fide* Churchmen to a substantial share in the control of Church affairs. This was only one of many resolutions petitions, letters and speeches on the subject, and Edward was not one to ignore the challenge. In February, 1886, he formally opened the House of Laymen, to be elected and sit concurrently with the Convocation. 'Laymen,' Edward said in his opening address, 'bring to bear on many problems living, everyday experience, a quick perception of social change, a persuasion that spiritual work which claims to deal with the nature of man should take cognisance of all such change, and ignore no fact; they bring fertility of resources, and suggestiveness as to overcoming differences, or as to approaching them from new sides. Clergymen are by education and life observant of, and will assuredly maintain, that unbroken thread of faith and administration that comes to us from the Divine beginnings of our religion. Each therefore gives the other scope and strength, distinct theory and working ideas...' And he brought in his beloved St. Cyprian by saying that he had promised the faithful laity that he would do nothing without their assent. Edward was sorry that the House of Laymen turned out to be mainly Conservative, with but three Liberals to 11 Conservatives in it among the peers, and the 19 or 20 members in the House of Commons were also all Conservatives.

Also in 1886 Edward introduced the Archbishop's Patronage Bill, the intention of which was to abolish the traffic in Livings. Edward himself introduced it in the Lords, where it was well received, and it passed a Select Committee successfully, but was never considered in the Commons, owing to the Dissolution which followed Gladstone's defeat on the second reading of his First Home Rule Bill in June – and the end of his third premiership. In 1887, Edward introduced another Patronage Bill which differed materially from the first one, but this one fell to the ground between the Lords and Commons, and was not introduced again until 1893. Its place was taken by the Clergy Discipline Bill, to which Edward zealously applied himself, and which was rewarded with better success in 1891 and 1892. It was made a Government measure in the Commons, with Gladstone's powerful assistance.

Edward's satisfaction with the progress of Church reform was lessened by his irritation with the heads of the Conservative Party. At the beginning he was not familiar with Parliamentary methods and he underestimated the difficulties in getting his Bills on to the Statute Book. He did not realise that there were in the Cabinet, owing to a Unionist Coalition, a number of politicians who were indifferent to the Church and its reforms; indeed, some were even hostile. He himself had a cordial relationship with Gladstone and was always consulted on Church matters, such as the appointment of a Bishop. As a Conservative himself he was bitter when a Conservative Government failed to acknowledge his right to be informed and showed what seemed to be a deliberate want of consideration. Another factor in his dissatisfaction with politicians was the fact that he was no diplomat. As a ruler he could act tactfully when it suited him to do so, but when he was confronted by influential people on equal terms, especially those who were indifferent to the questions he felt so keenly about, he found it difficult to meet their lack of sympathy with equanimity. He was inclined to take their attitudes too personally, and he sulked. The Radicals chastised the Church with whips, he used to say, but the Conservatives used scorpions. The latter party was in danger of alienating the sympathy of a large and influential body of Churchmen, which would be disastrous to the best interests of religion. Churchmen were not dependents whose support of the Conservatives was certain. Radical politicians at least tried to give the Church its due and recognised Churchmen as worth conciliating. Edward thus regarded the two main parties with mixed feelings – his instincts were Conservative, but his sympathies often leftward and his regard for Gladstone was very high. Still, at the end of ten years of hard labour in Parliament, through many disappointments, he could look back and say, 'They have not been in vain.'

At the end of 1885 Edward was ill with a fever which laid him low for almost a fortnight, during which he suffered from what he called 'sick picturesque fancies'. All his rest was uneasy – faces and groups appeared and reappeared in his disordered mind and could not be recognised. But by January 9 he was able to drag himself out of bed into another room, and two days later was allowed to walk out for half an hour in the garden. Minnie was the perfect nurse and everybody said prayers for his quick recovery. He was able to open Convocation in St. Paul's, driving from Addington and back and taking everything very quietly. Halfway through January the intense sense of weakness he felt had begun to recede and he increased the length of his daily walks so that, with Minnie at his side, he could manage to keep going for an hour and a half. He was able to prepare for a 'Quiet Day' in the College Chapel at Winchester at which nearly 80 public school Heads and Assistant Masters, 18 of them from Eton, were expected to attend. Edward prepared six talks based on his old Keble addresses, which were later published under the title *Communing of a Day*. When he arrived at Winchester on January 18 he went straight to Martin's grave on which he laid a cross of white flowers. All was in beautiful order, and the porter told him he regularly cleaned and oiled Martin's plaque and how his wife had bought a Bible and written in it 'In Memory of Martin White Benson'. 'The sky was still bright blue,' Edward wrote in his diary, 'while the moon made everything brilliant. But the light is only on the surface...'

The gathering was a great success and it was decided to make it a biennial event. All were determined to deepen the school life of the Masters in the hope that it would have its own effect on the boys – not that they would be stricter or more exacting with them, but would be themselves greater Christian examples.

The Queen opened Parliament on January 21. She now wore only a diminutive model of a crown, and the crimson and ermine mantle, being too heavy for her to wear, was looped around the Throne so that she had merely to sit down. Her own dress had grown a monstrous black silk train many yards long. After so many tall men had trooped in her procession before her into the House, Edward was almost startled by the smallness of the figure which followed them, though there was no figure more impressive or stately in demeanour. Minnie and the girls had seats in the gallery – Maggie particularly had a great taste for pageantry.

On the following Sunday Edward remarked on the loveliest snow landscape he had ever seen. Snow had fallen for 24 hours in such minute flakes that every tiniest twig was dressed and scarcely a dark particle of branch or evergreen leaf was visible. When Church was over a soft south breath had turned all to dripping water. Then the weather became dreadful, with 'mist, cold, snow-slush, queazy earth'. But Edward was able to have his first ride of the year, with Nellie beside him, along roads full of slushy ice. They stayed out for two hours and Edward felt renewed. A few days later he took his last walk round Addington before returning to Lambeth. 'I never saw sky, earth and trees so wet, soaking, sodden and weeping, and occasional cold showers, as if the clouds ran over in sheer helplessness. The swans are very happy in this melting of the ice. Voraciously hungry, but Madame won't quite eat out of my hand, though now very near it. The old fellow pokes me if I don't attend to him fast enough ... now it's calm evening with bronzy cumuli, bronzy beech tops, the old yew black and stiff and the cedars all in motion.'

On Monday, February 8, Minnie returned home from a drive with Mrs Davidson with a sad tale to tell. Their carriage had been stopped near Hyde Park Corner by a line of stationary carriages, one of which had had its panels and the back smashed and its dishevelled coachman had lost his hat. They had to retire by Stamford Gate, learning afterwards that the incident had been caused by a gathering of the unemployed in Trafalgar Square; a mob had marched through Piccadilly, smashing windows and wrecking houses, but whether the mob was composed of genuine unemployed or of the riff-raff which surrounded them was at first not clear. The next day it was announced that the rioting had been partly the work of thieves, roughs and idlers who had attached themselves to the legal demonstrators, and partly of the 'Revolutionary Social Democrats'. Edward blamed the new Government for failing to give clear directions to the police. 'Thus it is,' he commented sourly, 'to depend on the suffrage of the lowest.'

One of Edward's dearest friends, Henry Bradshaw, Cambridge University Librarian, was found dead in his chair at King's, on February 11. They had known each other for 36 years, and Edward described him as the gentlest, most sympathetic and painstaking of friends and a great Christian power in King's – a layman devoted to the Faith, and deeply read in all modern literature as well as ancient. He was so perpetually acquiring scholarship and accurate knowledge that he scarcely ever brought himself to write it down. He was, in fact, a great loss to learning.

Henry Bradshaw's funeral was both touching and impressive. Generation after generation of graduates, and down to the youngest undergraduate, were there, as well as many of Edward's contemporaries.

The windows of the Chapel, of which Edward knew every pane and displaced fragment, never glowed so brightly as on that day, so that the roof was not gloomy but like the outside sky.

On February 10 the new House of Laymen, Edward's own creation, met for the first time, with 100 members elected by the Diocesan Conferences. It possessed neither legislative nor originative power; in fact, it was for counsel only. Lord Selborne was the first Chairman, and he, absurdly, was not allowed to speak or vote. The Laymen had determined to follow Rules of Parliament which, differing as they did from Convocation, would be inconvenient, and Edward wondered whether they had unwittingly 'raised a Frankenstein'. But it would all come right, he decided, if the House learned a little modesty.

There is a mysterious passage in Edward's diary of March 11. 'All day have been in a cloud and out of heart because I thought quite early in the day that a mean slight was put on me by someone. If it is physical, it is very unpleasant and very closely tied up to the moral. If it is moral it undoubtedly has a physical effect. My mere thoughts derange several organs at least slightly. My feeling moves particles of matter rapidly and not through any secondary exertion of muscle...'

In May Edward introduced the Church Patronage Bill in the House of Lords in a speech that received compliments from both Lord Selborne and Lord Salisbury. The Bill was read a second time and referred to a Select Committee. On May 24 the Deceased Wife's Sister Bill was brought before the House by the Duke of Argyll. Edward spoke against it, on social rather than on scriptural grounds, and the Bill was thrown out by a majority of 22.

Another death of someone close to him occurred in July. This was Robert Hodgson Sidgwick, his father's first cousin and Minnie's uncle. Edward had got to know him when, aged 15, he had stayed at Skipton Castle. During walks and talks and the reciting of poems, Edward soon regarded him as both father and big brother. Robert Sidgwick was a devout Churchman to whom daily prayers and the weekly early Communion were necessary parts of life. As an example to his poorer neighbours to give up ostentatious and expensive funerals he directed that when he died he should be buried in a simple white deal coffin and drawn in the parish hearse, and he further ordered that only his children should attend the funeral; and that the difference between the cost of this simple service and the usual elaborate ceremony should be given to the poor; but when his own funeral was held he could do nothing to prevent the procession of people on foot and in carriages, the like of which had never been known in Skipton before.

During July Edward retired to Addington, feeling tired and dispirited, but a visit to Bamborough Castle in Northumberland soon put him to rights. He took the Castle, which was let during the summer, for two months, and installed the entire family there. The pleasure of the visit was enhanced when Maggie got her First Class in Philosophical Schools. He told her how he wished that Nellie could have had the chance of such an honour, but she said that no-one at Oxford had done so well as Nellie in so short a time. Edward was very impressed by the Castle, its stately aspect, the colour of the granite, the tapestries, pictures, library, armoury. 'We sit in the felt presence of past people.' Fred's comment was rather different. 'Marvellous place – ghastly chambers.'

Alnwick Castle, where they went for lunch, was less imposing than Edward had anticipated. He was startled to step through the low Gothic door, turn upstairs and find himself in an Italian lobby, with Justice and Minerva in colossal marble. The intricately worked ceilings were magnificent, executed by a young Alnwick man, trained by an Italian brought over to found a school of woodcarvers. The gem of the gallery was Bellini's picture of gods and goddesses 'eating and sleeping vulgarly'. Fred was impressed by the same picture, though he attributed it to Titian who, he knew, had altered it after Bellini's death. Fred also spent a lot of time before Poussin's *Ariadne*.

On September 16 Edward and Minnie paid a visit to the Farne Islands, on the only day out of ten which the sea permitted the trip. Edward decided oddly that its sanctity was unspoiled either by 'profanity or devoteeism', and tried to discover the remains of St. Cuthbert's Cell and Wall, doing a kind of personal archaeological 'dig' by observation, taking into account local legends and what Mr Cutting, who was in command of lighthouses and coastguards, told him. He preached to a few people in the Chapel, which was fitted up with the spoils of Durham. The only woman on the islands complained that it was very monotonous and Satan gave her a hard time by making her discontented. Edward told her that St. Cuthbert must have felt the same and that Satan often threw stones at him, an Archbishop. At that the woman felt better. If Satan treated God's servants like that, who was she to complain?

Another old friend died early in October. This was Dr. W.H. Thompson, master of Trinity College, Cambridge, the ideal of a don and scholar; at 76 'the last of the heroes'. His caustic remarks were balanced by his kindness. He had a large tranquil eye, a handsome olive face, thick eyebrows and curling lips. He wore a black velvet double-breasted waistcoat and a stock without a collar. 'I sate at Chapel,' Edward wrote, 'at the funeral in the place where dearest old Francis Martin sate when first I knew him. What noble heads then rose above the front of the Stalls as we gazed on them, knowing that there was intellectual greatness living over and with us – all gone. Westcott was just a Bachelor then, Lightfoot the year above me.'

Edward had a memorable day on October 3, though he did not say where he had experienced it. 'In the morning Mr H. preached the worst and worst expressed sermon I ever heard. In the afternoon he outdid even his morning self.'

He was still tired and overworked so in the same month he took Nellie for a short tour of Holland and Belgium, making extensive notes of every church and cathedral they visited, and his comments on the services they attended were both sorrowful and scathing. 'So strange that Devotion shall have again parted company with Edification, just as St. Paul reproved it for doing, and how strange that these glorious structures should be venerated still by the people who have robbed them of the greatest reverence by which alone could their work be carried on' – all that because Vespers had been replaced by the Rosary and Benediction. At the end of a heavy day doing the sights of Ghent he wrote, 'And now midnight. Goodnight to all the world. The Great Bear hangs in deep blue between the Beffoi and the Tower of St. Bavon, and the carillons chime sweet farewell to the day. Goodnight to all but God.'

Nellie spent her 23rd birthday in Bruges on October 10, but Edward forgot to mention it in his diary. 'There were crowds at Mass, Rosary, and Salut, of course,' he wrote, 'but Vespers were going on in truly majestic form in the Cathedral, the Bishop on his throne, many canons, vicars and scarlet little boys, copes, incense, and the most clear and pious singing with certainly not a dozen people. So now the really edifying worship of God is being left to the clergy. The Methodism of Romanism is as strong as our Methodism – plain, almost vulgar, with incessant repetition. It is driving out the inhabitants of the Church.'

After visits to Antwerp and Malines they went to Waterloo. They had studied the Battle well and walked to every point of both English and French lines and relived every moment of the conflict. The vividness of the whole was almost painful as the hours went by, and Edward's veneration for the genius and self-control of the Duke rose, as he said, to boiling point. 'The devotion of Christians to their religion has scarcely equalled the devotion of those soldiers in the battle,' he sadly reflected, 'death and suffering embraced with ardour for the cause, and that by the lowest of the people as well as by the heroes.'

Edward and Nellie returned home on October 16. '*Domum, domum, Deo Gracias.*' Then came a five-day driving tour in Kent, visiting 30 churches, finding only one church and its clergyman unsatisfactory. He received a warm welcome everywhere he went from church people who were proud of the church and content with their priest, and found the mass of the clergy certainly worthy of their place.

The rest of the year was spent quietly at Addington, entertaining visitors and coping with the rain and with the various little clouds which hung over his horizon. They included the presentment of the Canons of Lincoln Cathedral for using the Eastward position (this was to become a *cause célèbre* in later years); the menace of the Russian Government against the Assyrian Mission; a spreading agitation against the payment of Tithes; the proposal of the Bishop of Gloucester and Bristol to confiscate episcopal revenues and sell episcopal houses; and the vigorous and spiteful attack on the building of Church House from most of the national newspapers; and the wish of the Bishop of Sydney to be designated Archbishop.

He received a letter written by Lord Salisbury on behalf of the Queen to say that she wished a Jubilee Service in Westminster Abbey, at an altar on the spot where she had been crowned – 'but a very short service and without any sermon because the weather is likely to be hot and in hot weather she has a tendency to feel faint.' 'As if everyone did not know that she dislikes a sermon for its own sake,' Edward tartly remarked.

Just before Christmas he went with Nellie to see the four oldest women of the village. They were all so nice, affectionate and soft-mannered. Assured homes, pensions and kindness through generations had had a fine gentle effect. Some of them had lived in the village for 40 years and remembered four Archbishops.

On Christmas Day there was skating on the lake and work on the *Saturday Magazine* in the evening. But the thought of Sunday, the following day, was oppressive to all but Edward.

After Christmas there was a most cruel snowstorm – 14 inches of snow fell in six hours, preceded by two inches of rain and snow together. The sky was gloomy, and there had been a biting wind and choking fog by turns. The snow adhered to the branches and leaves of the trees, building up high on even the smallest twigs. Then it froze and every tip sparkled with an icicle. The grand ilex split into three, branches and trees in all directions were borne down by the weight, and the snow everywhere beneath the trees was positively strewn with small twigs as if there had been a rush-bearing with tree shoots. During the night there was a thaw and in the morning every tree was battered but clear of snow. 'In its effect,' Edward wrote, 'it is rather like my work (which goes on, however, without stint), nipping off with its big pincers so many amenities and edifications. I struggle on a little with Cyprian, however, and it keeps things fresh to some extent.'

CHAPTER SEVENTEEN

1887 DID not start well for Edward – 'a drear beginning,' he called it, and his depression meant that he was late in writing his diary. One of the Bensons' favourite maids, a quiet, religious girl, had been lying between life and death for almost three months, and they were all puzzled that she was still alive but was not improving. Then Nellie had been ill for five weeks, listless and with no appetite, and she too was not getting better. The weather was foul with constant rain and snow; no-one remembered such desolation. Bishops were opposing Edward's measures for reducing the Church's problems, and foreign Bishoprics were under attack from various sources; and Lord Iddesley, who had been a solid supporter of Edward's plans for foreign missions, died suddenly. The Tithe war raged in Wales, and a Canon Liddon had set himself up in opposition to Edward over the appointment of a new Bishop in Jerusalem to assist the Greek Bishop there, and was writing savage letters and anonymous articles (one of them called 'The Dead See') in the *Guardian*. But eventually things were calmed down by the appointment to Jerusalem of the Archdeacon Blyth of Rangoon, a sweet and saintly man about whom nobody could say anything but good.

It was a relief for Edward to attend the re-opening of the splendid Southwell Minster in Nottinghamshire on February 2. It had been five-and-a-half centuries since an Archbishop of Canterbury had officially visited those parts and Edward, rejoicing in the picturesque side of his high office, wore his scarlet Convocation robes. He was preceded by the verger of the Cathedral with silver mace, and the Rev. M. Fowler, Edward's Chaplain, carried the gold processional cross. Edward was delighted to be amongst ancient and noble buildings again and he studied its Norman features with an architect's eye.

Edward was much concerned with the great temperance movement that was a part of the social and moral climate of the time, but his interest went further afield than his own country. Early in 1887 he took the bold step of addressing Jonnikos, Metropolitan of Moscow, on the subject. 'We should rejoice to know,' he wrote, 'that there was a prospect of an early and common uprising both of the Russian and all other Churches of Christendom against the fatal increase of spirit-drinking which is causing much sin and ruin, both of soul and body, not only to the inhabitants of the several countries, but also to the native heathen races with whom for commercial relations they are brought into contact.' A year later he sent a friendly letter to the Metropolitan of Kief and through him to the clergy and laity of the Church of Russia on the occasion of the celebration of the 900th anniversary of the baptism of St. Vladimir, an event of the same importance as the baptism of Ethelbert by St. Augustine. The letter contained the remarkably vehement sentence: 'The Russian and Anglican Church have common foes. Alike we have to guard our independence against the Papal aggressiveness which claims to subordinate all the Churches of Christ to the See of Rome.' He received sympathetic answers to both his letters.

Queen Victoria opened the new People's Palace in May. 'We drove to Shaftesbury Avenue into the route, and back through Hyde Park. The whole way for so many miles was lined with tens of thousands of people, delighted, cheering, well-behaved. The warmth and loyalty grew more and more conspicuous as we drove eastward along the Mile End Road. The Queen's voice in the Hall was as clear and bright as ever, as she begins now, with lower lip a little protruding and the flesh round the eye falling, to look quite the old lady, and she was visibly more tremulous in both sinking and rising in her old stately curtsey.

'The sight of those mighty ribbons of human faces and forms haunts the eye still, and I shall never forget it. It gave one the strangest thoughts about cities, and races, and the numberlessness of man and the riddle of his future. It grew oppressive to have humanity so crushing into one's eyeballs. But the thought of communism, or socialism or unbelieving having hold on these people seems ridiculous in sight of this enthusiasm. It makes one shudder at the thought of what would be, if ever those were against us. That the Church, too, was not valued and even loved could never have entered the mind. The contrary was apparent. But the responsibility for these masses, where does it rest? They are not a church-going race – but less a chapel-going one. But there is a solemn, quiet sense of religion for all that in their sayings and doings.'

The Jubilee Service on the completion of the 50th year of the Queen's reign took place on June 21, and was a very different but no less remarkable function from the one at the People's Palace. A special police pass had been issued to Edward to allow his carriage to pass through the streets when all other traffic was stopped. He left Lambeth about an hour before the service in Westminster Abbey was due to start, but at the south end of Westminster Bridge a police inspector stopped the carriage and not even when Edward produced his pass was the man convinced that the Archbishop of Canterbury had the right to proceed. Edward's anger, not slow to rise, reddened his face as he boomed, 'Well, all I can say is, that unless you allow me to proceed, there will be no service today!' The inspector took the point and hurried off to make enquiries of a superior officer. He returned with profound apologies and waved the carriage on. So dignity was restored to the procession and the service started on time.

The ecclesiastical part of the celebration was regarded by all as deeply and convincingly devout. The Queen's manner was most reverent, though she looked anxious and her movements were stiff. Edward and the Archbishop of York wore purple Coronation copes embroidered in gold and silver with pomegranates, and the Bishop of London was in scarlet cope and ermine cape; Canons wore gold or crimson, chairs and stools were covered in velvet or white cambric. The Dean of Westminster read the Lesson and Edward read the first three prayers, later the second three. Kings and Princes sat on velvet settees, among them the Queen of Hawaii who was slightly ill-at-ease because she spoke no English. Arthur was Edward's usher, properly dressed in gown and gold buckles, walking with the mace through the glass door in the screen and so having a perfect view of everything that happened.

There was a congregation of 9,000 in the Abbey and all were well-behaved, Edward noted. So were the crowds outside. The numbers of little children and babies in their mothers' arms greatly impressed the Bishop of Iowa and the Americans in general. The public-houses were open until two o'clock in the morning, but the cases of disorder before the magistrates next day were fewer than usual.

Another memorable sight was the Riding of the Princes before the Queen's carriage as she drove to the Abbey – 32 of them, sons, sons-in-law, grandsons and great-grandson. After that came the Salutation, when first of all the Princes kissed the Queen's hand, then the Princesses; she stooping a little to kiss them on the cheek or forehead. Edward noticed the reverence with which the Crown Prince of Germany kissed her.

'Everybody feels that the socialist movement has had a check,' Edward wrote after the service. 'It is impossible they can persuade themselves that the multitudes are on their side. The quiet respectful attitude of the people, and their enthusiasm whenever the Queen appeared, are absolutely universal, and not a dog has moved its tongue.'

The following day Edward, Minnie and Nellie attended a great reception at the Foreign Office. The Papal Envoy was there and a large number of people who were presented to him, though not Roman Catholic, curtseyed as to a royal personage. 'At the last reception Buffalo Bill was the lion,' was Edward's sarcastic comment.

His birthday, on July 14, was the occasion for a mournful contemplation of his faults and inadequacies. 'I think the thing I marvel at first is the thinness of the partition by which He and He only keeps me from falling under so many ghastly temptations and propensities so terrible. The falls are sad enough and bad enough, and the character they reveal to me painful indeed. But the grace which keeps me one inch farther is simply more visibly alive and active in my most certain experiences, more prompt, more steady than I have any experience of among material things. Everything material is simply feeble; and everything personal is shadowy as compared with this personality under whose shadow I am allowed to dwell.

'And all this is the more extraordinary because of the hurry, hotness, aridity of the life I am obliged to live in London. The want of time to read and think, the shortness and distractions of prayer, seem to threaten one's very existence as a conscious child of a living God. And yet He is on my right hand and I know it.'

During July he went with Minnie and Maggie to Marlborough, where Fred was still at school, and preached in the Chapel, and was most impressed with the behaviour of the boys and the religious atmosphere in the Chapel. In the afternoon they walked in Savernake Forest and Fred read some George Herbert poems aloud in a most feeling way. Edward decided that Fred was a very manly and sweet boy. He was head of all athletics and had just received the English Poem Prize. His Masters considered that he should take a First at Cambridge.

In August Edward and Minnie took Easedale House above Grasmere in the Lake District for a family holiday. He remembered the time they spent there with great affection. There had been so many activities; walking, riding, climbing, endless discussions and some work done on Cyprian. Mr Little, Hugh's Tutor, was with them, and Arthur Mason appeared for a time, and they all read *The Merchant of Venice*. Unfortunately they had only been there a few days when Nellie developed pleurisy – a fact barely acknowledged in Edward's diary – and he was scarcely more interested when Fred became ill with jaundice after a strenuous climb with Beasley, his Marlborough Master and friend. Minnie had to be nurse while Edward entertained a succession of visitors. The Master of Trinity was one of them. His daughter had just died and the career of his brilliant son had been cut short by hysteria. Other visitors included Bishop and Mrs Temple, Henry Sidgwick and his wife Nora, and Lucy Tait.

Nellie recovered and was able to go for a drive. Then there was a long period of rain. Edward read the newspapers and found them very dispiriting. The Tithe Bill had been dropped; the Welsh Dissenters were growing more truculent; the Welsh clergy more necessitous, and the

Government more unsafe; and the feeling for Home Rule for Ireland showed, to Edward, an unexplained advance. The outdoor activities planned for the last part of the holiday were curtailed by more furious rain, so a new *Saturday Magazine* was hastily written. Fred was still poorly, Edward was not feeling at his best, and Hugh was not doing very well with his tutor. Edward insisted on braving the elements and went out in a hurricane which thundered and boomed along the slopes, the raindrops being as sharp as gravel. There were vast masses of inky cloud with savagely torn edges coming from the north-west, out of which poured lashings of rain. All the becks had risen and were foaming white. He descended by the black and rippled Tarn, though shielded from the worst of the elements by Sergeant Man and Tarn Crag.

On September 19 it was time to return to Addington, and the holiday ended with a great deal of quiet relief from everybody except Edward, who would have still been striding vigorously up hill and down dale, in spite of the rain, if he had had his way.

Edward went to stay with friends in Essex – the first time he had set foot in the county despite its proximity to London. 'Essex has at least the merit of not being coveted by Cockneys,' he wrote. 'When they have made Surrey a populous desert, they may take to Essex…'

After a most successful Church Congress at Wolverhampton on October 3 he went to Cambridge to meet Fred and see a second son into his rooms and his college – 39 years as near as possible to the day since he himself had arrived in such awe and doubt to begin a new life. But he found the secularised Colleges were not the same 'sacred homes' that they once were. Their increased showiness seemed to remove some of their claim to veneration. He disapproved of the shortening of gowns into jackets, and thought that the undergraduates he saw in the street had an almost comic look about them and were emblems of the lack of dignity and self-respect which Church homes lost when they became steps in worldly life. Fred murmured agreement, yawning inwardly at his father's pompous declaration. He was impatiently looking forward to the arrival of Eustace Miles, due to appear in four days' time, and to the fascinating opportunities that were to take up his energies and emotions for the next few years.

Socialism was still a menace and was beginning to scare people. Edward had been reading H.H. Champion on the subject. 'He contrasts the Lord's "Come unto Me all ye that travail and are heavy laden, and I will give you rest" with "the primate's £15,000 a year and two palaces", and my recommending to the East End poor "the alleviation of spiritual consolation". Of course I never did it in that bald sort of way, but if I had – are not the words a poor paraphrase simply of Christ's saying? And if they only knew what a small fraction of either money or space for anything except to work and the possibilities of work.' But it was all very well scoffing at the written word of fanatics – it was more serious when he learned of the mobs that were threatening London. Canon Rowley had told him how he had been walking about with the police in plain clothes and had been in the thick of disturbances. 'The police say they are not all the unemployed, but are made up of well-known thieves and villains. Nevertheless, many workmen who are in employ gave up their dinner hour to swell their numbers. It is all formidable, though the police take it lightly. But few consider where all this will grow.' Edward's not-well-thought-out remark, uttered years before, that London distress could be met by 'spiritual consolation' was being bandied about by agitators in their speeches to the mobs and had angered them so much that there were rumours of a 'visit' to Lambeth. There had been a perceptible change in the attitude to care of the poor around London. In previous years they had begged, but in a respectful way, and vicars in rich parishes had been able to relieve their distress. But then they began to demand and refuse to leave the doorstep until threatened with the police. Edward came to the conclusion that things would really go amiss until the genuine working-man chose to take matters in his own hand and put an end to the tactics of the agitators. He expressed no opinions about providing the unemployed with work, increasing low wages, fighting lack of incentive, and improving facilities and services for the out of work. He made no criticism of greedy landlords and rapacious employers. Nor did he comment on governmental lack of concern. He loved the working man when the working man loved him, and was devout; but he was scared of excess and things out of control. Not even prayer, it seemed, could do much to restore the old traditions of respect, and belief in the Divine way of ordering life.

On November 3 Edward had the immense gratification of being present and preaching the sermon at the consecration of Truro Cathedral, the building of which he had lovingly watched after he had left Cornwall. The building was finer than he had ever dared to hope. 'It has sprung to its perfect power and beauty,' he wrote, 'its magnificence of fittings and splendour of vessels out of a soil dry, cold and unwilling to bear it.' Truro was beflagged and festooned for the occasion. Cornwall's Royal Duke was again present, and in addition to the Archbishop, 20 other Bishops took part in the proceedings. Edward's gold crozier was borne before him by his Chaplain, and two scarlet-cassocked acolytes held up his train. Lord Mount-Edgcumbe, the Chairman of the Building Committee, presented the formal petition for the consecration. The text for Edward's sermon was: 'In due season we shall reap if we faint not,' and he could not resist a reference to St. Cyprian – *"Respondete Natalibus"* – "Rise to your birthrights!" Would he not say, rejoicing that the Church in Cornwall is her own again: Rise to your birthright, your English, Catholic, Apostolic, Christ-given birthright. Help, comfort, strengthen, revive, found...'

The Southern Rose, provided by Wellington boys, gave Edward great pleasure. The window, a replica of the rose window in Wellington College Chapel, was placed in the transept of the new Cathedral and, writing later to his 'dear Wellingtonians', he said that it was a joy which came to him very often to hear of the high tone, character and reputation of old Wellingtonians from all over the world.

Every day of that week the Cathedral was crammed with parishioners of every Deanery; labourers, fishermen and their wives, farmers – many of them Dissenters – all talked of their Cathedral, and were proud to give to it. Edward thought that the appearance of Bishop Wilkinson of Truro was perfect for the occasion. 'His very spare frame and face, his deep olive complexion and tight drawn skin, close to jet black hair, compressed lips, and deep, restrained, tender, devout eyes, are a very portrait of a believer and a Bishop.'

Fred's account of his visit to Truro was more laconic. On November 3 he wrote, 'Opening of Cathedral. Luncheon. Leave by 6 train. Arrive at Swindon 3 a.m.' Swindon at that hour of the morning probably lasted longer in his memory than the pomp and pageantry of the morning service.

It was only rarely that Edward attended the theatre, but on November 26 he went to Cambridge to see a University performance of *Oedipus Rex*, only because it was written by Sophocles, for whom he had great admiration. His views afterwards were apt and penetrating. 'The representation was beautiful and accurate. The music expressive, but too loud. There should be but two or three thin instruments. The words of the chorus were drowned deep. Iocasta was finely acted throughout. Oedipus swift and noisy till the last scene, in which his awful appearance actually seemed to impress himself and he rose immensely. It was with a real thrill, not soon recovered from, that I saw and heard him. The Greek Play always was to me the finest form of human composition – and it has gained by this sight of it.'

The winter of 1887 was spent at Addington and he was able to do a great deal of riding as the weather and soil were exactly to the hooves' tastes, and the stubble fields were all open. 'If it were not for this free riding in this perfectly restful country, away from all villas and roads, I do not believe I could healthily carry on this work, which lasts from 7 a.m. to 12.30 every night. I can never be possibly grateful enough for this quiet country home. No railway station, no villas, no-one to meet or see but the simplest people at the most rustic tasks. The conformation of ground which keeps the

London smoke clean away is a marvellous gift from God, and work early or late does not seem to hurt one at all as long as one has such air, such exercise, such sights.' But on Christmas Day he was depressed, thinking that his fretting, chafing and murmuring was the real reason why Hugh shrank from work and seemed set on life yielding him as much innocent fun as could be extracted from its hours. 'Church, church and walk with Arthur,' wrote Fred on Christmas Day and escaped into the writing of his story *Sketches from Marlborough*, on which he had been engaged on and off for some time. Soon after Christmas he heard that Perkins, a printer in Marlborough, had agreed to print it for him at his own expense. He finished the book the following April and it was published soon afterwards. In June he was despondent – only 101 copies had been sold. But that slight disappointment (the book, in fact, went into a reprint) did not put him off from deciding, once and for all, that his future was to be involved with writing. The bug had invaded his sytem and took relentless and permanent hold.

The year 1888 was full of interests and anxieties. The difficulties of the Jerusalem Bishopric were still not completely resolved. The prosecution of the Bishop of Lincoln for Romish practices was beginning to move. The Lambeth Conference – the gatherings of Bishops of the English, American and Colonial Churches – was to take place in the summer. And Edward's mind was continually occupied by questions which were arising with regard to the relation of the English Church to the Old Catholic movement, the position of which seemed to be half Roman and half Protestant. He was full of sympathy for those who had rejected Roman supremacy, but he could not give his unqualified protection without the pledges of recognition from the whole body of Bishops – which had not been forthcoming. So dignity and caution had to be his watchwords.

Edward and Minnie visited Winchester again in February and went over all the spots that were dear to them. They found that in a corner of the dormitory in which Martin had slept a little marble slab with his name on it had been put up by the boys and a new window had been opened into the court. A few days later he opened a Workmen's Club at the Oxford House in Bethnal Green, where the two woes, Edward said, were drink and early marriage. 'Self-restraint is a law which their betters have come to, and so surely can they. Their temptations are not really greater to any vast extent. They listened very patiently to this doctrine, and applauded it...' A month later he opened the Wellington College Mission in East Street, Walworth. He mingled with a crush of very poor people, so poor that many of the women's neat dresses had been hired for the afternoon. His concern for the poor and needy, confused as it was, was heightened when he learned of the conditions under which the foreign Jews who had fled to

England from oppression in Russia, Hungary and Poland worked. They worked from five or six in the morning until midnight, making worthless boots in sweatshops for about 15 shillings a week, eating stale bread for their dinner, and that they had to buy from their employers. 'Anything more sad, more abject, more dirty, more gentle in manners and more hopeless in tone, I have never seen. We hear today that 45,000 Jews are ordered out of Odessa. Where are they to descend? But to close ports against misery is what England is not capable of... This is a seething abyss of human wretchedness. It makes one more amazed than ever at the world's very existence...' Yet the members of the Sweating Committee in the House of Lords seemed to him half aghast at the very thought of finding a remedy. Apply factory acts to adult males? But that would affect Lancashire adversely. Higher wages and less work would mean trade would be driven from England and the Jews already in the country would then be unemployed; all very distracting considerations, Edward thought, before regretfully giving up the problem as insoluble. All he could do was to give the hungry and wretched the promise of eternal hope.

The Third Lambeth Conference, attended by 145 Bishops, was opened at Canterbury on Saturday, June 30, with magnificent pageantry arranged as meticulously as a stage spectacle after weeks of rehearsal. Then in Westminster Abbey there was an even more impressive ceremony and Edward preached for 45 minutes on the life and onward movement of Christianity. He was gratified that nobody fell asleep. Before the Conference actually opened for business on July 3, there was Communion in Lambeth Chapel with Edward as celebrant and the preacher was the Bishop of Minnesota. Lunch at the Palace, then the Conference began in the Library, behind closed doors. It had been made clear at the outset that the Conference was in no sense a Synod and was not competent to make binding decisions on doctrines or discipline. The deliberations came to an end on July 27, and a Farewell service was held in St. Paul's Cathedral before the Bishops dispersed to all parts of the world.

On August 21 he was returning with Nellie from the workhouse at Croydon down a rough lane when Nellie's horse stumbled and fell to her knees on the sharp loose stones. She plunged forward twice in attempting to rise, and then stood, trembling, obviously injured. She saved Nellie from being hurt, even killed, by lifting herself up although, in great pain, following her instinct rather than taking the easier course of just rolling over. They got the animal to a nearby stable and a veterinary surgeon suggested that the mare would have to be destroyed, which she was, after three months of unsuccessful treatment. 'Surely brutes must find something in the grave – some reward,' was Edward's heretical opinion.

The next Benson holiday was to Scotland. Edward and Minnie and

Arthur were only 'moderately comfortable' on the journey to Oban via
Stirling even though they had a bedroom, sitting-room and dressing-room
on the train, together with servants and luggage. They took a house at
Braemar, where Bishop Lightfoot of Durham and Professor Westcott (with
his four sons) were staying. Lightfoot's heart condition was giving concern
to his friends and his doctors considered that if he wished to live
comfortably for a few more years he would have to give up mental labour,
bodily exertion, stress and anxiety – most galling conditions to one who
had been so active intellectually, spiritually and physically. The rest of the
Benson family joined them at Braemar. Edward, Minnie and Nellie had
lunch with the Queen at Balmoral. She was very gracious, and agreed with
Edward that it was a shame that the Highlands were more thinly inhabited
than they used to be, and that the crofters were very poor and untidy. She
also spoke of the Bishop of Durham. 'I have known him so many years and
he is very clever indeed and very ugly...'

Fred developed a painful boil on his hand and had to have it lanced.
'Oh!!!' he wrote in his diary. The boys stalked deer, but without success.
Edward pondered on the strange fact that they should have taken to
shooting so strongly when he and both his parents had been like Buddhists
in their aversion to taking life, and held that it could not be reconciled with
'sport'. But there was a class in society who seemed to be kept strong and
pure through shooting, which preserved them from gambling and from
worse, from petty intriguing and from 'foppery' – so perhaps killing for
sport was acceptable after all; though the gamblers and fops who were also
good with guns rather spoilt his theory.

The family returned to Addington at the end of September. Edward was
in much better health, stimulated by the lengthy talks he had enjoyed with
his friends, though he was still very anxious about Lightfoot's health. At
the end of October he went to Bournemouth to see the Bishop who was
staying in a pleasant and comfortable house, with two chaplains, two
nurses and a doctor looking after him. He had undergone an operation at
exactly the right moment, though it would be months before the doctors
could declare if it had been fully sucessful. He was very weak and able to
work on literary projects for less than an hour per day, but existed
otherwise on readings, prayers and hymns said and sung on his behalf.
The impish side of his nature had not changed. 'He does not see how he
can at present attempt to convert Pope Leo XIII,' his Chaplain wrote to
Edward soon after his visit, 'but he will be glad to do anything which your
friends can suggest in this direction.'

But Lightfoot lingered on until December 21, 1889 – a telegram from
Bournemouth gave Edward the news of his death. In his diary he wrote, for
once simply and sincerely, '47 years of a friendship which never had one

hour's interruption, and of which every hour was uplifting. There never was a life taken before the Throne more charged with perfect service – as unselfish as it was solid. And he laid it daily and hourly before God. To think that I have been allowed to have this man as my bosom friend since I was 14 – I have had the thought of him always as part of myself in whatever I thought and whatever I had to do – even when there was no talking or writing about it. I think the thing which I care for almost most in life as a token of blessing is that he told the men at the great King Edward School dinner that I was "*praecordialissimus*" to himself always. All the people keep writing to me to tell me that he is a loss to Christendom, to the Church, to the world, and so he is, but I cannot rise to be sorry for *them*. "What am I to do, what can become of me?"' he finished, freely translating from Aeschylus. 'I feel frozen...'

At the funeral at Durham and Auckland, Westcott, the other member of the trio of schoolboys who had planned to revitalise the Church, threw the earth upon the coffin. Two days afterwards Westcott preached 'the most perfect sermon' at Westminster upon Lightfoot.

Edward received a copy of the new Wellington College Hymn Book in October, 1888, the original of which he had compiled during his Wellington days. His idea then was to include only hymns that were poetical in themselves or else the best renderings he could get of very famous hymns or those marked with great associations. Next he wished to assign hymns to days and hours so that special associations should, on the recurrence of days and times, return to the boys involuntarily and awaken thoughts, memories and ideas which would strengthen, perhaps reclaim.

'I have heard that it succeeded,' Edward wrote. 'Young officers leaning against bulwarks humming and whistling tunes have recognised each other as old Wellingtonians – in the Himalays it has been so. And in the bush S. spent his 21st birthday going through all his old favourites. "Why, that is the Tuesday morning hymn," said a young soldier. "You are an O.W.!" These things I thought useful and timely.' The new version of the hymn book was three times as long as the first, more a repertory than a brevarium, but Edward hoped it would still act as an introduction to young soldiers who spent their spare time whistling in the bush.

Archbishop Tait's youngest daughter Agnes, died in December, 1888. Edward felt it very deeply. He had married her to the Rev. John Ellison only a year before. 'Her beauty, her wonderfully light abundant hair, her sweet voice which used to ring through Lambeth Chapel so true, her delicate touching manner made her a singularly endowed brightness. And there she sleeps – the church full of friends from all distances...'

On the last night of the year there was a midnight service in Addington Church. 'So full of fears, misgivings, anxieties, perplexities,' Edward wrote afterwards, 'such sorrows threatening, such sorrows present, such openings for great mistakes, such possibilities for hostility gathering *in cumuli* on the horizon – the clergy so depressed – I dare not write the utter emptiedness of confidence. I can only look on mutely – and grant that it might be steadfastly – to Thee who has led me *a juventute mea usque ad hanc horam*.' Another descent into the blackness of depression was not the best way to begin a new year, and his spirits were not lifted by compiling a list of all the problems that faced both himself and the Church: Temperance, Purity, Slavery, the wretchedness of the poorest classes at home, their ignorance and wildness and false friends; Patronage and its mischiefs; Clergy Discipline; the failings of the Missionary Societies; the repression of slavery in Africa; the Turkish threatenings of the Assyrian Mission; Natal and South Africa – and the disgust of churchgoers in the colonies at the way in which their Bishops forsake them to return to England; and, looming up into the foreground, the trial of the Bishop of Lincoln.

The Judicial Committee of the Privy Council, with the Bishops of London, Salisbury, Ely, Manchester and Sodor and Man, acting as assessors, had decided that the Archbishop of Canterbury had the authority to try Dr. King, Bishop of Lincoln, on certain charges of irregular and unlawful ritual brought against him by the Church Association. The great ecclesiastical suit opened in the Library of Lambeth Palace on Tuesday, February 12, 1889. The charges against Bishop King were: the use of lighted candles on the Communion-table or the re-table during the Communion Service when not required for the purpose of giving light; mixing water with the wine during the Communion Service, and subsequently consecrating the mixture; standing during the Consecration prayer, facing east with his back to the people so that they could not see any 'manual' acts; adopting the eastward position during the previous part of the Communion Service; having the hymn *Agnus Dei* sung immediately after the Prayer of Consecration; making the Sign of the Cross with uplifted hands before the congregation when pronouncing Absolution, and also when giving the Benediction in the Communion Service; and drinking the water and wine at the cleansing of the sacramental vessels after the Communion Service in the presence of the congregation.

It was all taken most seriously, as though the future of the Anglican Church depended on the outcome, and the trial created the deepest interest. Long before 11 o'clock on the opening day crowds besieged the gates of the Palace and policemen had to keep order both there and at the entrance to the Library. At the end of the great hall there was a dais, with a slightly elevated chair for the Archbishop, and the assessors sat on either side of him – to his right his Vicar-General, Sir James Parker Deane Q.C., and the Bishops of Oxford and Winchester. On his left sat the Bishop of

London and next to him the Bishop of Salisbury. The Bishop of Rochester joined them when he had returned from a trip abroad. Edward was attended by two domestic Chaplains and his private secretary. Between the Bishops and counsel there were tables for the Press; the general public were kept behind a barrier. In a recess to the right of the dais four women, all dressed in black, could be seen in the shadows. They were Minnie Benson, Mrs Davidson, Lucy Tait and Lady Deane.

The court opened with a prayer and two collects by Edward; then Dr. King, who had been called one of the holiest and most beloved of English Bishops, read his protest against trial by the Archbishop alone, and demanded to be heard in Synod before the Metropolitan, with comprovincial Bishops. The argument about that lasted for several days, then the court adjourned.

Proceedings were not resumed until May, when Edward announced, after taking advice, that he was of the opinion that he possessed sole jurisdiction under the old Canon Law, and rejected the Bishop of Lincoln's plea. Edward's decision did not go unchallenged. Dean Church, in a *Guardian* leader, called his claim 'a large order'. It was a position new and strange to contemporary experience, he said, and though it seemed constitutional and reasonable it gave everyone who was affected by it a good deal to think about. The words were mild but serious, coming from such an important figure.

The trial dragged on month after month and all Anglican England was agog. The Bishop of Lincoln availed himself of the most eminent counsel; the prosecutors were also ably represented. Details were argued over at great length, for days at a time. The objections raised to the constitution and jurisdiction of the court were subjected to rigid examination; and the evidence that 'certain men' were sent to Lincoln from London to spy on the Bishop's celebration of the Holy Eucharist was firmly established. Edward thought this a dreadful thing for the Church Association to have organised.

When the trial was over Edward had to prepare his judgement. He worked furiously at it. His dressing-room at Lambeth was stacked with books of Lituriology. Libraries were ransacked for anything that might be useful, and lists of references were made to be worked out in the British Museum. But, with so much work of other kinds to disturb his concentration, he chose to complete his judgement far away from London and took most of the family to the Rieder Furca Hotel, above the Aletsch Glacier, opposite the Bel Alp, in August, 1890. Minnie had taken Maggie to Aix for treatment for her rheumatism. They had to put up with bad weather for most of their stay, but Fred managed an ascent of the Jungfrau. Edward finished his work and packed the result off to the printer. Then he could relax and did not return home until September. On October 4 he finished the final proofs. It had been very stressful work; like exploring a labyrinth, he complained. What made it painful to write was the knowledge that the topics were so infinitesimal in comparison to others which should have been uppermost in the minds of Churchmen. 'It is agonising,' he wrote, 'to be working at candles with my Nellie so ill overhead.'

On November 21, 1890, in a court crowded to suffocation, Edward delivered his judgement. It took him five hours to read, and the tense silence during his reading was broken only once by applause which was quickly suppressed. The judgement, a masterpiece of compromise, was given in Edward's best voice, solemn and clear, bristling with learning and very intelligible. In brief, Edward's conclusions were: the mixing of water with wine during the service (though it was no ecclesiastical offence to do it beforehand), the concealing of the manual acts from the communicants, and the making of the Sign of the Cross in the Absolution and Benediction were declared illegal practices, innovations that must be discontinued. The administering of the chalice, mixed before the service, the eastward position in the first part of the Communion Service, the singing of the *Agnus Dei*, and the presence of lighted candles on the altar were all declared to be legal.

Edward's speech contained some weighty comments. He deprecated as 'not decent' the action of religious people intruding on the worship of others for purposes of espial; he deplored 'the incongruity of minute questionings and disputations in great and sacred subjects which diverted time and attention from the Church's real contest with evil and building up of good'. And he reminded his hearers that 'public worship is one of the Divine institutions which are the heritage of the Church, for the fraternal union of mankind. The Church, therefore, has a right to ask that her congregations may not be divided either by needless pursuance, or by exaggerated suspicion, of practices not in themselves illegal.'

One passage in his speech was particularly welcome to his supporters. 'The tenor of the Common Prayers is openness. The work of its framers was to bring out and recover the worship of the Christian congregation, and specially to replace the Eucharist in its character as the communion of the whole Body of Christ. By the use of the mother tongue, by the audibleness of every prayer, by the priest's prayers being made identical with the prayers of the congregation, by the removal of the invisible and inaudible ceremonial, the English Church as one of the special works in the history of the Catholic Church restored the ancient share and right of the people in Divine Service...'

Among those who were impressed by Edward's knowledge and wisdom was the Bishop of Rochester. 'The emphatic statement that no sacrificial value is attached by the theologian of repute to the eastward position ought to take the sting out of the judgement's toleration of it,' he wrote in his diary. 'If we expect toleration for ourselves we must give it to our neighbours, who do not deserve to be called Roman because they light candles and turn to the east. We can no more prevent the subtle but growing influence of the artistic and the objective elements in the public worship of the present time by denouncing it as Popish than we can prevent Erie from going down the Niagara Falls by shaking a walking-stick at it.'

Other Bishops agreed with Rochester. Dr. Harvey Goodwin of Carlisle said in a sermon that the moral effect of the Archbishop's judgement would be of the weightiest kind, and it was his belief and hope that it would tend to the settlement of doubtful questions and the pacification of the Church. The Bishop of London, Dr. Temple, took a broad and philosophic view. He pointed out that the principle adopted by the Court was that nothing was to be added to the form prescribed in the Book of Common Prayer. The Bishop of Exeter advised his Diocesan Conference that the judgement made for both liberty and order. The Bishop of Ripon said, 'The anxiety lest the pure reformed attitude of the Church of England should have been altered was a groundless anxiety.' The Bishop of Wakefield joined in the chorus of approval. 'I rejoice that the learning and acumen of the Archbishop have been approved by the highest legal authority, and that the Supreme Court has set its seal on His Grace's fairness and impartiality.' The Bishop of Gloucester spoke of the judgement as 'learned, lucid, vigorous and impartial, and withal peace-making and tolerant'. Lord Halifax, as mouthpiece for the English Church Union, expressed his satisfaction.

But there were opposite opinions, both from the Church and the Press, and some of them were very hard-hitting and made Edward fear that an appeal against his judgement might upset it. One of his chief opponents was Dr. Ryle, the Bishop of Liverpool, who regarded the judgement with surprise, pain and dislike, and thought that the gulf between Evangelical Churchmen and other schools of thought would become wider and deeper than ever. The Evangelical Press was also divided. *The Record* displayed courage in pointing out how it had always deprecated the action of the Church Association which had originally instigated the prosecution of Dr. King, and compared the judgement favourably with previous judgements of the Judicial Committee. *The Rock* adopted an opposite opinion and spoke of 'the bathos of judicial trifling'. *The English Churchman* was more pronounced. In its view a blow had been struck at the stability of English law and the maintenance of order among the people – a serious wound had been inflicted on the Church of England. In the opinion of the *Church Intelligencer* it would have required a bulky pamphlet to enumerate all the mistakes and erroneous suggestions of inferences involved in the judgement.

When he had weighed up the value of the various opinions defending and attacking his judgement, Edward did a bold thing. He issued a pastoral letter upholding his own judgement as Church law in such a way that if the opinion of the Judicial Committee had been adverse it would have brought Church and State at once into a strained relationship. Happily the crisis was averted and the Lambeth Judgement was upheld on all counts. Those who may have anticipated a dangerous collision had their fears removed. Edward satisfied himself that Dr. King would obey the judgement in every particular and no penalty was imposed on him.

Edward's standing in Church and country was never higher. Months of toil and anxiety had brought peace to the Church. The moderate party received the result with unfeigned relief and the judgement had not so gone against the High Church party as to threaten disruption. The permission of lighted candles, of the use of a mixed Chalice, of the eastward position, and the refusal to condemn the singing of the *Agnus Dei* were clear and substantial gains for the High Churchmen. The requirement that the manual acts should be visible and the prohibition of ceremonial mixing of the cup were not very sympathetically accepted, but banning the Sign of the Cross in the Absolution and the final Benediction attracted less unfavourable notice than the other prohibitions. The Church Association received no sympathy; serious and moderate Evangelicals warmly welcomed a pronouncement so full of toleration. Dr. King's appeal was heard in June and July, 1891, before the Judicial Committee of the Privy Council who delivered judgement on August 2, 1892, dismissing it, and thus bringing an end to the whole affair. No kind of punishment was meted out to the Bishop of Lincoln, who loyally accepted the verdict of the Committee, and his friendship with Edward remained as loving as it had ever been.

At the beginning of October, 1890, when Edward was finishing his judgement, Hugh was at Cambridge for an assembly of freshmen, Arthur at Eton, Edward, Minnie and Maggie were visiting friends, and Fred and Nellie were alone together at Addington for a few days. They had a wonderful time, free from rules, conformity and religion, playing games with Beth, riding, playing tennis, lazing, discussing anything and everything – it was an idyllic time that Fred never forgot. Then he had to return to Cambridge; the parents returned, and he and Nellie parted with regret, though they made plans for Christmas.

About the middle of the month Nellie fell ill. She caught diphtheria from a contact in the village, and after a short illness she died on October

27. She was 27 years old. 'Her passing was as sweet and serviceable as all her days,' Edward wrote. 'But, though she was the bond of love to her brothers and all, we are learning to say "*O Quanta Qualia*" without shrinking.' On October 29, the day of her funeral, he added, 'My Nellie to the earth of Addington – the width of the love manifested to her – by every creature. Sacrament in the chapel – servants – men.' Despite his grief, and constantly as he missed Nellie, it was not the same dark and desperate feeling that he suffered when Martin died, and he was able to talk easily and lovingly of her from the day of her death.

Nellie faced death with courage, even welcomed it as a new experience. 'I wonder what it will be like. Give them all my love,' was the last note she wrote to her mother when she was unable to speak. Her brothers had arrived at Addington in response to telegrams, too late to see her alive, but were present at the burial in Addington churchyard on a bright autumnal day. 'Gay, adventurous and brave,' Arthur called Nellie. If the Benson siblings had voted on the most popular of their family Nellie would have come out top of every list, and when she died each felt that a special companion and confidante had gone; and the Bensons' corporate life began to disintegrate. The gap in the family circle grew wider, paths were diverging and intimacy losing its glow. Unsentimental affection was still present, but sometimes violent criticism pulled them apart.

In November that year Christopher Benson, Edward's brother, died at Wiesbaden at the age of 54. Edward went out to the funeral and was touched by the evidences of esteem in which Christopher had been held – he had been a true 'Lay son of the Church', devoted to it both spiritually and materially. After returning home Edward and Minnie stayed quietly at Addington until it was time for his Lincoln judgement, and after its delivery they visited Windsor as guests of the Dean, soon to become Bishop of Rochester; then they went to a cottage at Reigate, lent to them by Lady Henry Somerset. The year ended sadly with the death of the Dean of St. Paul's and that of Archbishop Thompson of York. Edward went to the latter's funeral at York Minster, which he described as a beautiful and tenderly sung service, then to Bishopthorpe, the Archbishop's Palace, for another service in the ugly little parish church, different from but just as thrilling and comforting as the one in the magnificent Minster. As the service was ending he noticed that a little breeze swept a heap of hurrying brown leaves down into the gravel one by one among the wreaths, and a little snow fell in light tiny crystals.

CHAPTER EIGHTEEN

I N the New Year of 1891 the earth was iron-bound in frozen snow and had been for weeks. The only good thing about it was that it was possible to toboggan gloriously from the top of Fir Mount right over the path to the garden. Nellie, who would have been at the centre of the enjoyment, was not forgotten for a moment and her laughter rang like a bell in all their hearts. Edward had not been able to ride for several weeks and was feeling restless. It had been the coldest, hardest, duskiest and foggiest weather he could ever remember, and day after day the air was grey with the smoke of London, and the smell of London was in his nostrils, and the snow was black with the smuts of London. 'This is progress,' was his sarcastic comment, 'for it was never so seen before.'

His depression was made worse by the refusal of Bishop Wilkinson of Truro to come to a decision about resigning his seat. He was ill and not likely to get better. He was unable to carry out his many tasks without suffering terribly before each one, yet was reluctant to give up his life's work. His doctors had tried, without success, to persuade him to go, but his brain was becoming fuddled and he stubbornly refused to listen to their advice. Edward was sorry for the old man, but impatient too, and relieved when the doctors decided that they would let the Bishop carry on until Easter, then bring matters to a head. Such a contrast to the man he had seen and admired at the consecration of Truro Cathedral – Edward sorrowed at the change.

In February he was tired of inaction and rode with Maggie in Hyde Park in a fog as black as night. All the street lights were lit although it was daytime. They rode up to the Albert Memorial and to Queen's Gate. It was much lighter in Kensington, but they returned to night in Westminster; there were a few other black ghosts riding in the Row too. Edward and Minnie naturally remembered Martin's death on February 10, but they were not able to go to Winchester until the 12th, when they found that the faithful porter and his wife were still taking care of Martin's plaque, after 13 years. Edward preached at the Regent Street Polytechnic on February 15 to 1,500 young men on how to read the Bible. He had heard a rumour that the Bishop of London was going to withdraw his licence and close the Polytechnic on account of the jealousy and opposition of the clergy of the neighbourhood who thought that their choirs and congregations were diminished by the flourishing college. But, Edward argued, the place itself would go on just the same and its frequenters would still frequent it – only they would be in the hands of Nonconformity instead of the Church. 'Who is as blind as my servant?' he sighed.

In March he founded the Mary Eleanor Benson Gift for the Parish of Lambeth, in accordance with Nellie's dying wish. She had left £2,000 to be used for the project. Nellie had spent most of her pocket money in helping poor (but respectable) girls, and finding them good homes, and employment in shops and domestic service. The Deed provided for the application of the Trust's income to continue the training, outfitting and convalescing of poor girls, the first preference being given to the members of her own Bible class. Later in the month a new Eagle Lectern was placed in Lambeth Chapel in Nellie's memory. It was presented by the Duchess of Bedford and others of Edward's Class of Ladies, and the inscription bore the words 'In the midst of death we are in life'.

Edward's 'Class of Ladies' or the 'Lambeth Penitents', as they called themselves, had been formed by a number of zealous and influential women who were anxious to stop the rot that they claimed was ruining London – a rot that the Prince of Wales, leader of the 'Marlborough House Set', with coarse and vulgar behaviour, was responsible for.

They had asked Edward to speak to the Prince about the harm he was doing to society and this had put him in a quandary. He disapproved as much as anybody of immodesty and immorality, but when it came to admonishing the Prince of Wales, with whom he was on very friendly terms, he hesitated, and decided that it was not his business to lecture the Prince on hearsay reports of his private life – charges which could not substantiated without opening up many cans of worms. His suggestion was to hold weekly prayer meetings at Lambeth at which the faithful could pray for the reform of the rakes, gamblers and drunkards. With that the ladies had to be content, and the meetings were started. The Princess of Wales was invited to attend but the Queen would not give her permission. 'Religion was not a thing to be mixed up with life,' she said tartly.

The Penitents did not achieve anything dramatic if, indeed, anything at all, but at least they were trying; and Edward's conscience was fairly clear.

Edward recorded in his diary that the Clergy Discipline Bill, on which so much effort had been spent the previous year, had passed its Second Reading and was due to run the gauntlet in the Commons. He had noted the ill-natured reception given to Bishop Temple, Bishop of London, when he spoke in favour of the Bill, and was indignant on his behalf. 'It is painful, very painful, to see the Lords always so unappreciative of the Bishop of London – the strongest man, nearly, in the House, the clearest, the highest-toned, the most deeply sympathetic, the cleverest in principle – yet because his voice is a little harsh and his accent a little provincial (though of what province it is hard to say) and his figure square and his hair a little rough, and because all this sets off the idea of independence, he is not listened to at all by these cold, kindly, worldly-wise, gallant land-owning powers. Some day his force and goodness must carry them.' In April he wrote again about the Bishop, who had spoken in the Marriage Law Amendment Bill. 'There is something sickening in seeing the House of Lords with its regulated tones and silken manners, which are well able to express if they chose kindness and sympathy and chivalry, utterly unaware that they have greatness and strength in the Bishop of London. They talk, they look, they laugh at any allowance against himself which he makes. But I cannot but believe that if he would only speak a little oftener he must impress even their complacences.'

Edward continued to fill his days (or have them filled for him) by matters great and small – interviews, conferences, committees, business in the House of Lords, meetings, services and sermons. Thursday, March 19, was a typical day. At 11 o'clock he presided over a meeting of the Ecclesiastical Commission; this was followed by an interview with the patron of Wootton about an extension of the parish. After lunch there was a conference with Lord Herschell, then a meeting with Sir Frederick Goldsmit and Isabella Bird on the Assyrians and their Mission. Later the Assyrian Committee met at Church House, then the Church House Committee met. Then he was off to the Lords to move the Report and amendments to the Clergy Discipline Bill. The next day he was equally busy – a meeting of the Beverley trustees, followed by a ceremony in the Library conferring the Lambeth degree of Mus. Doc. on one of his clergymen. There was a service in Lambeth Chapel at 3.30 p.m., then the House of Lords claimed him for an hour. At 5 p.m. he addressed a public meeting of people interested in the Lambeth Savings Bank. Edward working under enormous pressures was Edward at his best; there was no time for black thoughts or despair. It was at Addington where he was more able to relax that coughs and colds took their toll and where his gloomy presence prevailed.

On March 5 Archbishop Magee took his seat in the House of Lords for the first time as Archbishop of York; on May 9 he was buried at Peterborough, his former Diocese. Edward could not be present; he was at the funeral of Thomas Hare, his 82-year-old brother-in-law, a Bencher of the Middle Temple. Eleanor, Thomas's wife and Edward's sister, had died in February, 1890, after a long illness. Edward, Charles and Emmeline

(Mrs Woodhouse) were the only ones still living from Edward White Benson and Harriet Baker's large family. Charles, however, was to die in 1893; Emmeline outlived Edward.

In April the Bishop of Truro resigned. His health improved immediately and he took up his work with a new alertness before he finally vacated his See. April 25 was the anniversary of Edward's Consecration in 1877 and of Lightfoot's in 1879. His friend Randall Davidson became the Bishop of Rochester on that day too. In June and July Edward had a severe attack of influenza. He only wrote a few entries in his diary and spent the time gardening in a desultory kind of way. One of his few letters was to Bishop Davidson, in which he said that he had not been trepanned, as far as he knew, but the surface of his brain had been absorbed about half an inch in depth, so that his thoughts, words and deeds belonged to a remote past. 'I assure you, influenza is nasty. Thought, affection, devotion, sensation, will, memory – all smoothed down with a flat-iron.' But he was well enough to be present at the laying of the Foundation Stone of the Church House by the Duke of Connaught and to speak in the House of Lords in favour of the Free Education Bill.

Another family death occurred on August 3; that of his half-uncle, the Rev. William Jackson, who had been devoted to Edward's father and his study of chemistry. Jackson had ordered in his Will that he should be cremated and Edward disapproved but could do nothing about it, except to be absent from the ceremony.

In August it was time for another family holiday and, with Lucy Tait, they crossed a rough Channel and arrived at Chur by way of Basle, then went on to Pontresina. 'Year after year,' Edward wrote, 'the rolling and advancing stream of travel is acting to make nations more like each other in Europe. I see manners and tones becoming more alike – certainly vast changes since 1852. I think there is less and less apparent recognition of Divine presence in our daily affairs. Certainly less in forms of speech.' From Pontresina they walked, rode and climbed, visited churches and cathedrals, explored the valleys and made copious notes on the fauna and flora of the neighbourhood. Edward was often depressed – nobody could tell why, except that he received a batch of letters from England, one ungentleman-like, he hinted, one rabid, and one from the Prince of Wales on the subject of gambling. On principle the Prince was against it, but gave plausible reasons why sometimes it was not wrong. Edward felt that 'receptivity' was much decreased by the crowds of visitors they saw every day. The glories of the mountains were fast becoming merely spectacles, he thought, and ceasing to be sanctuaries.

He and Lucy went to the Languard Valley which was extraordinarily bare and desolate. 'The last few trees are long dead, pine trunks standing gaunt against the great traces of stones, which are crusted with ancient greenish lichen – here and there tufts of darkish purple monkshood are intermixed with brilliant yellow arnica – marmots whistled and a few stonechats chipped. A marmoset came on us suddenly to his horror and darted to and from among the stones with his beautiful feet and long curved tail, quite beside himself till he suddenly tilted himself into his hole. Another stood up and caught sight of us at the mouth of his burrow, whistled and dived instantly. The Albriz was very fine with the glacier in his lap; the Layou peak above to the left – a cold, unfertilising stream wandered to the edge and threw himself over – pale browns, pale greys, pale greens, and steep slopes and precipices everywhere.'

During the Pontresina holiday, Fred and Hugh had a most frightening experience on the Pitz Palu, one of the Bernina peaks. They planned to climb to the top on one side and descend on the other, but on the way down a fierce wind caused snow from the rocks to be hurled against them, so that they staggered and slipped. Hugh appeared to collapse, and had to be carried by their two guides along the ridge, while they tried to find shelter. They poured brandy down his throat, but it only revived him momentarily. Fred followed the little procession for an hour as they gradually climbed down, sometimes seeing the guides with their burden, then losing them when they were hidden by the rocks; so he did not know whether Hugh was alive or dead. When they had escaped from the wind into the sunshine he found the guides roaring with laughter and Hugh quite drunk, trying to sit on the point of his ice-axe. The brandy had had a delayed effect on the 19-year-old youth not used to strong drink. They did not return to the hotel until Hugh had sobered up, and Fred was spared the terrible task of announcing to his father that his youngest son was dead. 'Hugh tired today, after being as well as possible last night,' Edward, who had not been told about the brandy incident, commented, 'and declaring as if he had walked 100 yards only, appears today to have had a kind of collapse and seems very poorly.' He went on to complain about his sons' smoking habits and that in the evenings, after meals, and at other times, they were lost to him in the smoking rooms they had set up. But he did not think he could be expected to learn to smoke at his age in order to keep them company.

Gradually Edward felt stronger, calmer. He had a good week of reading, particularly of Homer, and he managed to send a good many sheets of Cyprian to the printer. He also corrected the proofs of a book that Nellie had written about her social work which he was having privately published. Fred had to leave the party on August 27 to start his work in the city walls of Chester, looking for Roman inscriptions on the tombs of the legionaries once stationed there. Cambridge had given him £40 as the nucleus of a subscription. This was after he had gained his Tripos in Archaeology and was given an open scholarship to King's. Fred had little time for the Romans because they were not Greeks, but he thought the task would fill up the autumn nicely and might yield material for a fellowship dissertation. Edward was delighted with Fred's success and urged him to stay at Cambridge to take a Theological Tripos with a view to ordination. He desperately wished that all his sons would enter the Church, but Arthur, firmly established as an Eton Master, had shown no signs of wanting to change his job. Fred was absolutely sure that he had no vocation and wanted to become an archaeologist, though a career in writing was fixed at the back of his mind. Edward did not try to dissuade him, but inwardly was sad. His hopes were now centred on Hugh, due to enter Trinity after failing his examination for the Indian Civil Service; and Edward's heart was gladdened when his youngest son did finally decide to enter the Church.

In October Edward attended the Church Congress at Rhyl when the question of Welsh Disestablishment, which was becoming urgent, was discussed. There was a large preponderance of Welsh Parliamentary representatives there, pledged to Disestablishment; the Nonconformist bodies were united on the subject; and the rising tide of Welsh Nationalism, uncertainty as to the attitude of the English Church, and the Irish precedent – all combined to create fear, even despair, in the hearts of Welsh Anglicans. Edward gave a powerful and moving speech to a large assembly that was the turning point of the whole controversy. He ended by saying, 'But, you, who are our eldest selves, the foundation of our Episcopacy, the very designers of our sanctuaries, the primaeval British Dioceses from whom our very realm derives its only title to be called Great Britain, I come from the steps of the chair of Augustine, your younger ally, to tell you that by the Benediction of God, we will not quietly see you disinherited.' The speech produced a profound sensation – its militant vigour combined with stately dignity undoubtedly contributed to the collapse of the movement favouring Disestablishment, at least temporarily. Agitation, both for and against, rumbled on for another four years until, in 1895, the Bill to introduce it perished with the Government that gave it birth; and in all the anxious work of those years Edward was guide and mainstay of the opposition.

At the end of December another foreign holiday was planned, this time to Algiers, with Minnie, Lucy Tait, Maggie, Fred, Canon Hutchinson, and his daughter Amy. As usual, Edward started out in a gloomy sorry-for-himself mood, not improved by the wretched journey from Paris to Marseilles – 'foodless, sleepless, crowded transportation, owing to the mismanagement of the agent.' He went on to describe a pain he felt in the evening. 'It was not a satisfactory pain but it was an acute pain, of which I am not certain that I know the source, which in the evening gave me some little torment. Fred read aloud everyone's favourite piece from *In Memoriam*. *In Memoriam* was inexpressibly dear to me for the best part of my life. It came out just when my mother and my sister Harriet died. I sank into it and I rose with it; and tonight among their very nice talk of it, my two children's views of it were throughout what I had taught. There was nothing in early life I so longed for as to lead my children along those ways and kindred ways in other poets. It had been done, and yet they were quite unconscious of my having any keen, deep interest in it, still less the passionate and absorbing interest with which it has gone with me through the valley and the shadow of death. I could not be silent throughout.'

They arrived in Algiers on the first day of January, 1892, gliding into the port through a sea of glass. The plan was to stay only a short time there, then travel through North Africa to Tunis, seeing Roman cities en route. In this way Edward was able to give such a vivid description of Carthage in his Cyprian. It was also his first contact with a race as alien as the Arab; and the extraordinary power of their religion and their devotion to it impressed him very deeply. They left Algiers for Setif on January 11. 'After it's dark tonight we shall never see it again,' sighed Lucy from her window overlooking the bay.

They pursued an eastward route as far as Tizi and passed through the great Haut Plateau. They visited Constantine, Tebessa, Timehad, Tagaste (where Augustine was born) and Biskra before reaching Carthage. Edward filled page after page in his notebooks, and his diary swelled with descriptions of the countryside, the desert, the Arab towns with their shops and colonnades, Roman viaducts, tombs, theatres and temples. He was in his element, and dragged the others for miles in this direction and that. They all professed profound interest, but privately they were less than enthusiastic about the rigours and the tiring expeditions, especially those on foot. At the hotel in Biskra Edward received a telegram announcing the death of the Duke of Clarence, the eldest son of the Prince of Wales, a weak and self-indulgent young man who was reported to be involved in the Cleveland Street scandal and at one time was even suspected of being Jack the Ripper; but Edward called him 'a good-hearted, sweet-tempered young Prince, not over clever, but one who could not put up with anything he thought wrong, who would have lived purely and reigned peaceably.' He wished to return home at once, but the Prince of Wales wired him that he was on no account to curtail his holiday. The telegram was followed by a letter expressing such heartbreak that the jovial rake could not possibly have felt, written in conventional but not entirely sincere terms. 'It has pleased God to inflict a heavy crushing blow upon us – you know what a happy family party we have always been – so that the wrenching away of our first-born is a sorrow – the shadow of which can never leave us during the rest of our lives. On this day month he was to have married a charming and gifted young lady… His bride has become his widow without ever having been his wife…' The Princess May of Teck 'could not realise that he is gone and is walking restlessly about', but happily she soon rearranged her affections and became engaged to Prince George, the second son, instead.

The Bensons arrived in Carthage on January 22 and stayed there for nine days. They sketched and walked, lunched with the city's nobilities, explored the Arab quarter, the Phoenician and Roman graves, visited museums and found a mass of Christian inscriptions. Edward explored Carthage and its environs on his own, the rest of the party could not keep up with him, seeking to capture Cyprian in his old haunts and follow his life by what he left behind. Tireless, indefatigable, he was enraptured with everything he saw – he had reached El Dorado. 'I cannot conceive how any human creature can be disappointed with Carthage, one of the most magnificent situations in the world,' he wrote. He was taken around by Père Delattre, head of the Order of White Fathers, who was a fount of information about the old city and its history, and Edward was charmed with him, his red beard and blue eyes. The whole pilgrimage was an experience he never forgot, and his work on Cyprian was greatly improved by treading in the saint's footsteps. He even found the place where he was martyred, in a corner of what was then the English consul's garden; and he also discovered his burial place which had a modern cross which Edward felt to be not in quite the right place. Edward wished he could stay and organise an archaeological dig in order to get nearer still to his beloved saint, but time ran out and at the end of January the exhausted family (except Edward, still in a state of exhilaration, and Fred, who had left the others in Tunis in order to go to Athens, by way of Malta and Brindisi) arrived in Marseilles after a frightful journey of 42 hours, and were able to fall into bed in Paris in the early hours of Sunday morning. Then it was back to the Clergy Discipline Bill and further attempts to bring the Church Missionary Society into line, opening exhibitions, visiting Lambeth Workhouse – and burying his beloved dog Watch, who was nearly 20 years old. The grave was dug on the lawn at Addington and a stone erected bearing the words *Esne Vigil* – 'to remind us to watch and, though vainly, to ask him if he live yet?'

CHAPTER NINETEEN

THE year 1892 continued to be as busy and stressful for Edward as all other years had been since he became Archbishop, and one of his chief problems was the opposition to the Church of England which the working classes were expressing with more and more fretfulness. Minnie and Lucy went to a meeting at which Tom Mann was the speaker and returned glowing with enthusiasm for his exposition of the 'Religious Basis of the Socialist Movement'. They were struck with Mann's natural eloquence and power – and with the religion which he asserted for himself and claimed for most workers, 'though it is not,' he said, 'the religion of the Churches.' Edward was unable to comprehend anything that departed from the status quo of the Anglican religion; and deviance from the rules and rites of the Establishment disturbed him greatly. Even though he could dimly see the force of the emotions behind the calls for justice and freedom by people like Mann, he was determined to try to bring them to reason and persuade them to return to the Church's fold.

About a June visit to Wellington College for Speech Day, he wrote: 'All about the place I found everything which I had so thought out and worked out with such pain and grief sometimes, and designed with such care, just as commonplace to everybody as a gravel walk. But a gravel walk is good walking. There is a certain pleasure in finding one's memory extinct in one's lifetime…'

In August he left Addington for a visit to Yorkshire with Maggie and Lucy Tait. At Skipton he found it strange to see that the once so beautiful Airedale with its copses and ridges, clear streams, grey stone farms and small villages that he remembered from boyhood had grown into one dismal connected street. 'What can people do but be Radicals who see Nature's beauty daily disappearing and man doing nothing that is not ugly around them,' Edward wrote. Then he was overwhelmed by a flood of memories. 'I realise more and more how much the associations here with my dear old aunt and my father and my own cousins entered into and guided my boy life. The thought now of rushing after "Mr Christopher" down the slope from the Castle gate for early church at Christ Church, the sauntering up with Robert along the churchyard wall, the many sage, shrewd and true church sayings of John and the mystic interpretation of Christopher, and the talks with my dear old aunt about past generations when I was 15 – all these things are symbolic to me now.'

Stonegappe was almost a ruin – walls falling, trees felled, the garden a wilderness, the lawn a field and the rooms, once full of the vigorous presence of John Sidgwick and his wife, were bare and dirty, the walls and ceilings beginning to crumble. The village priest was nothing but a peasant, the choir was unbaptised and the people knew nothing of Missions. Edward was dejected and forecast that he too would soon be in similar ruins.

They went on to Keighley by train and found that smoke was eating up everything. They drove over Barden Moor and from Wharfedale to Nidderdale, from Bolton to Pateley Bridge, then to Dacre and Low Hall, where Robert Benson had lived. They saw old Christopher Benson's tomb in Pateley Bridge old churchyard and inspected the Church registers. There the first Christopher Benson appeared in 1556, and his son's baptism, marriage, and baptism again of his child. Edward felt very proud of those independent old Dalesmen of so many centuries whose love of country life lived on in him, and he was glad to think that many others of their qualities lived on too, for they were the strength of the land in peace and war.

In October Edward was ill, depressed by the weather. In November he presided over a conference at Lambeth on the duty of the Church to the aged poor – the members were in favour of such duty, fortunately. The rest of the year was spent at Addington. 'Arthur, Fred, Hugh, all home. Delightful. What could be more perfect than these three with Maggie, except the certainties about the other two.' He recorded an accident while riding. 'My horse fell heavily with me in a deep lane rotten with all these rains and trodden into dough. Neither she nor I the least hurt though she on her knees and I on my shoulder.' Then he had to bring God into the accident. 'Sometimes I think that such a departure from this world would be the most enviable. Perhaps that is fear of pain. Choose Thou.'

In 1893 the most determined effort at Disestablishment which occurred during Edward's Primacy was initiated but, as usual, when that sort of danger was imminent, his spirits rose to battle with it. Colonial Church policy in Natal, with the suggestion of merger with the South African Church, had also to be dealt with by patient conciliation and Christian democracy. Pressure was heavy on Edward and he needed a change. At the right moment, out of the blue, he received an invitation from Lady Crawford for him to take Minnie and Maggie to visit her at her Villa Palmieri in Florence; and the friendship that quickly sprang up between them gave him much delight and was a great help in later years. Lady Crawford had two daughters, Lady Mabel and Lady Jane Lindsay, and they too proved to be congenial companions, and became almost as dear to him as his own daughter; and Lady Crawford herself was like a mother who had earned affection and respect. 'We have been in the Queen's favourite villa entertained like Queens,' he said. He spent day after day visiting churches, galleries and museums, and riding far into the country; and his delight and interest were revealed by his full and enthusiastic diaries. He revisited the Villa in the spring for the next three years, each time receiving joy and friendship.

Three weeks of lovely weather at Addington in April gave Edward further rest and refreshment. His work on Cyprian prospered, and he was able to demolish a backlog of correspondence. The weather was bright from morning till evening; all foliage was out a month before its time, and flowers which usually succeeded each other all bloomed simultaneously. Then it was back to Lambeth, with meetings to protest against Disestablishment, work on the Patronage Bill, and to arrange a great meeting in the Albert Hall on the Defence of the National Church. 8,000 people attended on May 16, and more than once they rose to their feet to cheer a speaker. Edward thought it all looked like one of John Martin's pictures, *The Day of Judgement*, perhaps. 12 speakers, including Lord Selborne, the Duke of Argyll and the Bishop of Durham, spoke with great force. There was only one dissident voice. A cry of 'False!' rang out once but was immediately stifled. Edward opened the proceedings, although he was suffering from a hoarse throat, and gave a great rallying cry. 'We have England and God's Church and we mean not to go down. We do not stand or fall together, we stand. By God's Grace we advance. Our call is not to perish together, but to prevail. Our foes are human. Our foes have hearts. And the Church (that is we) must so live and labour and love, that there shall be no resisting her.'

The feeling throughout the country was against the Suspensory Bill, a preliminary measure in the attempt to disestablish the Church in Wales, and there were shoals of petitions and letters. 'But what we have to do,' Edward wrote, 'is to press on with a strong continuous force for the Church as the mover in all good things, a mainspring without which the works of goodness would cease.'

During May, 1893, Edward's weighty preoccupation with Church matters was punctured by a family event which forced him briefly to descend from the heights to contemplate with amused amazement the achievement of his son Fred, for Fred had become an author and had published a book which within weeks had become a runaway bestseller and had brought the name of Benson into the consciousness of thousands of people who would not have connected it with an Archbishop. The name of the book was *Dodo* and it had had a somewhat chequered career. In the early 1880s Fred and Maggie had collaborated on a story which bore some resemblance to the later work, but their inspiration had dried up and the idea had been discarded. After he had taken a First at Cambridge Fred again began to tinker with the first draft of the novel with a heroine who was both fascinating and heartless. He wrote quickly and without pausing for self-criticism, his enthusiasm taking him over the hurdle of the absence of plot. There were minor characters who circled around the central figure and occasionally clashed with her, but he could not call up development, depth of feeling or interplay of character. His intention was to make Dodo reveal herself by what she said rather than by what she did, which therefore required no comment; an original idea which at the time Fred was not capable of sustaining successfully. Dodo was rich, attractive and adored in society. She flirted and smoked and outraged her peers, and she talked incessantly. But she never changed – neither events nor people had any impact on her; on the last page she was the same Dodo she had been on the first, and after a few weeks Fred found that he had lost direction and did not know what to do with his exasperating creation. He felt disinclined to spend any more time on it and decided instead to concentrate on his archaeological studies.

After his six weeks work excavating the town walls of Chester were over and his funds exhausted Fred returned to Cambridge to write up the results of his work. On an idle impulse he took out the incomplete manuscript of Dodo and his interest was rekindled; but before resuming writing he decided to get an expert opinion on what he had already done. He sent the roughly written manuscript, full of erasures and illegible interpolations, to Minnie and asked her to pass it on to Lucas Malet for judgment.

Lucas Malet was Mary St. Leger Kingsley (1852–1931), a daughter of Charles Kingsley and friend of the Bensons since the Wellington days when Minnie had found such happiness on her visits to the family at Eversley. Charles Kingsley had died in 1875, and the male bonding between Edward and Charles had necessarily come to an end. But Minnie, Mrs Kingsley and Mary had continued to have a warm relationship. Mary married the Rev. W. Harrison, the rector of Clovelly, in 1876 and began a career as a novelist, calling herself Lucas Malet.

But Lucas Malet did not actually appear in the saga of Dodo immediately, because Minnie did not send the manuscript to her, but to Henry James, in October, 1891. He replied coolly, making it obvious that the story fell far short of his literary ideal. 'Make yourself a style,' he wrote. 'It is by style that we are saved.'

Fred swallowed this humiliation and went on with his writing. Several months later Lucas Malet did receive the re-written and tidied-up manuscript, and criticised it kindly and honestly, though ruthlessly, suggesting where to cut, where to revise and how to give the characters vitality. Fred was inspired sufficiently to revise the story thoroughly and he finished the second volume in the autumn of 1892. Methuen, the first publisher to whom it was submitted, accepted it immediately.

'*Dodo* is out,' Minnie wrote excitedly to Maggie, 'and I have sent you a copy. Your father had the first copy and has positively read some of it.' Another letter followed. 'I have been reading *Dodo* again, and it's binding. I think it is cleverer than I thought. Now the world's eye is on it, and it is that majestic thing, out.' It does not seem that Edward, the most unliterary of men, exerted himself unduly to finish *Dodo*. It was surprising that he started the work at all, but he did, and became greatly puzzled that a son of his, a scholar and an archaeologist, could write such nonsense. Still, parts of it were quite amusing, he conceded, in a shallow kind of way, and it certainly showed application on Fred's part to have written so much and succeeded in getting it before the public in hard covers. He wrote to Adeline, Duchess of Bedford, a strong-willed lady he greatly admired, 'I have just met Lord Halifax who says everybody is talking of nothing but *Dodo*, that it is most diverting. I cannot understand the source of this apparent knowledge. Fred is going to see the original, they having exchanged letters. What a cross-built world!' and with those words Edward ended his participation in his son's literary endeavours, though there was an amusing follow-up that concerned Ethel Smyth, of whom Edward heartily disapproved. Her opinions were outrageous, her dress unconventional and she lacked femininity. When *Dodo* was published she became unexpectedly welcome at Lambeth and was invited to dinner. To her mingled terror and gratification Edward almost embraced her, and all through the evening he was over-solicitous. When she was leaving she asked Minnie why the Archbishop had been so amiable. Minnie explained that he thought she might have been hurt about the composer, Edith Staines, the character in *Dodo* that she had obviously modelled for, and had tried to make amends for his son's offence. In fact, Ethel had been pleased to be included among the socialites that Fred had parodied. She considered that Edith Staines was the one decent character in the book, and was not hurt at all.

Up until *Dodo*, Ethel and Edward had not been 'two dewdrops destined to roll into one', as Minnie put it. She stood in deadly awe of him. She found his beauty disconcerting, his office deeply impressed her, and she was affected by the fact that he was seldom quite at ease. The sight of his majestic form approaching the tea-table scattered her wits completely, and nervousness made her do stupid things. It was found expedient for her to be smuggled into Lambeth by back entrances and herded into a side room. But Ethel bore Edward no ill-will, in spite of his rudeness, and thought it flattering in a way to inspire so intense an aversion; the situation was more exciting than disagreeable.

There is only one recorded incident of Ethel standing up to her tormentor and coming off best. It was at a dinner at Addington when Edward, forced by Minnie to take her into the dining-room, looked at her as though she were a toad. He asked her opinion on some ethico-musical point, kept carping at her answers and finally said, 'I really don't know what the drift of your argument is, as I have been wholly occupied in noting the fact that you have used the expression "that sort of thing" seven times in one minute.' But Ethel stuck to her point in spite of continual exclamations of 'That is bosh!' The chaplains were white with amazement and Minnie and Maggie were acutely uncomfortable. Then Edward declared, 'I will discuss music no longer.'

The next topic was a liturgical work that Ethel had been reading and which Edward had called 'unfair'. When she asked in what respect he considered it unfair he stared at her in disbelief at her impertinence in questioning his judgement. 'Do you mean historically unfair?' she persisted.

'Pray what may historically unfair mean?' said Edward.

'I mean unfair as to the use the author makes of historical elucidation, for as a layman, unversed in rubrical history, I cannot judge of his methods of employing it.'

'I should have thought it patent to anyone that the book is untrustworthy,' Edward said loftily.

Thereupon Ethel quoted an important argument of the author's which turned on the particular use of a particular rubric in the Missal. 'Is that so?' she said innocently.

'It would take an expert a week to decide that question,' was Edward's scathing answer.

'Just so!' Ethel's voice rose with triumph. 'Hence my remark that a layman cannot be expected to judge of the historical fairness of the book!'

It was a distinct score for Ethel, and all Edward could mutter was, 'That is very true.'

It was flattering in a way to be such a very red rag to such a bull and because she had had the satisfaction of putting him in the wrong Ethel liked him better and was less frightened of him from then onwards. The next day Edward's penitence was touching – he insisted on taking her into luncheon on his arm. 'I might have been Adeline, Duchess of Bedford!' she boasted.

In 1893 Ethel Smyth's *Mass* was performed in the Albert Hall to a very enthusiastic audience, though the Press greeted it with scorn and patronage, and Bernard Shaw was his usual witty self. 'She writes indiscriminately, with the faith of a child and the orthodoxy of a lady. Her *Mass* belongs to the light literature of Church music. It repeatedly spurts ahead in the briskest fashion, so that one or two of the drum flourishes reminded me, not of anything so vulgar as the Salvation Army, but of a crack cavalry band. Much of the orchestral decoration is very pretty. The work, as a whole, is fragmentary, but it is very far from being utterly tedious and mechanised like Dvořák's *Requiem*. Above all, it is interesting as the beginning of what I have so often prophesied – the conquest of popular music by a woman.' Edward had overheard Ethel playing parts of it on the piano at Addington and remarked that it appeared that God was not implored but commanded to have mercy. Maggie said that she understood that what had been aimed at in the *Christe Eleison* was an expression of intense terror. 'Indeed,' said Edward. 'I can only repeat that to me it sounded like orders issued in an extremely peremptory manner.'

CHAPTER TWENTY

AFTER the excitement of Fred's literary endeavours had subsided Edward became involved in the preparations for the wedding of George, Duke of York, to Princess May of Teck, former fiancée of the Duke of Clarence. It took place on July 6, 1893, and 'the sight of the Chapel in brilliance was impressive. Not a uniform but was traditional, not a ribbon or medal but had a great scene or period in history, a conquest or a battle, at its birth. The finest thing of all was the Queen's entrance. Lord Carrington, the Lord High Chamberlain, was not at the door to receive her – Lord Brendellsane (Lord Steward) declared to me it was sheer dawdling. I could scarcely believe my eyes when the Queen entered the Chapel by the lower end and began to walk up, alone. The Duchess of Teck and her grandson of Hesse were behind her. On she came, looking most pleasant, slightly amused, bowing most gracefully to either side, her black silk almost covered with wonderful lace, and a little crown with chains of diamonds on her head, walking lame with a tallish stick. She looked Empire, gracious Empire; was helped on to the footpace by her grandson, and sat down in her chair looking so gallant and commanding and kind too.

'The Lord High Chamberlain had expressly arranged with me to have no address. The Duke of York spoke to me especially of his wishes to have none. As I was finishing breakfast after our Communion in Chapel came a note from the Queen commanding me to give one. At 11 a.m. I had to have it and in that space I had to write an address of this sort and write it out...'

Some days after the glitter of the royal wedding came the simplicity of a large gathering of the poor, halt and blind of Lambeth, in the Palace Guardroom. There were songs and other music, the picture gallery served as a tearoom and a service was held in the Chapel. 'The Lambeth poor are a remarkable example of a survival of real old country ways and country feelings,' Edward wrote, 'a great simplicity and a great deal of sense and unspoilt care for the place in which, and the walls under which, they have lived. There are still oddities of dress among them and when the Taits came to live here the women still wore the long hanging ringlets which had passed away elsewhere. Many have lived here 30 or 40 years in the same little houses. But now the little houses and little people are passing away and huge factories fill "the Element with poisoned steam".'

This was not the end of Edward's activities that summer. His youngest brother, Charles, with whom he had had little contact over the years, died after a short illness, and he went to the funeral in North Wales. He attended the Governing Body of Charterhouse School in July, and in the same month presided over a meeting of the Society of Antiquaries. He celebrated the Quingentenary of Winchester College and in his sermon made a touching reference to the death of Martin, 15 years before. In August the whole family, with the exception of Fred, who was in Greece, went to Switzerland for a month, but Edward returned home early in September to attend the debate on the Second Reading of the Home Rule Bill in the House of Lords.

'The seats were absolutely full, not another peer could have been seated. There was a thick body of them standing between the rail of the Throne and the Woolsack. The peeresses' gallery was quite full and the dresses most rich. The strangers' gallery full to the top and all the ambassadors. There were 20 Bishops. Lord Cranbrook spoke with the utmost fire. The Bishop of Ripon really held the House captive with his moderation, his happy quotations, his wit and perfect skill. Lord Salisbury was very fine. The voting was tremendous – the wretched 41, so many of them Gladstone's new creations, and the other side 419... The majority of 34 which passed the Home Rule Bill in the House of Commons was therefore put under wraps. No-one knows what Gladstone will do next. No-one seems to mind.'

On September 17 at Addington he was very relieved that there had been so much rain during the night, the first for many weeks. 'No season has in my life been like this. The grass is brown everywhere amd has grown so little that cattle cannot be sold, for no-one has any grass for them. Some fine trees have their heads quite bare while the rest is green – new catkins have come out on hazels and there are roses and red haws on the bushes at the same time. Honeysuckle is again in flower. The sunsets have been too magnificent – burning red in flaring waves, while the sky has been covered with the most delicate white threads against the purest pale azure. Horses seem all to crawl till they get to some ground where there is a breath of air. Rabbits do not appear at all by day. The swallows are beginning to muster.'

At the end of October Edward delivered his Charge, *Fishers of Men*, to the Diocese of Canterbury in his Third Visitation. His indomitable friend, the Duchess of Bedford, had had a strong hand in its composition, taking out everything that 'offended her finest female sense'. The Charge was also given at Ashford, Maidstone and Croydon. His characteristic hopefulness, his view of the great position and opportunities of the Church, even in time of danger to her establishment, was never more marked, and everybody who heard him was both impressed and uplifted. It may be regarded as Edward's last will and testament to the Church he loved so much and served so faithfully. It covered a number of important subjects, the Parish Council Bills, Christian Socialism, spiritual power, modern devotionalism and finished with an indignant outburst against Roman Catholicism and 'fingering the trinkets of Rome'.

On the day her father was in Canterbury, Maggie delivered her third lecture to an audience of 100 working men in Croydon. The subject was 'The Indirect Effect of Strikes' and for an hour afterwards she was plied with questions, some foolish, some complicated, by Socialist workmen, but they were all good-natured. One of them finished up by saying,' Whether we agree or not, Miss Benson has answered us fairly and squarely.' They asked her to return with another lecture when she was free of other commitments. 'The Croydon Socialists! Isn't it a triumph!' Minnie crowed in a letter to Arthur. Maggie and Fred went off to Athens in November for five months. 'How shall we get through it and not get hardened with such absences,' Edward wondered.

Fred's *Six Common Things*, a book of short stories, was published towards the end of the year. He had written them hastily in Greece, after *Dodo* had been accepted. The book was published by Osgood McIlvaine, a rather obscure firm, and it slipped quietly into oblivion. But Edward read it and in December wrote to Maggie, 'I like his "commonplaces" immensely, all but Mrs Naseby. I shouldn't care to read some of them aloud, and he has kept clear of suggesting that you should cry. Tell him I'm always thinking about him. What is his exact work just now? Thank him for his letter.' He could not write to Fred himself then because his arm had developed rheumatism and it was necessary to ration letters severely. 'As people who have to control their expenses begin with their subscriptions, so I have left off letters of affection and friendship,' he told her.

On November 18 Hugh was 22 years old. 'Most thankful to God for his healthy development of spirit and the sweet way in which life for the Church is opening upon him,' Edward noted with satisfaction.

Edward showed his interest in the working classes by visiting the Working Men's College in February, 1894, and distributing certificates of proficiency to the students. He told them of his friendship with Charles Kingsley, who had been associated with the College, and how he had also heard of its progress from F.D. Maurice, whose great name was a perpetual inspiration in the work. And he was pleased to find that Plato's combination of physical and intellectual excellence as an indispensable element of education had been adopted by the College. 'Colonists,' he said, 'frequently implore me to provide clergy who are not mere scholars and students, but men who can also ride, swim, play tennis and cricket.'

A great deal of Edward's time was devoted to the cause of church schools. He spoke on the subject at the annual meeting of the Canterbury Diocesan Education Society and later, in June, at a meeting of the National Society, urging on the clergy the great necessity of being constant and regular in visiting their schools, and he quoted some remarkable statistics which proved that with the decline in religion in the schools of Victoria (Australia) there had been a moral deterioration in the character of the people.

The organisation for the diffusion of Church knowledge, initiated in 1893, developed healthily in the years that followed. It had met with a warm and enthusiastic response and Edward was determined that it should not disappear without trace, especially as the Disestablishment measure was about to surface. But there were possible dangers in the movement's development – one, that a Church Party in the House of Commons would be a dangerous innovation; so would a political party in the Church. Resistance to measures designed to separate Church from the State should not be an arbitrary rallying to some battle-cry, but an intelligent resistance of Churchmen to what they considered an unnatural and undesired divorce. At a meeting held at Lambeth on May 5, 1894, it was decided that the campaign should concentrate on Church people carrying on personal conversations in their own neighbourhood; the diffusion of a knowledge of the facts and truths about the Church by leaflets; the creation of an Intelligence Department to circulate true information through the Press; and the holding of public meetings. These were carried out by a Committee of Laymen representing the Provinces of Canterbury and York, aided by a Ladies' Central Committee and large General Committees. There was to be a Church Committee in every parish. 'It will be a large business if God prosper our work,' Edward wrote, and it seemed that God did approve for within a year over 5,000 parishes each had a committee in full working order.

Edward was concerned lest this new Church Knowledge organisation should interfere with the valuable work of the Church Defence Institution, and finally, in 1896, there was an amalgamation which Edward brought about after endless meetings and private interviews. The composite body was known as 'The Central Church Committee for Church Defence and Church Instruction'. In time its activities grew less onerous. The Church walked warily in times of quiet, but the Committee was there at hand to walk boldly in times of trouble.

Welsh Disestablishment reared its head again in March when in the Queen's Speech it was stated that an Evicted Tenants' Bill was to take precedence over all other measures. This pleased the Irish party and Lord Swansea who, in a meandering speech, said that the Church was doing more harm than good in Wales. Lord Rosebery, the Prime Minister, was also woolly and imprecise in answering a question about the future of the Home Rule Bill, and the whole session was one of muddle and indecision. Edward could only sigh and wish that all his hard work in drafting Bills and amendments would bear sweeter fruit in the future.

On returning home Edward drew up a Manifesto on Disestablishment, signed by all the Bishops, against the Welsh Suspensory Bill and protesting against the dismemberment of the Church of England. It was respectfully received by the leading papers, a novel departure from their usual practice of damning with faint praise. Then there was the Deceased Wife's Sister Bill to fight. The Second Reading was defeated in the Lords by 129 votes to 120, which was reasonably satisfactory, though not conclusively so.

Ember Week was a very happy time for Edward. He had the wonderful happiness of ordaining his own son deacon in Croydon Parish Church. Hugh had passed First Class in the Universities Preliminary Examination. 'His pre-eminent interest in theology,' Edward wrote, 'and the singleness and eagerness of his character, give us beautiful hopes of his humble service to God and the poor. He begins indeed among the lowest at Hackney Wick in the Eton Mission. We are unspeakably indebted to Dean Vaughan in training our Hugh. When you multiply such a debt as this by the number of men for whom he has done the same, I doubt whether the Church owes so much to anyone at all. What is greater than the formation of Ministers for the spreading of the Kingdom?'

CHAPTER TWENTY-ONE

IN the Autumn of 1894 the question of English Church policy in relation to the Church of Rome began to assume a tremendous importance to Edward who, as chief official of the Reformed Church, stood in a unique and delicate position to the Church of Rome. On one side he was pressed to enlist the co-operation of Romanists in England in many social questions, but on the other he was bound to listen to the large section of English Churchmen who were vehement advocates of complete isolation from Romanists, whom they regarded as traitorous and unscrupulous foes; and Edward was urged to denounce their actions at every opportunity. There was the desire for Reunion on the part of a great number of people who abhorred fundamentalism, and against that the fear of the threat of Reunion by the ancient and oppressed Churches of the East who rejected the falsification of doctrine of the Rome they knew. Such was the position, official, social and ecclesiastical, in which Edward found himself, and it became imperative for him to consider afresh his former predelictions and principles in the greater debate.

Edward himself had from boyhood felt deeply antagonistic towards what he considered the errors of doctrine and the arrogant claims of Rome. Principally he was moved by doctrinal questions, feeling a peculiar horror towards rendering the Virgin Mary part of the homage due only to the Lord. He was occasionally heard to mutter that he could almost believe that Rome was Antichrist, and he said of Roman reasoning that it produced the stupefaction of reality in him. 'It seems to belong to a world where reasoning is a mere sequence of words, and the Bible has another Gospel in it.' The influence of Bishop Wordsworth, a noted opponent of the spirit and teaching of Rome, had greatly influenced him in his formative years, and his own historical studies, especially the life of Cyprian, served to confirm the total absence of foundation of the Roman claim. But he was more concerned to establish the true historic position of the Church of England – of her Evangelic doctrine with its English and not Roman ritual, of her Apostolic Ministry, of her peculiar mission, and of the unsurpassed knowledge and the keen insight of her Reformers.

He denied that he feared Rome. 'The ancient Church of England is with us,' he said. 'I do not fear that the Italian Mission will make anything of our clergy or of our people.' Yet he always stressed the necessity of a constant resistance to Roman propaganda. He was amused that when he hesitated to be associated with a charity, or to speak at a social function, the promoters always said, 'We hope to get Cardinal Manning.' 'Just as,' Edward pointed out, 'when the dog won't eat his dinner we call out "Puss, puss!"' He was also amused, though irritated, when the question of who took precedence, he or Cardinal Vaughan, came up.

Some of his opinions about the Roman Catholic Church were harsh, unwaverinng and, indeed, ungenerous, but Edward never changed or concealed them. When he was appointed to the Primacy he refused to send a formal notification of the fact to any member of the Roman Church, and he declined to send the Pope a present on the occasion of his Jubilee, even though such an act of personal kindness might do something to heal the schism between the two Churches. To Canon Mason, who suggested the idea, he wrote, 'It is the Pope's business to eat dust and ashes, not mine to decorate him.'

Yet Edward did have a deep-rooted desire for a true and enduring reunion of Christendom, and for that reason he shunned any hasty compromise or shallow patching-up that would stand in the way of genuine peace. 'The aspiration after unity,' he declared, 'must take account of the Eastern Churches, of non-Episcopal Reformed Churches on the continent, and among the multiplying populations of the New World as well as of the Christianity of Asia and Africa,' – a vast task indeed, a dream whose fulfilment was infinitely far off, but which he worked to build, slowly and surely.

The idea of practical rapprochement between the two Churches was brought very prominently before him by Lord Halifax in 1894. Halifax was a rather undistinguished figure generally, but passionate in his desire to see Reunion achieved. He was the son of the first Viscount Halifax, a former Chancellor of the Exchequer and Secretary for India, and father of the future Viceroy of India, Foreign Secretary (noted for his appeasement of Hitler in Germany), and Ambassador to the USA. Edward had met the Viscount when he was President of the English Church Union and had liked him very much as a truly religious man, though he thought that in the aims and tactics of the ECU there was something very far from 'heavenliness'.

Halifax had often discussed the possibility of Reunion with a French priest, the Abbé Fernand Portal, later a Professor in a Theological Seminary at Cahors. They agreed that the decree of Papal Infallibility was a serious obstacle to any reconciliation, but if both sides desired it, the prospect was by no means hopeless. The Abbé published a pamphlet in which he reluctantly concluded that English Orders were invalid, though it was written in a most conciliatory spirit. Another theological writer, the Abbé Duchesne, came to the opposite conclusion and stated that the Roman Church had never condemned the Anglican Ordinations, and that the reordination of Anglican priests was a mere question of practice and would solve the problem. This was followed by a letter to the Abbé Portal from Cardinal Bourret attacking the position of the Anglican Church, and this led to the Bishop Salisbury publishing a letter endeavouring to explain the Anglican position and to correct some of the errors into which the Abbé and Cardinal Bourret had fallen.

This toing and froing of arguments and explanations could have continued as long as the patience of the writers lasted, but matters were brought to a head in the summer of 1894, when the Abbé Portal himself came to England, and Lord Halifax wrote to Edward asking if he might bring the Abbé to see him so that he could judge for himself the very favourable dispositions entertained abroad about the Church of England and the great desire of the Romans to know more about it. 'Life is so short,' he wrote, 'and the divisions of Christendom are so disastrous to souls, that any little thing we can do to become better known to one another is a thing one thanks God for.'

Edward agreed, though with reservations, to see the Abbé in Lord Halifax's company; and the two men paid a courtesy visit to Addington for a 'working breakfast'. The question of reunion with Rome was only alluded to in a general way; there were no references to any practical measures. Edward was careful to avoid any compromising statements; his view from the first seems to have been that an attempt was being made from Rome, working through the genuine enthusiasm of Halifax and the Abbé, to compromise him as the official chief of the Anglican Church, and he was determined not to utter a word that could be construed as an apology for the Anglican position. He would not compromise the status of the English Church, he would not stand at the bar of Rome, he would not give up the truth won back after a long struggle.

While the Abbé Portal was staying with Lord Halifax he met the Archbishop of York, the Bishop of Peterborough, the Bishop of Lincoln and Edward's friend Westcott; and he attended services at several churches, mainly of the High Church persuasion. Then the Abbé went to Rome, where his pamphlet had been studied with great interest, and he was received by Cardinal Rampolla, the Secretary of State at the Vatican, and by the Pope himself. To the Pope the Abbé suggested that a letter from him to Canterbury and York might open communication and lead the way to meetings between Anglican and Roman theologians on the question of Orders, and discussions on other points of difference. The Pope expresssed interest, and Cardinal Rampolla gave the Abbé to understand that his letter was to be taken as an indirect step towards ascertaining the feelings of the English Archbishops. He also told the Abbé that the Pope would ask the Abbé Duchesne to prepare a memorandum about his views on the subject of English Orders. The Abbé was so impressed with the importance of the Cardinal's letter that he hurried back to England to see Lord Halifax. Edward was staying in a house lent to him by Dr. Warre, Headmaster of Eton, near Dulverton in Somerset, when he received a letter from Lord Halifax saying, 'I have had a very important communication from the Abbé Portal which I think will both please and astonish your Grace very much. I have some very wonderful things to tell your Grace.' Halifax did not mention that he would be accompanied by the Abbé Portal, and if Edward had known the nature of the communication which was to be made to him it is doubtful whether he would have agreed to the meeting.

The three men met at Dr. Warre's house, with Canon Mason present to take notes. The Abbé could only speak French, and his joyful news, which turned out to be not so joyful, was frequently interrupted by Edward for explanation and comments. The story was not as straightforward as Edward and Lord Halifax had believed it was going to be. The Abbé had given the Pope a most enthusiastic report on what he had seen in England – that the Church was at the head of the intellectual movement, that there was a great feeling for union and that many people were praying for it. He described the English services and ritual and other features of English Church life, and waited breathlessly for what the Pope had to say in response. He was overjoyed when the 85-year-old Pope said in an impassioned way, 'How gladly I would say me *Nunc Dimittis* if I could make the smallest beginning to such a reunion!' Then he promised to write the proposed letter to the English Archbishops. 'Come back to the Vatican in two days' time when it will be ready,' he promised. But the letter was not ready. The Pope's advisers had persuaded him that it would be incautious for him to write in person; and he had been given less enthusiastic accounts of the state of the English Church than the Abbé had provided. Instead, it was decided that Cardinal Rampolla should write a letter to the Abbé which he was not to publish, but which he might show to whom it was concerned; and he was told that the Pope intended to commission the Abbé Duchesne to examine at length the question of Anglican Orders. If the Cardinal's letter was well received the Pope would then write in person.

So that was the joyful news and Edward did not think much of it. The Abbé could only express his disappointment that his original plan had been reversed, but he insisted that a great step had been taken nevertheless.

Edward was critical from the beginning. He said that the Romans were trying to commit him, when the Pope had not committed himself, that Rampolla was but a Minister whose words could be disavowed, while it would be impossible for him to employ an agent whom he could disavow. It was the duty of Rome to take the first step, and he would be put at a disadvantage if he wrote to the Pope when the Pope had not written to him. Edward then brought up every objection he could think of in order not to have to give way an inch; and he finished up with the point that Cardinal Rampolla's letter (which he had not yet seen) was only written to a private person, and that he could only take notice of it accordingly.

The arguments on that point alone lasted half an hour, and it was obvious that Edward was getting tired, especially as everything was conducted in French; and Canon Mason felt that the Archbishop was not doing himself justice.

When at last the letter was produced Edward read it and said wearily that it was a nice letter but very general. It contained several expressions offensive to Anglicans, and Infallibility was by no means the only thing that stood in the way of Reunion. A state of mutual misunderstanding had been reached, so the Canon took the two guests out for a walk until lunchtime while Edward had a short rest.

Lord Halifax and the Abbé were gloomy as they strolled about the grounds, feeling that Edward had been unnecessarily obstructive. Canon Mason tried to explain that it was only his honesty that made the Archbishop seem to be against the Abbé's proposal, that he would not allow anybody to give the Pope the impression that Reunion would be easier than it would. But the meeting had been a profound disappointment, and Edward's distrust seemed to his visitors to be exaggerated. In view of some recent utterances of Cardinal Vaughan, who had become Archbishop of Westminster in 1892, and the subsequent publication of the Papal Bull condemning English Orders, Edward considered himself justified in feeling that it would not be prudent to write the suggested letter to the Pope. He thought he was being entrapped into committing himself to some statement that might damage the Church of England; and the meeting ended on a cool note.

Lord Halifax, however, was not one to give up easily. Two weeks later he wrote an impassioned letter to Edward asking him if he would write a private letter that he, Halifax, could take to Rome, a letter that would speak of peace and union; and he enclosed a letter he had sketched out that he hoped the Pope would reply to. His arguments, born of his intense desire for Reunion, were persuasive, and he even went so far as to remind Edward that Dante had assigned the lowest place to those who, having a great opportunity, refused to take it; but Edward was not to be drawn further into the intricate affair. Even after Halifax had visited Addington he could not be budged. 'Halifax is like a solitary player of chess,' he wrote, 'and wants to make all the moves on the board himself on both sides.' He decided to take no notice of Cardinal Vaughan's speech in which he insisted on the necessity of absolute and unqualified submission on the part of the English Church to the Church of Rome before reconciliation could be thought of. Such a declaration would put an end to anything that might have been projected, but Edward decided to close it in silence, and as far as he was concerned the rest, for a long time, would be silence.

But he had not reckoned with Lord Halifax's persistence. In December he wrote to Edward, urging him again to write a letter that might open the door the slightest bit ajar to a favourable view of Anglicanism by Rome. Edward's reply was as uncompromising as ever. 'I really cannot accept your letter (the one Halifax proposed to take to the Pope). It omits safeguards which I had used. It inserts phrases which would compromise me extremely in England, and which do not represent my views. I am afraid that you have lived for years so exclusively with one set of thinkers, and entered so entirely into the usages of one class of churchmen, that you have not before you the state of religious feeling and activity in England with the completeness which anyone attempting to adjust the relations between Churches ought to have. It is impossible for me to accept private assertions as to what is going on. It is equally impossible for me to adopt the part of a secret diplomatist among the Councils of the Church.'

Edward could not have been more blunt, and with that Lord Halifax had to be content. And he was content until the following March, in 1895, after he had delivered an address at Bristol on the subject of Corporate Reunion, a copy of which he sent to the Bishops and Archbishops. He received another off-putting letter from Edward, who insisted again that it would be impossible for him to frame or approve any answer to a question which had not yet been asked; the only concession he would make was to point out the gain that would accrue to Christendom if the Church of Rome would take pains to understand the history and principles of the Church of England; and he promised that his attitude would be favourable towards any genuine and generous attempt to understand the facts of the Anglican position. Beyond that he would not go. Rome had to admit the possibility of error on her part and admit as a fact the genuineness of English Orders.

In April, 1895, staying with Minnie at the Villa Palmieri, he met Halifax face to face to hear about the latter's interviews with the Pope, Rampolla, Duchesne, Vaughan and others; and there seemed to be a chink of light in the darkness – a chink that was extinguished two days later when the Pope's Apostolic Letter appeared. It showed no recognition of even the existence of a Church of England.

Halifax continued to press his case, polite but insistent; Edward continued to stonewall, polite but stubborn. In his speech at the Diocesan Conference in the summer of 1895, and in a Pastoral Letter which he wrote in September, he was bitter against a 'certainly friendly advance made from a foreign Church to the people of England without reference or regard to the Church of England, apparently in total ignorance of any Church with any history or claims, and offered this reunion with a parade of methods of worship and of rewards of worship which was totally alien to the feelings of a nation which had become readers of the Bible, and who could never admit that such things had any attractions for them. It is the duty of the laity as well as the clergy to preserve in purity a loyalty to the Faith and practices which characterise the Reformation.'

The Pope eventually appointed a Commission to investigate the subject of Anglican Orders, which was a step in the right direction. At least he had recognised that there was an Anglican Church, but unfortunately the course taken was not one which Lord Halifax and the Abbé Portal had recommended because the Commission was composed exclusively of Roman theologians. The reason for the change in emphasis was undoubtedly due to the malign influence of Cardinal Vaughan. The Commission finished its sittings in June, 1896, and in September the *Apostolicae Curae* was published, and, as was only to be expected, English Orders were declared entirely null and void.

Edward, assisted by a number of Bishops, was working at a draft reply, but his involvement in the whole grave and delicate controversy was brought to an end by his death in October, 1896. His last words on the subject were noble and unequivocal. 'Our Holy Orders are identical with those of the whole Catholic Church. They are in origin, continuity, matter, form, intention, and all that belongs to them, identical accordingly with those of the Church of Rome, except in one modern point of subjection to the Pope. There is not a break anywhere in our orders, sacraments, creeds, scriptures, spiritual gifts, in all that compacts and frames to "holiness" of the "one Catholic Apostolic Church" of the ages.'

To show Edward's desire for a unity which would be a unity in truth, not in mere uniformity, the words with which he ended his book on Cyprian could not be more fitting. 'A true unity has to take account equally of Christ's Prayer and of Christ's Laws; of the Prayer which he offered over the Sacrifice of Himself, and of the Laws which our Creator impressed on the intellectual existence of our race. One centre we have, but the approaches to it are infinite.'

CHAPTER TWENTY-TWO

H UGH had drifted into the idea of taking Orders as the line of least resistance, though when he started to study theology seriously he discovered it was the one subject he really cared for. At first he only looked forward to being a country clergyman with a beautiful garden, an exquisite choir and a sober bachelor existence, though such a shallow ambition eventually transmuted to something more noble.

The Dean Vaughan whom Edward praised so highly was the Dean of Llandaff and the Master of the Temple, formerly the Headmaster of Harrow, and an Evangelical by training and temperament. He had collected about himself an informal band of young men to whom he gave a daily lecture. They lived in lodgings and attended the Cathedral services, but there was no regular discipline, and Hugh was very happy at Llandaff. One of his dreams was eventually to set up a small community, on the lines of Nicholas Ferrar's at Little Gidding, to be run on devotional and mystical lines. Hugh had few urges toward a pastoral life and his community was to exist as a fortress of quiet for the encouragement of its members' individual impulses; discipline and action were not to be the main considerations. In a way his ideas were a throwback to the scheme which his father and Westcott had planned when they were schoolboys – an institution in which married priests and their families could lead a common life with common devotions; though in Hugh's case it was not likely that there would be much chance of the inmates expressing their independence.

Hackney Wick, where Hugh began his clerical work, was a large and poor parish which had been adopted by Eton as the venue for its Mission. Money from the school was poured into the parish, a magnificent church was built and a clergy house and clubs were established, all under the direction of St. Clair Donaldson, who became Archbishop of Brisbane. Hugh's work was principally to help run the boys' clubs, talking with the boys and joining in their games of football and cricket; not a congenial occupation for someone of Hugh's artistic nature, whose mind was full of poetry and mysticism. He did not have a robust interest in the young, although he could be frank and charming to them, but he became more and more convinced that the way to lead boys to religion was not to share their amusements, but to create a strong central nucleus of Christian instruction and worship. His time, apart from his clubs, was very full: visiting the sick, producing childen's plays, helping at a ladies' settlement, conducting funerals and taking services; and he gradually came to the conclusion that the adjuncts of worship were not adequate to awaken the sense of the personal and intimate relation between man and God. He needed to fit some definite form, rite and symbol to religious emotion, and Confession was one form of Catholic doctrine he thought about a great deal, though he wondered whether that and other rites might become invested with mechanical sanctity instead of being the symbols of grace. Hugh was ordained as a priest in 1895; and he then made a full confession before a clergyman, thus divesting himself of the last shackles of evangelical thought. But it was not until after Edward's death that he began to consider becoming a Roman Catholic.

Maggie, who was 28 in 1893, began to suffer from rheumatism and her doctor advised that a winter abroad in the sun might help. So she travelled out to Athens first to be with Fred and later to go with him to Egypt. She enjoyed Athens tremendously and became very popular with members of the Legation, with Fred's archaeological friends and with the Queen of Greece, who asked her if the English aristocracy behaved as oddly as they did in *Dodo*. In Athens she occupied herself with sketching, going on expeditions, attending lectures at the Archaeological School, and taking lessons in German and modern Greek.

And while Maggie was beavering away at her various occupations Fred was falling in love with Regie Lister, a younger brother of Lord Ribblesdale, and a Secretary at the Legation; a charming and effeminate young man who had a genius for friendship. They undertook expeditions together round Athens, wandered in the Peloponnese for three or four days at a time, sleeping in indescribably dirty inns and searching for the Temple at Bassae.

Lord Alfred Douglas stayed with Fred in his rooms for about a week and they found each other pleasant and entertaining. Fred met him again at Luxor, and with Robert Hichens, author of *The Green Carnation*, and Reginald Turner making a vivacious quartet, they travelled up the Nile together, quoting bits of *Dorian Gray* and having a lively and cheerful time.

In January, 1894, Maggie and Fred went to Egypt and up the Nile as far as Aswan. At the bazaar they saw Sudanese, Nubians and Bedouins. 'They are the most beautiful people,' Maggie wrote to her mother, 'with such a step and great wild fearless eyes – the little children are so perfectly beautiful too – you would rejoice in their bare limbs – they don't mostly wear anything except a strip of leather and beads – sometimes not that – but you get to regard dress as a European prejudice.' But in spite of the excitement and beauty of Egypt, Maggie decided that she preferred the green fields and grey skies of England, and began to make plans for what she would do when she returned home. 'Do you think I could lecture in London?' she asked Minnie. 'I want to finish the illustrations of my book, then do you think I might undertake a short course, or would it interfere too much with dinner-parties and London in general? I ought to settle down.' Maggie had taken on Nellie's social duties, but found them more irksome than her more placid sister had done.

After a summer at home she was back in Luxor by Christmas 1984 and was warmly greeted by the Arabs she had known. Her own special donkey-boy almost wept to see her again. She took up excavating at Luxor seriously early in 1895 and it became her absorbing interest for the next two years. She got permission from the Ministry of Antiquities to excavate the Temple of Mut in the horse-shoe lake at Karnak (though the Museum of Gizeh could claim anything it liked out of the finds). She wrote a book about her work in conjunction with her new best friend, Nettie Gourlay, who joined her to help with the work. Fred was there too, spending the winters in Egypt in between visits to Greece, working for the Egyptian Exploration Fund. Greece had cast a spell on him that transported him into the dawn of the civilised world, but Egypt had a sinister mystery that appealed to another side of him, his imagination ever ready to be seduced by the malevolence behind the ordinary. Every time they went up the Nile in a post-boat Fred found a quiet corner and wrote his Greek story, *The Vintage*, which appeared in 1898, while the smell of Egypt was working on his subconscious mind and making ready for *The Image in the Sand*, which was to lie dormant until 1905. He tried to forget *The Rubicon*, which Methuen had published in 1894, and which had earned him the most scathing criticism any novel could ever have had. It was a bad book, Fred was the first to agree – its plot preposterous and the characters paper-thin, but it was no worse than scores of others of its type. The success of *Dodo* was the cause of the critics' savage onslaught on an innocuous little effort, that deserved only pity, then oblivion. *The Judgement Books* was the only other book of Fred's published in Edward's lifetime, and that was a failure too. 'The decline of Mr Benson continues,' said the *Saturday Review*. But Fred was not discouraged. He worked steadily on *Limitations* and *The Babe, B.A.*, neither of which exhausted him.

Apart from her rheumatism Maggie suffered from congestion of the lungs and was often laid low with the sort of depression that Edward would have recognised. She had to avoid chills and fatigue, but in spite of her disabilities she crammed her days at Karnak with unceasing activities. The English archaeologists were willing helpers in deciphering inscriptions and Fred was given the job of general supervisor, responsible for arranging where the cleared earth should be put and making a plan of the temple to scale. At sunset, when the day's work was over, Maggie worked at her book, *The Venture of Rational Faith*, or wrote her animal stories, and she, Fred and Nettie Gourlay played picquet, and games with pencil and paper. The culmination of the exploration was finding the image of Sen-mut himself, also a superb Saite head, a statue of Rameses of the Exodus and a scribe of the eighteenth dynasty. Maggie was also instrumental in solving a 4,000-year-old mystery. She found that the name of Sen-mut and his deeds as temple architect had been defaced on hieroglyphic inscriptions and the name of King Tuthmosis III, nephew and successor of Queen Hatshepsut, had been superimposed. On one tablet the deletion was not quite thorough and it was discovered that Sen-mut was but a common man, with no ancestral records. He had himself confessed to an affair with the Queen, thus causing a great scandal and so, when both he and the Queen were dead, all mention of him and his achievements had to be erased. A later theory about Sen-mut maintains that it was the Queen herself who had his inscriptions defaced because he was getting too ambitious. He put little statues of himself in her temple, and even built one of his own next to hers.

At this time some letters from home made them uneasy. Minnie was worried about Edward's health – he was overworking, as he had been for years, but was getting more tired more often; he had attacks of breathlessness if he did anything very strenuous and had a sense of oppression in his chest. He was looking his age, his face more lined and a stoop more pronounced. But his doctor's report was not alarming and Minnie's fears gradually slipped away. She was always a worrier, she confessed.

Maggie continued to find exciting objects – some huge lion-headed statues, and baboons crouching in a small chamber in the temple. Fred remained an eager assistant when he was not busy with his own work for the Egyptian Exploration Fund. He and Maggie became the greatest of friends. He declared that when she was really well he would advertise himself as a companion to an invalid lady. 'I will recommend him highly,' Maggie told her mother.

Arthur, a prosperous and well regarded Housemaster at Eton, suffered periodic depressions and announced that he could not stand the work for another term, but he always did; and in addition produced several volumes of verse and book after book of meditative essays that became very popular. With Hugh at Hackney Wick, Fred was the only one of Edward's sons who had not settled down to a proper career. Archaeology fizzled out when his grants from Cambridge dried up and he failed to get a Fellowship for any of the work he sent in. The Law, the Church and the Army were obviously all impossible for the dilettante Fred and in desperation Edward suggested education. 'Why not become an Inspector of Schools?' he said. Fred gave a half-hearted assent, privately and stubbornly registering his determination to become a writer. He collected a number of testimonials from his tutors and sent them off with his application form, but the education office was not impressed and decided to carry on without Fred's help. He was not cast down, and Edward could not at the moment think of any other position towards which he could direct his errant son.

By March, 1896, Edward had almost come to the end of his work on Cyprian, and was sending his final notes to the University Press. It struck him that he had been working at the book for at least 30 years. 'I pray God,' he wrote, 'bless this Cyprian to the good of his Church. If he bless it not I have spent half my life in building hay and stubble and the fire must consume it. But, please God, may it last.' He added later, 'If ever it sees the light many will think it a very odd book. Folks are edified in such different ways. But it has edified me, which is what I began it for.'

At the end of March he went to the Villa Palmieri, with Minnie and Lucy. He went to a service in the Roman Catholic church and was impressed in spite of himself. 'Why,' he wondered, 'when the Church of Rome has services in which Christ alone is set forth, so visibly crucified among us, without a syllable that is not Christian and Scriptural, no sound but of Christ and His Sacrifice for us – why is it she is elsewhere given over to a lingering paganism and to worship as frivolous as that of the rosary? And to doctrines as antichristian as the infallibility?'

The first reference he made to his breathing difficulties was after a ride to Monte Senario and back, when he was relieved not to have had any problems. The family returned home on April 24, Edward spoiling for battle in the House of Lords and at Convocation. His days continued to be full of speeches, conferences, debates, dinners, confirmations, and visitors, and his tiredness at the end of a long day was more apparent. But 'I walk better and am better on such a glorious day', he wrote on a sunny day in May.

On May 20 he went with Convocation to Windsor. The Queen had said that she could not attempt to read her address but she made a neat and lively extempore speech. She sent for Edward to see her in her own room afterwards and spoke very tenderly of Prince Henry of Battenberg, married to her daughter Princess Beatrice. The Prince had died at sea of fever caught in the Ashanti compaign. The Princess cried a great deal and said she was going to dedicate her future only to the Queen. 'She is certainly a brave woman,' said Edward, 'and cleverness doesn't matter in the long run.'

One Monday in June was one of the gloomiest days that Edward could remember. The Education Bill was dropped by the Government. It would have been a really great measure. But even with a majority of 274 in the Commons they could not carry it because they had wasted their time on small affairs which they imagined would be non-contentious – reckoning without Sir William Harcourt, former leader of the Lower House, whose lukewarm support of the Bill led to Lord Rosebery's resignation in 1896. The Deceased Wife's Sister Bill, which Edward opposed, was passed by 142 to 113 votes. 'I spoke like waving a pocket handkerchief from a sinking craft,' said Edward. His efforts were useless against those of the Prince of Wales, who was in favour of the Bill, the only piece of legislation he had ever taken an interest in, and who persuaded several new peers to vote for it. 'Balfour,' Edward went on, 'has really collapsed – a triple stroke for the Conservatives and the Church. He is interested in everything but politics. He reads no papers, does not know what is the business of the House when he gets there, and takes no pains to cultivate his "boys".' There was also trouble over the proposed amalgamation of the Central Church Council and the Church Defence Institution. It was not until the following day that Edward cheered up slightly when he remembered that it was the 37th anniversary of his wedding. '37 years of blessings with two such piercing sorrows – such noble children – such goodly works allowed and assigned – such blank inadequacies. *O Bone Domine.*'

In July the House of Lords passed the Third Reading of the Deceased Wife's Sister Bill by a larger majority than it had the Second Reading and Edward, forced finally to admit defeat, foresaw a vast change in the minds of the Clergy towards Disestablishment on the grounds that Church principles could not live in association with the modern English state. 'We work henceforth for its disassociation, it is now the only freedom,' they would say.

The Queen held a Garden Party at Buckingham Palace on July 13. 4,000 people were present, and as it was very hot the silk in umbrellas and parasols heaved gracefully through the grounds like the waves of the sea. The Prince of Wales, after glancing Edward's way several times, approached him and held out his hand diffidently. 'Will you shake hands with me?' he said. Edward replied, '*Vicisti,*' at which the Prince laughed heartily but without comprehension.

On July 14, his birthday, Edward started a Committee for caring for the religious condition of deaf mutes.

Towards the end of the summer of 1896 Fred left Egypt for Athens then went on holiday to Capri, an island that so enchanted him that he began to form plans for another and perhaps much longer visit. Maggie also left Egypt for a cure at Aix-les-Bains, but in August all the Bensons were together at Addington: Arthur was going to Scotland, but called at home first; Hugh had a holiday from the Mission; and Maggie was deeply involved in writing up the results of her digging at Karnak, and writing frequent letters to Nettie Gourlay, her 'dearest', falling out and making up again as lovers do. For a few days the family was united for the last time, with no clouds over the summer skies. All was harmony, peace and nostalgia.

CHAPTER TWENTY-THREE

EDWARD had decided to devote part of his annual holiday to a visit, partly personal and partly official, to Ireland, being anxious to give the Church there, which had passed through such difficulties in consequence of being deprived of her property by the Act of 1869, the encouragement and support of his presence. On September 17 Edward and Minnie crossed over from Holyhead to Kingstown. The weather was tempestuous and the travellers felt the full brunt of the storm. The boat was nearly two hours late. Lord Plunkett, Archbishop of Dublin, was their host and they stayed with him at Old Connaught, on the borders of County Wicklow, spending the first two days sightseeing. They travelled to Dublin by rail and on September 20 Edward made an eloquent appeal at a public meeting held in the Metropolitan Hall in Dublin, on behalf of the Kildare Cathedral Restoration Fund. On Sunday he attended divine service in Christchurch Cathedral, and in the afternoon he preached in the National Cathedral of St. Patrick, and on Monday he visited the Church of Ireland Training Centre in Kildare Place and made visits to several places of interest, including the Library where they saw the Book of Kells. On Tuesday he gave a sermon at the re-opening of St. Brigid's Cathedral in Kildare. For 250 years the building had been an unsightly and neglected ruin, but had been restored at a cost of over £10,000. After the ceremony he and Minnie were walking back to the Deanery when there was a sudden burst of wind and rain. Edward had no umbrella and Minnie hastily opened her own and tried to shelter them both. Edward ducked. 'You may put out my eye, dearest, if you please,' he said, 'but don't spoil my new hat!'

They stayed with Lord Plunkett until Saturday, then left for Armagh to visit Dr. Alexander, the Archbishop. While they were there, Dr. Alexander's second son died unexpectedly in Norfolk and he had to leave his guest hurriedly. Edward's farewell was tender and touching. He gave the Benediction and kissed the archiepiscopal ring. A week later they were in Londonderry where, replying to an address presented in the Cathedral, Edward expressed his admiration for the courage with which the Church of Ireland had coped with the enormous difficulties of Disestablishment.

He was struck by the peace which prevailed among different-thinking people in Ireland, and trusted that it would continue. During the tour he was in especially good spirits, his many speeches were in his best vein and his conversation at various dinner tables was vivid and lively. He had not had a period of depression for a long time, and the family had noticed and commented on his cheerfulness and gentleness.

On October 8 Edward and Minnie arrived in Belfast for a brief visit as guests of Lady Shaftesbury at Belfast Castle. The next day he managed to pack 3,000 people in a meeting at the Ulster Hall, and when he rose for his last public speech it was the signal for the entire audience to rise and cheer. They were due to leave for England the next day and on the pier at Larne an address was presented to him by the Rector of Larne, read with difficulty under a flaring station light. Edward's reply was charming. 'You must allow me to thank you in the briefest possible terms on behalf of Mrs Benson and myself for your kindness in meeting us at this last moment with such loving words. We have just come from Belfast, where we met with a very cordial reception at the hands of the Irish Church, but I did not expect that we should be carried down to the very shore, and that we should hear an address expressing such affectionate sentiments read before we left Ireland ... I only came to Ireland to enjoy myself, and to re-open that magnificent old Cathedral about which so many memories cling; but all through my visit I have received the greatest kindness and unforgettable hospitality ... I do hope that the future will draw our respective Churches closer and closer. You have learned to live not only in adherence to the principles of your Church, but you have learned to live in peace with all men. Permit me again to thank you for so affectionately bidding us "Goodbye" in such tender terms.'

Edward and Minnie crossed to Stranraer on Friday night, then took the train to Carlisle, where they stayed the night after seeing over the Cathedral; on Saturday they arrived at Hawarden in Cheshire via the midday London and North-west express on a visit to Mr and Mrs Gladstone. They intended to spend Sunday there, hoping to recuperate a little from overwork and over-travel, and expected to be back home on Monday. At Addington only Fred and Maggie had been left and even they drifted off in different directions, visiting friends, leaving Beth as usual to hold the fort. Fred drifted back again to spend another night at home in order to welcome his parents' return.

After warm greetings from the Gladstones, whom they had not seen at Hawarden before, Edward and his host, who had retired from political life in 1894, almost immediately settled down to talk about the Pope's Bull, which had come out while the Bensons were in Ireland. They managed to disagree with the Pope's strictures against Anglican Orders for three hours, both men full of animation and excitement. There was more delightful conversation at dinner and when the Bensons retired for the night Edward was still full of talk; Minnie had never seen him more active or serene. During the night the torrential rains had ended, snow had fallen and revealed Hawarden as a very beautiful place. They went to early Communion in the village church, and after breakfast Edward went upstairs to begin a draft of his reply to the Pope, and was almost late in joining the churchgoers in the hall. Minnie noticed again how well and happy he was looking.

He had to stop frequently on the way to church to recover his breath, but this was not unusual. He was shown his seat next to Mrs Gladstone with Minnie on her other side. Mr Gladstone had stayed at home to avoid the intense cold. Edward smiled when Mrs Gladstone asked him if she should move her husband's hymn-book and shook his head, and he was still smiling as he stood through the Exhortation, though he raised his hand to his eyes as if he were testing his sight, and a deep flush spread over his face. As he knelt for the Absolution his head suddenly sank on to his book and he began to breathe loudly and harshly. Then he seemed to lose consciousness.

Minnie moved across Mrs Gladstone and went to him; others pressed around and a doctor in the congregation tried to discover signs of life. He was carried down the church path to the Rectory and put on a sofa in the library. After several vain attempts to revive him all left the room but Minnie. Later he was arranged in his robes and his hands crossed on his breast. Everyone said how strong and kingly he looked, not a bit as though he were dead, but smiling in his sleep. Mr Gladstone was greatly shocked, but he was able afterwards to say in a firm voice, 'He died like a soldier.'

Fred received a telegram at Addington, and Arthur at Eton, though neither missive said explicitly that Edward was dead. Hugh did know the truth and told Arthur when they met at Euston Station. Fred summoned Maggie, and on Monday they all met at Hawarden. They found Minnie shaken and silent, outwardly self-controlled. Edward's coffin was covered with a magnificent white embroidered pall, later used for Mr Gladstone himself two years later, and was taken to Canterbury Cathedral to await the funeral on Friday, October 16. It left from Sandycroft Station on a bright October day, with early frosts yellowing the woods. All down the line, at the principal stations, clergymen stood bare-headed. Canterbury was reached when the sunshine had given way to darkness and drizzle, and the coffin was taken in a hearse through crowded streets. All that night, and the following day and night, Edward was watched by his friends who had loved him. The coffin rested in the Martyrdom Chapel, and bore only a wreath of white flowers from the Queen and a white cross from the Gladstones. 'I am stunned by the awful news,' the Queen telegraphed to Minnie. 'My heart bleeds for you; but my own sorrow is great, for I was so fond of the dear, kind, excellent Archbishop. A terrible loss to us all.'

In the Cathedral there had been an early celebration of Holy Communion, mainly for family and friends. When the doors were open at midday a great crowd of sorrowing people poured in. At the appointed moment the Bishop of Dover entered the Chapel the coffin was raised on the shoulders of the pall-bearers and carried slowly through the cloisters and in at the West door, round which the space was kept clear by lines of troops to prevent the thousands of people gathered in the bitter wind and rain from creating chaos. The procession seemed never-ending. 400 clergy were followed by Rural Deans, the Mayor and Corporation of Canterbury, Edward's private secretaries, invited Church dignitaries, members of the Houses of Parliament, 30 Bishops, the choir, Canons, Minor and Honorary, the Archbishop of York, the Archbishop of Dublin, and Hugh Benson: then came Edward's coffin, his family, the Duke of York representing the Queen, and representatives of the Prince of Wales, his wife and other members of the Royal Family. At the rear of the procession came the private mourners, who included Edward's domestic chaplains and members of his household. Though the Nonconformist Churches and the Jewish Community were represented there was no sign of a Roman Catholic.

The choir sang the 90th Psalm, and the Dean of Canterbury read the Lesson. Then followed Gounod's *Send out Thy Light and Thy Truth*. The processsion reformed and marched down the nave towards the north-west end of the Cathedral where, beneath the tower, was the open grave. The hymn chosen was '*Quisquis valet numerare*'. The Duke of York laid the Queen's wreath on the coffin, sentences were read by Canon Mason and the committal prayer was offered by the Dean of Winchester. Hugh led the congregation in the Lesser Litany and the Lord's Prayer, and the Archbishop of Dublin said the concluding prayers. The choir, without organ accompaniment, sang 'Thine for Ever, God of Love', a hymn that Edward had joined in barely two hours before his death, at the early service in Hawarden Church. Then came the *Nunc Dimittis*, the Archbishop pronounced the Benediction from the altar, Stainer's sevenfold 'Amen' echoed through the Cathedral, the organist played the 'Dead March' in Saul, and the service was over. Minnie and the family returned to the house of the Bishop of Dover, who had given it up for their use for the day.

Memorial services were held all over the country, as well as on the Continent and in America. A public meeting was held in London soon after the funeral, at which the Prince of Wales was present, to consider what form the Church's memorial should take. It was decided to place a recumbent statue of the Archbishop in Canterbury Cathedral, and devote the balance of the fund to the completion of Truro Cathedral. Tributes to

Edward poured in from the pulpit, the Press and the platform, full of rich Victorian hyperbole. According to these sources he had been wise, kindly, firm of purpose, far-seeing, charming, fatherly, boyish, a creative genius, heavenly-minded, prudent, bold, diligent, courteous, patient, single-hearted, devoted, dignified in diction and demeanour, a statesman, a leader, a brilliant scholar, a true Christian gentleman – and much more.

Bishop Baynes of Natal, a former chaplain, was one of the few people who ventured on a picture that was fuller and truer that most that were being painted by friends and colleagues. He mentioned Edward's days of reaction, days when the cloud would settle on his nearest and dearest relationships, when there was thunder in the air and the storm would burst. Then woe to the unlucky one who happened to act as a lightning conductor. Edward could be terrible in his wrath and at those times his chaplains and family wished for the power of David's harp. But little of this side of Edward's nature was allowed to seep through into the outside world.

The widowed Minnie was now 55 years old, a squat, fat little woman, her round face redeemed by a lively expression and a friendly smile. Since her marriage at the age of 18 all her life had been dedicated to her exacting husband. 'I must not think of being at ease,' she wrote in her diary, 'but of suiting my ways to his feelings, and this without a shadow of thinking that my ways are better than his, although I like them better.' The shy, inarticulate girl-wife of the Wellington days had become a self-possessed hostess; she had managed two large establishments most efficiently and entertained a great number and variety of guests with a full range of conversational topics. She was not interested in ecclesiastical affairs, a fact which Edward would have been surprised to learn, and had none of the conventional accomplishments, though she was a great reader and an even greater letter-writer. Now she could give her curiosity and quick perceptions full rein, no longer answerable to another person.

Two letters from Arthur to Fred, written in August and September, 1925, are illuminating, making clear the real relationship between Edward and Minnie, as seen by at least two members of the family from close at hand over many years, dramatically exposing the differences in character between them. The tributes to Edward after his death included many referencess to Minnie as his truly loving helpmeet. Her whole life was wrapped up in her husband and children, people said, and he knew and appreciated her unfailing attention and devotion; they were the perfect couple. But Arthur wrote in very different terms. 'I have been present at talks at Addington when Papa's hard displeasure about some trifle was intolerable. On the other hand I used to think at the Addington meals, that Mama was dextrous in reverting to subjects which always rubbed Papa up the wrong way. It was a case of real, natural incompatibility. Mama was an instinctive pagan, hence her charm; Papa was an instinctive puritan with a rebellious love of art. Papa on the whole hated and distrusted the people he didn't wholly approve of. Mama saw their faults and loved them. How very few friends Papa ever had. Some old ones like Bradshaw – sort of tradition, but how he drifted away from Bishop Wordsworth and John Wordsworth and Wilkinson. He disliked feeling people's superiority. His mind was better and stronger than his heart and his heart didn't keep his mind in check. It was a fine character, not a beautiful one. He certainly had a tendency to bully people as he believed from good motives. Mama never wanted to direct or interfere with people and I think was the most generous and disinterested character I have ever known. But her diary is very painful to me because it shows how little in common they had and how cruel he was.'

Fred had made a similar comment in his Marlborough diary of January, 1887. 'E.C. (Edward Cantuar) is brutal sometimes to M.B.' He replied to Arthur's letter and Arthur wrote again with further comments on their parents' disparate characters. 'I expect it would have been better for Mama to have taken the line you suggest. But on the other hand Papa was a very difficult person to deal with, because he was terrifying, and remembered things, not very accurately, because he remembered the points which were in his favour and forgot the points which were not. Mama forgot everything, or if she remembered, forgot the sense of resentment. Then he wanted, as you say, obedience and enthusiasm. Mama never claimed either exactly, but got both. Then Papa cared intensely about details, and details never interested Mama; and one must remember, as you say, the other side – and Papa's affection, when it rose to the surface, was very revealing indeed.' Such an assessment, in such direct and obviously deeply-felt language, was necessary to agitate the soothing balm which the world had poured on to Edward's character. Nearly 30 years after his death his personality had the power to disturb memory and cause resentment on Minnie's behalf.

Arthur's own estimation of his father's qualities, written soon after Edward's death, is well thought out and admirably clear and perceptive. His own life, as well as those of his mother, brothers and sisters, had been scarred subtly and irrevocably by the strongly contrasted strains that existed side by side in his father; and it was to Arthur's credit that he could emphasise the undoubted sincerity, courtesy and gentleness that Edward could display as well as the petulance and bullying that the family had suffered from for so many years.

Edward was a stern puritan, Arthur wrote: severe, strict, with a natural and deliberate love of discipline. He hated luxury, waste, worldliness and idleness. He disapproved of much innocent pleasure, and the lighthearted youthful cynicism which proceeds from pure ignorance of the world was to be sharply reproved. So was all graceful, indolent trifling with the serious side of life. To the outer world he often seemed to have more of the master about him than the priest; he had more respect for strength than sympathy for weakness. He could give a strong and tender sympathy, but was more disposed to correct faults than to penetrate motives or allow for shortcomings.

At an early age he had to share responsibilities with his mother over younger lives, and after her death had to bear them alone, far sooner than most adolescents and young men have to; and that burden, allied to the piety of his father and the influence of Prince Lee at King Edward's School, had given him a religious gravitas that normally comes much later in life, and had also given an impetus to the pomposity that grew in his late teens.

Edward made friends without much difficulty, but his friendships were apt to deepen or diminish in proportion to the reserves of strength and feeling that the person possessed. He asked so much from those he admired and was so sensitive to their defects that his friendships were sometimes strained or even broken, and only a very few remained from youth to old age. The vitality which was one of the most striking elements in his character enabled him to give himself to the minutest details of life so that for the moment they were the only things worth doing; and this detailed attention that inspired all things gave a sincerity and careful courtesy which made them not easily forgotten.

Looking back through Edward's life one sees him as the idolised son of a home circle which never questioned his will. He was intensely absorbed in culture, in the aesthetic side of religion, in sacred and classical art, but was without any very deep sympathy with humanity, and he was imperious in claiming love from others as his right. Through much of his life he showed little of that simple love of others, the patient waiting upon others' needs, the pleading desire for another's happiness, the spirit that rejoices more over the penitent than over the just, the spirit of humblest self-sacrifice; in short, the spirit of Christ.

He had presented to the Church and the country a genuine nobility, loftiness of purpose, purity of aims and transparent sincerity; able to present profound truths simply. He had been a born leader, a master touching the keys, solving difficulties and inspiring allegiance in both the mighty and the meek. But to himself he had admitted a crushing sense of inadequacy and an inability to bear the awful responsibilities that weighed down on him; and the loneliness and desolation in his innermost being sent him flying to an utter dependence on God's Will, without doubt or question. The world saw him as a great man, he saw himself as a sinner, his family saw the greatness and the deep flaws.

CHAPTER TWENTY-FOUR

AFTER Edward's funeral the family, though drained emotionally and physically, had to leave Lambeth Palace and Addington Park quickly, for the sake of the next Archbishop, who was to be Randall Davidson. Before they decided where to settle down a foreign trip was arranged, partly to recover from their recent shock and partly to plan for their future away from the pressure of everyday trivialities. Minnie and Lucy Tait went out to Egypt to join Maggie who had planned to spend the winter there for the sake of her health and to carry on with her archaeological work. Hugh, recuperating from an attack of rheumatism, joined them, and Fred was to follow later when he had supervised the clearing of Lambeth Palace, an immense task which involved sending most of their furniture, pictures and carpets into storage. Then, in an almost empty room, in a mournful and deserted palace, he worked on the appendices and final proofs of Edward's book on Cyprian. It was eventually published in 1897. Arthur was credited as the editor, though it was Fred who had done most of the work in preparing it for publication; and Maggie had played a great part in the final draft. It was a month before Fred was free to join the others at Luxor (Arthur had remained at Eton, having little inclination for foreign travel). Maggie was still excavating at Karnak and Minnie and Lucy hovered in the background. Fred helped Maggie, and Hugh went out shooting quail. In the evenings Maggie wrote up her notes and Fred continued with his Grecian novel, *The Vintage*. Hugh quickly became bored and left the family for a tour of Palestine. Then Maggie fell ill with pleurisy and nearly died.

When she had recovered sufficiently to be removed the family returned to Cairo and from there went to Helouan for a week for swimming and sunbathing. There Fred developed a slight sunstroke and had to stay in bed for a few days. The others returned to Cairo and Fred supervised the packing of Maggie's antiquities when he was feeling better. He took a swift post-boat to Cairo but while on it was suddenly struck down by intense pains. In Cairo the doctor diagnosed typhoid fever and Fred had to undergo a long and severe illness which left him very weak. As his condition improved Lucy Tait went down with the same disease, but in a more dangerous form and for a time it was touch and go with her. Eventually the exhausted family was able to leave Egypt.

Minnie came through the 16-week period of stress and tension with her usual courage; and then had to find somewhere to live, a task she dreaded. Maggie had gone to Aix again and Fred to Capri to complete his convalescence. When they returned they found that their mother had rented for a year a comfortable Georgian house in Winchester, close to the Cathedral, with the river, the golf course and country club nearby. The surrounding countryside was very beautiful, the town placid and drowsy. The interior of the house soon looked like a miniature Lambeth Palace.

For a few months life in Winchester was ideal: and foreign travel, excessive heat, sandstorms, chaos and crises became no more than memories. Maggie grew stronger and regained her enthusiasm for writing. Minnie and Lucy Tait remained soulmates: and it was about this time that 'Ben', Lucy's pet name for Minnie, replaced her given name. Her children accepted the nickname, though they still called her Mama. Fred was busy writing. Arthur and Hugh spent the first Christmas in the new home and they all filled the time with the familiar pursuits that had made their earlier years so enjoyable. But without Nellie, of course, things could never be the same.

As the spring of 1898 approached Ben realised that she was feeling bored. When Edward was alive there had been two large establishments to administer. Now all there was to do was call on new acquaintances, go for drives and choose menus. Her occasional trips to London only heightened her sense of inadequacy. The spring was chilly and Maggie's health received a setback when damp weather affected her rheumatism. She gradually grew jealous of Lucy Tait, whom she imagined had taken her place as daughter of the house, and a distance stretched uncomfortably between mother and daughter. As a gesture of defiance she took over the running of the household and dealt with things as her father would have done, critically and with undue attention to detail. In a strange way she became a reincarnation of Edward, and Ben was forced to look on, worried but uncomprehending.

Fred was asked to administer a fund initiated by the Duke of Westminster, and directed by the Red Cross, for the relief of Greeks made refugees by the Graeco-Turkish war of 1897, and was out of the country for a few months. Before returning to Winchester he visited Capri and shared the Villa Cercola with John Ellingham Brooks, estranged husband of Romaine Brooks, the artist, and became further enamoured of the lazy, sun-drenched life of the island, becoming part of the homosexual contingent that had taken over Capri almost completely. He was enjoying himself hugely when letters from Ben made him return home in a hurry. He found that Maggie's depressions were getting worse, resembling the blackest of their father's moods, and a tendency to masculinity in her nature was beginning to show. Ben had decided that they must leave Winchester before the family disintegrated.

After much searching they found a house called Tremans, near Horsted Keynes in Sussex, between Ashdown Forest and the Sussex Weald. The lease was bought and Tremans became the Benson headquarters for the next 20 years. Part of the house had been built in the 16th century and there were oak-panelled rooms and great open fireplaces. The gardens, which were on different levels, led down to a brook; there was an avenue of pine trees, yew hedges, farm buildings, barns and a bowling green. The books, heavy furniture, pictures, parrots and animals survived another move which Fred again had to supervise. Arthur's boarding-house at Eton took up all his time, or so he claimed, and Hugh was too occupied with his religious concerns to help. He had given up a comfortable curacy at Kemsing and had joined Canon Gore's House of the Resurrection at Mirfield in Yorkshire.

Lucy Tait, whose money had helped to buy the lease of Tremans, did good work among the poor of Lambeth once a week, and she took a small house in Barton Street, near Westminster Abbey, which became a *pied à terre* for the Bensons when they wanted to stay in London. Maggie became happier and more active; she took over the gardens and was responsible for all the livestock. But Fred refused to rejoice too soon; he could not help but be apprehensive about his sister. Perversely, when the rest of the family, especially Ben, began to sun themselves, he was the one to become bored and restless. He was 32, settling into a dry middle age, so he supposed, and missing out on life. His days were shallow and lacked purpose, and he missed male companionship. After three months he went to Bayreuth with a family friend, discovered Wagner and worshipped him for the rest of his life. Back at Tremans he grew increasingly dissatisfied with life and a barrier grew between him and his mother. He sulked and she brooded and the first year in the new house dragged to an unhappy end. Finally Ben wrote to him a letter full of love and understanding, releasing him from all his obligations one of which was a promise to his father to live with and look after his mother, and Fred left Tremans in the autumn of 1900 and took a small flat in Oxford Street. He could now enter more fully into the activities of London's smart set – the old families and the aristocracy, but also the new-rich and the vulgar. Arthur never approved of Fred's 'flashy' friends and his involvement with the extravagant and outrageous hostesses of the day.

Fred continued to write with phenomenal speed, and a lot of what he turned out was shallow and unworthy of his talent. He spent some of the winter months in Switzerland to perfect his skating, and in London he became indispensable when society ladies needed someone to liven up luncheon or dinner parties, or when a personable young man was needed at a stately home weekend.

For the next five years, up to the summer of 1906, life at Tremans was leisurely, free from the crises that had made Winchester finally unbearable. Maggie had benefited most from the move; her depressions disappeared, her spirits soared and her activities in the house and gardens increased. She fortunately had two good friends to sustain her – Nettie Gourlay and Gladys Bevan, and she and Ben were reconciled; and in a much larger house it was easier to avoid Lucy Tait.

Ben, now over 60, also felt rheumatic pains in damp weather, and her eyes tired easily, but her youthful mind and vitality were not impaired by the passing years. Lucy Tait continued to be her confidante and lover. She could talk to her freely, grumble about her ailments, analyse all the weaknesses of her nature (extravagances and love of over-eating being the worst), convey her misgivings about Fred, and know that she would receive sympathy and consolation.

In 1903 Arthur resigned his Mastership at Eton and went to live in Cambridge, intending to devote his time to writing. Then, unexpectedly, he was offered a Fellowship by Magdalene College (principally because he could afford to go there without pay), and was elected in October, 1904. After living in rooms in College he moved into the Old Lodge, which he made spacious and comfortable and he lived there for the rest of his life. In 1915 he was elected Master of the College, a post which he held until his death in 1925. During his Cambridge years his books of poems, essays, novels and critical works appeared regularly and achieved a wide readership. They were urbane in tone and tenuous in substance; too light for philosophy, though more than journalism. He wrote them easily and with pleasure and they brought to him a great deal of money. His diary proceeded apace, eventually reaching over four million words.

While Fred was 'playing with his earls and countesses', as his mother put it, Hugh was struggling with his conscience at the House of the Resurrection and putting tentative steps along the road that led to Rome. His longing for shelter and security overrode his demand for the right to be fiercely individual. He was still the same Hugh who was unwilling to bend to others but in the end the need to be curbed by benevolent authority outweighed all other considerations. In the autumn of 1903 he went to the College of San Silvestro in Rome for instruction and was ordained nine months later. If Edward had been alive there would have been thunder and lightning as well as heartbreak, but Ben, though disapproving of the defection, believed that Divine Will had been at work and felt that she could not question it. Hugh, now a Catholic priest, threw himself into parish work in Cambridge, preaching to great acclaim and writing slapdash propagandist novels with great fervour. His novels, shrill and heartless as they were, made him a lot of money. In 1911 he became private chamberlain to Pope Pius X.

The most traumatic experience of Hugh's life began when he met Frederick Rolfe, self-styled Baron Corvo, after reading *Hadrian the Seventh* in 1905 and fell under the spell of the unbalanced poverty-stricken, vindictive megalomaniac. Hugh was dazzled by Rolfe's frenzied words, and infatuation blinded him to the man's excesses. They decided to collaborate on a book about St. Thomas of Canterbury, Hugh to do most of the writing and Rolfe the research; but, predictably, things did not go smoothly. Late in 1907 the project began to flag. There were mutual recriminations and Hugh's feelings for Rolfe cooled. The book was abandoned and Rolfe became Hugh's implacable enemy, sending him abusive postcards and letters of calumny to Arthur and to Hugh's Bishop. Hugh was shattered by what he learned about Rolfe's private life but was willing to become reconciled. Rolfe, however, refused every friendly gesture and the relationship ended in farce, each lampooning the other in a book. In 1908 Hugh gave up parochial work and bought a small manor house at Hare Street, near Buntingford in Hertfordshire, and settled down to writing, gardening, painting, reading, instructing converts, and investigating psychic phenomena; a placid life broken by preaching tours of America and Rome. His life was so full that he had no time for emotions. He remained, as he always had been, exasperating, dogmatic, eccentric, unloving.

Maggie's long-threatened troubles began in the late summer of 1906 with moods of great depression, tiredness, nervousness and worries about her health; and she developed a harsh and critical attitude towards her home and family. Ben realised that some sort of dread struggle had begun and that Maggie was doomed. She fought against her demons but her condition deteriorated, though, during the few occasions when she achieved a temporary serenity, she finished her book, *The Venture of a Rational Faith*, saw her friends and wrote cheerful letters. She went to Cornwall for a month with Nettie Gourlay and Beatrice Layman, then stayed with Gladys Bevan in London. She went to see Fred, who was then living in Oakley Street, Chelsea, and insisted that there was nothing really wrong with her. She did not tell him that she had nothing to cling to, that she was convinced that she was going mad and that neither friends, family nor religion could help her.

Back at Tremans she found that Ben and Lucy were away; when they returned Ben realised with horror that Maggie's wild-eyed condition meant that a crisis was at hand. The family doctor in London was telegraphed for and he arrived in the evening. During dinner Maggie collapsed completely; the quiet, self-controlled Maggie turned violent and threatening and though what actually happened is unclear the episode terrified Ben and her friends. Consultants were brought in; cerebro-meningitis, delirious mania or blood poisoning from influenza were tentatively mentioned as causes of her outbreak. She was removed to a private home for the insane run by Sisters of Mercy at Burgess Hill, and for the next ten years she was never out of medical care. When the fierceness of the first attack had abated she was moved to a private asylum at Roehampton where she developed a new delusion – that Ben w conniving with the doctors to prevent her from going home. Whenever Ben visited her she was assailed with bitter accusations and eventually she stopped going. Instead she wrote long and loving letters which Maggie insisted were lies and would scribble furious comments on them.

In late 1910 Beth's health began to give cause for concern. She was 92 years old. She died the following May in Ben's arms, and the whole family mourned, remembering her with tendeness and gratitude. 'Her life of long service is one of the most beautiful things I know,' Arthur wrote. Every mention of her, in letters and diaries, comments on her solicitude and her simple goodness; the Bensons regarded her almost as an institution, changeless and immortal. Only Maggie was unable to attend the funeral, though she grieved with the rest of them.

Fred was Maggie's most constant visitor; Arthur and Hugh somehow found it difficult to make time. He went to Roehampton every week when he was in London. He found that there was occasional clarity behind the delusions and with his cheerfulness and charm he often broke through the veil; then they would talk about their childhood days and laugh again over incidents that had amused them. But Maggie could never shake off the conviction that lies were being told about her and plots being hatched. In 1913 she had been transferred from the Roehampton asylum to live with a private doctor in Wimbledon, and in the summer of that year she escaped from the house and made her way to Victoria Station and found a train going to Horsted Keynes. She managed to walk the two miles from the station to Tremans and arrived home exhausted. She was allowed to stay the night as she seemed quite normal, but when the cab arrived to take her back to Wimbledon her mood changed and she spat out the usual accusations to Ben. That was the last time she saw Tremans.

Gradually she weakened, and in August, 1915, she had a heart attack. After that, curiously, the delusions disappeared and she saw things and people as they really were. Fred took Ben to see her and they talked again as members of a family; the years of miserable separation might never have been. 'She was just her old self,' Ben wrote, 'and most affectionate.' But Maggie was losing hold of life. In the spring of 1916 it was clear that she had only a few more days to live. On her last evening she saw Ben alone and they spoke, not of suspicions or estrangement, but only of love. 'Well, I have had a happy day,' she said to her nurse and died in her sleep. She was buried beside Nellie at Addington.

Maggie's death was poignant, but there was a touch of farce about Hugh's, which occurred in 1914. His health had declined soon after the outbreak of the First World War when he suffered from breathlessness and chest pains. He was worried enough to promise to cut down smoking, and when 'fake angina' was diagnosed he had to lessen his work load considerably. After preaching at Salford in October he became really ill with pneumonia and congestion of the right lung. He was given the last rites by Canon Sharrock of Salford Cathedral, made all the responses and even corrected the Canon when he stumbled over a word. The next day he insisted that it was all a mistake and that he was not going to die, but soon he changed his mind again and realised that there was little time left. With Arthur and the Canon he joined in the responses to the prayers for the dying, though he stopped the Canon once or twice to give Arthur some last minute instructions about his estate. Almost his last words were, 'You will make certain I am dead, won't you?'

Fred found Hugh's will and read the special instructions for his burial. He wanted to be buried in a brick vault in his garden and asked for a chapel to be built over it. The coffin was to be made of light wood so that, if he had been buried alive, he could break the top, use a duplicate key to the vault and so make his escape. If this was not practical a vein in his body was to be opened before he was buried. Fred saw that this latter was done, and the breakable coffin and the duplicate key were not required. Later, however, a chapel was built over the grave in the garden.

In June, 1909, Fred, aged 42, met a young man of 23 with whom he was to establish one of his firmest friendships in a life full of romantic interludes. This was Francis Yeats-Brown, son of the late consul at Genoa, who had been an officer in the King's Royal Rifle Corps before joining the Bengal Lancers, where he had been for three years. He was staying at his father's castle at Portofino, and soon he and Fred were inseparable, walking, swimming and rock-climbing together, writing and talking about art, life and literature.

Francis returned to India in 1912 and Fred visited him there, staying for several months. Illness caused his return home, and a tumour on a kidney resulted in an operation for the removal of the organ in 1913. He convalesced at Tremans, but he was never again as strong as he had been, and he had to cut down on skating, tennis and golf. He was at the Villa Cercola on Capri in the summer of 1914 and left the island hurriedly when it became apparent to him that war was inevitable. He was too old to enlist as a soldier so became attached to a branch of the Foreign Office; his job was to collect material about the enemy's position in Turkey and to write a book exposing the German plans. Later he wrote another book about German crimes which was circulated among the neutral countries. Then he turned to Poland and its involvement with Germany and Russia. During the four years of war he turned out four books in which he tried to disentangle the confusion of European relationships.

In September, 1915, Fred left Oakley Street and moved into a large house in South Kensington: 25, Brompton Square; and there he would return after his work in the Foreign Office, shut himself up in his study and forget the war for a few hours. He wrote several novels, but the most important and the most popular was *David Blaize*, a story of school life, sentimental in parts, but essentially a true picture of adolescent passions. The effect of this book on the reading public was electric, and Ben was moved to declare that it was the only book of Fred's that she approved of without reservations.

Up to the middle of 1917 Arthur felt completely at home at Magdalene. His income from his writings was substantial and a Swiss woman admirer of them had given him £40,000, an immense fortune in those days. He made many gifts to the College, and financed Fellowships and Exhibitions. He was elected to the Council of the Senate, became an Alderman of the Cambridge Town Council and a Liveryman of the City Guild of Fishmongers. He enjoyed the committees and syndicates, receptions and degree ceremonies, succumbed to the boyish charms of countless undergraduates, and relaxed in the company of old friends such as Percy Lubbock and Monty James.

Suddenly he began to have vivid and grotesque dreams, accompanied by severe headaches. Bromides did not work and the attacks increased in frequency and violence. He fell into an abyss of hopelessness and agreed to go to a nursing-home for the mentally sick at Ascot. After some months of rest, sedation and massage he felt some relief. In 1918 he began to write his diary again, but he had a relapse and put the work aside for another two years. More months of depression followed, and for six years he woke up every morning to struggle against nausea with life and everything connected with it. His condition was not helped by Ben's death on June 18, 1918, at the age of 72. She had become very frail and very deaf, but still possessed the indomitable courage she had always shown. The glamorous phase of her life had been the 14 years she had been mistress of Lambeth Palace and Addington Park when she had moved easily with diplomats, politicians, churchmen and other people of distinction. Her letters had gone out to the great and the humble. She had been revered by Gladstone and had had an affectionate relationship with the Queen. When Edward died she retired into obscurity but continued to wield influence with her letters. Hugh and Maggie died and Arthur was shut away in his own dark world, but Fred was cheerful and supportive and she and Lucy Tait had been inseparable for nearly 30 years. Ben had reached her final emotional fulfilment with Lucy. They addressed each other in extravagant terms and shared the great Victorian bed in which all her children had been born.

Fred disposed of the remainder of the lease of Tremans, sending much of the contents to auction. Charlie Tomlin, the houseboy, became Fred's manservant and stayed with him for the rest of Fred's life. Fred retired to his house in Brompton Square until some time in 1919 when he was offered and accepted the sublease of Lamb House in Rye, formerly occupied by Henry James. When the lease came up for renewal Fred and Arthur decided to share it, and it was arranged that Arthur should live there during university vacations and Fred for the rest of the year. Arthur found the house a delightful haven and continued to produce volumes of essays and reminiscences. Fred's output was also prodigious.

Soon after the end of the war Fred, now over 50, began to suffer from arthritis, which got slowly and insidiously worse. He had to give up golf, swimming and skating, and instead played chess, took up bird-watching and playing the piano. In 1920 his first 'Lucia' novel, *Queen Lucia*, appeared; soon after this came a book of family biography, *Our Family Affairs*. Arthur's health began to improve in 1920 and he was able to give up the security of the nursing home. In April of that year he wrote to Fred thanking him for being so wonderfully good to him throughout his lengthy illness and promised that he would never forget his kindness. Arthur returned to Cambridge for the Lent Term, and at Easter he was back in Rye. In 1922, he and Fred went to Blakeney in north Norfolk to watch birds, and in his diary he moaned about his abject misery. He was a sour and cantankerous companion, thus convincing Fred that he really was better.

But it was not until 1923 that Arthur admitted that his depression was really vanishing and at the age of 61 he began to look forward again to a life of productivity and the companionship of engaging young men. He hoped to make up for the wasted years with an orgy of creation. His diary had already passed the three million word mark. His disabilities – increasing weight, troublesome legs and neuritis – mattered less to him than the joy of his restored mental powers.

Fred returned to Capri, for the last time as it turned out, and found everything changed: people had died or moved away and there was creeping Fascism everywhere; and John Ellingham Brooks, though poor and friendless, was unwilling to take up Fred's offer for him to stay at Brompton Square or Lamb House. When Fred left for home they never saw each other again.

Arthur, having bounced back into Cambridge with his old powers recharged, became his familiar acerbic self, employing delicate malice when someone needed to be deflated and enjoying tilts with his best friends. Some of his young men had married and became less attractive to him, but in 1923 their places had been taken by the handsome and charming George Rylands, who dominated his thoughts and dreams as no-one had ever done before. The intensity of his feelings eventually began to fade and Arthur brought his last grand passion to a dignified end. Noel Blakiston was to stir his heart, but briefly and not violently. Shortly before the end of the Lent Term of 1925 he began to be troubled by severe pains in his side, accompanied by shivering fits. Pleurisy was diagnosed and he retired to bed. There he suffered a heart attack. Fred was present. 'I'm glad you've come...' Arthur gasped, and died just after midnight on June 17. A memorial service was held in Lambeth Palace Chapel two days later.

Fred was now the last of the Bensons; 58 years old, looking rather soldierly with his clipped grey moustache and short neat hair, but his eyes were as bright and blue as ever, and he was still a friendly, gossipy host. He had to spend many days at the Old Lodge, disposing of its contents – thousands of books, the diary, overflowing cupboards, boxes and drawers, and the heavy furniture, so he was glad to get back to Rye.

Arthritis had now taken a tenacious hold of his hip joints and he was never again to know freedom from pain, and he had to hobble about with the aid of two sticks. All the remedies he tried, from the orthodox to the wildly experimental, failed. Finally X-rays revealed that his condition had reached an advanced stage and he resigned himself to wearisome invalidism. Even bird-watching had to be given up; chess and the piano continued to take the place of physical activities. Writing, of course, was as necessary to him as breathing, and entertaining friends was almost as important. The garden at Lamb House was another preoccupation, and in a secret little enclave he sunbathed and wrote his books. He went to London infrequently and avoided large social gatherings. The eligible bachelor of Edwardian society had become quiet and withdrawn. The loss of his physical energy had coincided with the decline of his desire for experiences and love affairs, though in the frail, tired body something of the old Fred was still embedded.

In 1924 *David Of King's* appeared; a continuation of the story of the friendship between David Blaize and Frank Maddox when they were both undergraduates, and it was as popular as *David Blaize*, appealing to the same audience; nostalgic and elegiac, it comforted those of its readers who would never again know the pain and rapture of growing up.

Fred had a large number of friends in Rye, one of the closest being Canon Fowler, the Vicar. Francis Yeats-Brown was a frequent visitor. With Fred's help he revised the frequently turned down *Bengal Lancer*, which was finally published in 1930. George Plank, the artist, was close, and Radclyffe Hall and Una Troubridge became friends when they went to live in Rye. Dame Ethel Smyth was an occasional visitor to Lamb House, and Fred kept up with Eustace Miles, with whom he had collaborated on books on sport and keeping fit.

Although Fred continued to write his society novels, and the Mapp and Lucia books still appeared at intervals, in them the standard of comic writing constant, the invention never flagging, the characters as scathingly accurate as ever, he turned more and more to serious writing, chiefly biographies, and his studies of Drake, Magellan and Alcibiades were well received. *Spook Stories* and *More Spook Stories* established him as a ghost story writer of the first class. More family history was revealed in *As We Were*. *Charlotte Brontë* was considered to be the model of what a biography should be. *King Edward VII*, *Queen Victoria*, *The Kaiser* and *English Relations and Daughters of Queen Victoria* were perhaps too hagiographic to be really truthful. The best books to come out of this later period, apart from those mentioned, are *Paying Guests*, *Secret Lives*, *The Inheritor* and *Ravens' Brood*, the latter the most bizarre.

In 1933 Fred, a highly respected member of the Rye community, became a magistrate and dispensed justice with firmness, fairness and impish humour. Later that year he received an invitation from the Town Council to become Mayor of Rye. He was staggered, highly honoured and slightly amused; and agreed. He chose as his Mayoress Mrs Jacomb-Hood, the widow of an artist friend. He took great pleasure in all the pomp and ceremony associated with the office, and was amazed to find himself happily involved in unaccustomed duties. He was re-elected in 1935, in which year he also became Speaker of the Cinque Ports, and in 1936 agreed to become Mayor for the third time. An event in 1938 that gave him enormous pleasure was his election to an Honorary Fellowship of Magalene College, and he was equally proud to have the Freedom of the Borough of Rye conferred on him.

Fred started to write his last book of memoirs, which he was going to call *A Few People*. Unusually, he found the writing heavy going; he was less fluent than he had ever been, and the first draft needed much revision. He also started to suffer from the black moods that had so devastated Edward, Arthur and Maggie, though he was never as seriously affected as the others, and it was the constant pain of his complaint, being displeased with his work, and the feeling that life was no longer worth living, that brought on the depressions. But only Charlie, his servant and friend, knew about the undercurrents of apprehension and gloom; to his friends Fred was as affectionate and entertaining as ever. In a much earlier semi-autobiographical novel called *Up and Down*, Fred had tried to put into words what he felt about the visitation of the Thing. Neither Edward, Maggie nor Arthur had ever chosen such expressive words, even though they had all experienced its horror. 'But when I woke the Thing was there ... there was a blackening poison that spread and sprouted like some infernal mushroom of plague. I found that I did not care for anything any more; there was the root of this obsession ... it was all one, for over all and in all was the blackness of the pit of clouds ... within me was a centre-point of consciousness that only wailed and cried out at the horror of existence ... when I went up to bed the nightmare yelled out and smothered me. At one moment I was nothing set in the middle of cosmic darkness; at the next I was cosmic darkness itself, set in a microscopic loneliness, an alpha and omega of the everlasting midnight...'

Towards the end of 1939 Fred began to lose both appetite and weight. He felt tired when he should have been vigorous, his voice grew hoarse and he was troubled by a persistent cough. He saw a specialist at University College Hospital in London, where an exploratory operation was performed, and throat cancer diagnosed. Before anything could be done to alleviate his condition he died on February 29, 1940, a few months before his 73rd birthday. Though friends had called during the ten days he was in hospital, only Charlie Tomlin was at his bedside at the end, as loyal and supportive as ever.

A Few People, retitled *Final Edition*, was published towards the end of 1940 and the reviews were unanimously enthusiastic. Fred had written the masterpiece he had always dreamed of writing – the last testament of a charming, intelligent and civilised man, rich in human anecdote and zest for life. The Benson story had been told for the last time by somebody who had lived through it all, the difficulties of life with his father and the joys and travails of Ben, Nellie, Maggie, Arthur and Hugh.

LAST WILL AND TESTAMENT OF EDWARD WHITE BENSON

Edward's will, dated 1891, with codicils 1892 and 1893, consists of over 4,000 words of an almost impenetrable legal jargon which would defy anybody but a senior judge to make head or tail of, and almost every bequest was hedged about with so many conditions that getting to the nub of it is like fighting one's way through a jungle. It seems that Edward was unwilling to let the humblest teaspoon go unaccounted for and that he was determined to control as much as he could, from beyond the grave; and it was clear that he looked upon Minnie's possible remarriage with great displeasure. The words 'so long as she remains my widow' occur almost every time she is mentioned; it is as though he expected that Minnie already had her next husband waiting in the wings. He appointed Minnie, Arthur and the Bishop of Dover as executors and trustees, and the latter received £100 as a token of gratitude. Minnie was left £500 to be paid immediately after his death, and all his clothes, wines and liquors, housekeeping provisions and other consumable stores. His Aunt Mary Anne Chavasse continued to receive the annuity he had been paying her, and Beth was given an annuity of £45 a year. If any of his brothers and sisters were living at his death they received a book, engraving or small article in personal remembrance; his Uncle Alfred Baker, Canon Hutchinson and Lucy Tait were equally rewarded. His domestic Chaplains got £10 each to buy a remembrance, and there were small legacies to his steward, bailiff, porter, head coachman, housekeeper, wife's maid, head housemaid and valet; other servants benefitted to the tune of £5 if they had been in his service for five years.

To his successor in the See of Canterbury, for the use of the Chapel in Lambeth Palace, he gave his sacramental vessels, the eagle lectern, altar cloths, linen, engraved glass water cruet, and Litany Stool, and to his Chapel at Addington the screens, panelling, parquetry, carpets and stained glass windows. The Archbishop's Library at Lambeth received some of his own books which bore his arms and bookplate. Arthur was the recipient of all family letters, papers and manuscripts, the family miniatures, seals, buckles and rings; and the four children received his watches, jewels, and trinkets, though Minnie could have the use of them as long as she remained his widow. Every son in Holy Orders could have up to 200 books from his theological books, but if only one son was in Holy Orders then he could chose 300 books.

After debts, expenses and bequests the residue of his personal estate went to Minnie ('so long as she remain my widow'). Arthur received his Silver Salver, two candelabra, his Silver Declamation Cup and the silver cup left to him by Francis Martin, and to Fred went the plate left to him by Prebendary Wickenden (his godfather). The four children shared the residue of his plate, books, engravings, prints, pictures, works of art, household goods, furniture and other articles of household use and ornament, the selection to be made alternately according to priority of birth. The value of such choices were treated as an advance on account of their respective shares of his residuary trust estate – except for Maggie, whose choices were to be her absolute property.

Arthur and Hugh received £5,750 each, but Fred only £4,250 because he was already possessed of property to the value of £1,500. Maggie received £6,250. Then the ultimate residue stayed in trust for the four children equally.

A large part of the will dealt with the provisions he made for possible grandchildren, if they reached the age of 21 and did or did not marry. Maggie's heirs came in for special consideration. A codicil of 1892 deprived Arthur of £1,000 of the £5,750 legacy as he had already had the sum in advance; and a further codicil of 1893 dealt with investments, the value of which were to be used for the reparation of Lambeth Palace and Addington Park, the Assyrian Mission, the income of some poor benefices in the Diocese of Canterbury, and a fund for payments of an Honorarium to Honorary Canons; each of the above sums were to be recorded as 'Archbishop Benson's Gift'.

Edward, with his obsession for detail, must have experienced great satisfaction in drawing up a will which was designed to ensure that a maximum number of people would remember him; though it was perhaps surprising that he left nothing to Wellington College, Winchester School in memory of Martin, or Truro Cathedral; nothing to the poor of Lambeth; and not even a memento to some of his oldest friends such as Bishop Westcott, Arthur Mason or Randall Davidson. To the end of his life Edward White Benson was a complicated human being.

Selected Works of
Edward White Benson

1856   The Book of Rugby School, by E.M. Goulburn (Chaps. 1–3 by E.W.B.

1859   Sermons preached in Wellington College Chapel.

1870   A Memorial Sermon preached after the death of J. Prince Lee, first Bishop of Manchester.

1872   Work. Friendship. Worship. Three sermons preached before the University of Cambridge.

1874   Boy-Life: Its Trials, its Strength, its Fulness. Sundays in Wellington College, 1859–73. New edition, 1883.

1878   The Cathedral: Its necessary place in the Life of the Church.

1885   The Seven Gifts. Addresses to the Diocese of Canterbury in his primary Visitation. Macmillan. 225pp.

1885   Municipalities. An Address delivered to the Birmingham and Midland Institute.

1889   Christ and his Times. An address to the Diocese of Canterbury in his second Visitation. Macmillan. 240pp.

1890   Judgement. Read and others v. the Lord Bishop of Lincoln, in the Court of the Archbishop of Canterbury, November 21, 1890.

1891   Living Theology and other Sermons. Sampson, Low. 225pp.

1893   Fishers of Men. Addressed to the Diocese of Canterbury in his third Visitation. Macmillan. 166pp.

1897   Cyprian: His Life, his Times, his Work. Edited by A.C. Benson. Macmillan. pp xxxvii + 636.

1899   Prayers Public and Private, being Order and Forms of Public Services, Private Devotions, and Hymns, compiled, written or translated by Edward White Benson. Edited by Rev. Hugh Benson. Isbister. 274pp.

1899   The Apocalypse. An Introductory Study of the Revelation of St. John the Divine. Edited by Margaret Benson from the mss. Macmillan. 168pp.

1904   God's Board: Being a Series of Communion Addresses. Edited by Margaret Benson. Methuen. 233pp.

INDEX